Lost in the Here

A True Story

Melinda Dame Wilferth

To order additional copies of this book, contact:
Xlibris Corporation
1-888-795-4274
www.Xlibris.com
Orders@Xlibris.com
48089

LOST IN THE HERE

CONTENTS

DEDICATION

This book is dedicated to my daughter Blake, who demonstrated incredible strength for her young age; to John Wilferth, whom I will always love; and especially to my Lord Jesus, my Savior.

THANKS

I would like to thank my editor and dear friend Harvey McCloud for his assistance in helping me to put my experiences into words, and for his encouragement throughout my year and one-half journey of writing this book.

Dear Reader

I want to take you on an amazing journey, one unlike any you've made before. I warn you, it will be heartrending at times. But I hope you'll stay with me all the way, because it's also a journey full of love, humor, and courage.

The courage is mostly that of my husband and hero, John Wilferth. John is a loving father, a lover of life, a man with a hearty smile. He is also a very intelligent man, a financial advisor with a master's degree in business administration and a law degree. But something terrible happened to him on Easter Sunday, 2003, when he experienced a devastating neurological event called *status epilepticus*.

I am going to take you back to that terrible day when John was gripped by a brutal seizure while watching a basketball game on television, and through the five horrendous hours it took before the worst of the attack was over. You will also be there with me when, two days later, John woke.

Let me ask you this: Have you ever noticed a pattern in the sand as you walked along a beach, then later passed the same spot and found it gone? Maybe it was a name or a face that someone had drawn with a stick, or a series of small terraces created by the shoreline breeze. But when you returned, you found that the wind had blown it all away or that the waves had washed it into oblivion. All that information, all that reality, gone in the space of a few hours.

Well, that's what happened to John after he woke from the seizure. And not just once, but over and over. Except in his case, the designs in the sand were actually patterns in his brain. And what happened was that the neurons that kept the patterns in place didn't work right anymore. So when he tried to revisit the recent past, even if it was just an hour or two away, he found that the patterns laid down in his brain had disappeared. As ephemeral as designs in seasand.

What happens to a vital, successful man who loses his short-term memory function? How does he converse with others, maintain a demanding job, or find his way around in the world? How does he even retain a strong sense of who he is?

As you'll discover, one thing that happens is that he experiences reality differently from you and me. The present moment—what's here right now—becomes almost everything for him. The ties that anchor him to yesterday, the previous hour, or even a few minutes ago quickly disappear. It also becomes very difficult for him to make plans, even for the very near future, because he can't remember his plans from one hour to the next. As a result, with only the most tenuous connections to the past and the future, he feels perpetually stranded in the present moment.

Lost in the here.

How does a man cope with that kind of insult to his mental integrity? That's what most of this journey, this true story, is going to be about—the two years that followed John's seizure. What you will discover as you walk with John is a man who refused to be defined by the sudden violation of his mind. You'll come to know a man who fought, flailed, and used every ounce of mental energy he could muster to stretch the bars of the mental cage he found himself occupying—a man who had to re-invent himself to gain a measure of hard-won success.

But this isn't only John's story. It's about our entire family's journey as we faced these great challenges together. You'll also walk beside me in this book, and learn how I did some stupid things and some not-so-stupid things as I tried my best to empower my husband, making crucial decisions on the fly, often not knowing what was right or wrong. And you'll meet others. From my daughter Blake, who, despite her young years, did our family proud with her efforts to understand and care for her John-daddy. To a bevy of German doctors who injected John's head with stem cells, claiming that they would heal him.

Please understand that this isn't a story about superheroes for whom everything turns out wonderfully in the end. It's about fallible human beings who often stumble as they confront horrendous problems and who sometimes feel overwhelmed by their situation. But it's also about people who know how to laugh as well as to cry, and who simply will not give up.

There is one superhero in the book, however—God. For this is also a story of faith. It's a faith that sometimes wavers as it's tested again and again. But it's also a faith that grows and matures into a deeper understanding of what it really means to trust in God and to give a problem to Him fully. I hope that you will see God's light shining throughout this book, even as we traverse the darkest places.

I wanted to tell you our story not because our lives are any more important or worth knowing about than any others. All lives are important, and all lives are worth knowing about. But I think that some who accompany us on our amazing journey may find experiences and lessons in our story to inspire them as they confront obstacles in their own lives.

One thing I know for sure is that you're going to find here a very remarkable man. And yes, I will make this pun because I make it in love and in truth: you will find this man John—this man who forgets—to be, in himself, unforgettable.

CHAPTER ONE

BREATHE!

I know now that it can happen anywhere, at any time. It can happen while you're engaged in the most ordinary activity, the most ephemeral thoughts floating through your mind.

It can happen, for example, while you're lying on your bed on an Easter Sunday afternoon, just reading a book, and you become aware of a few grains of sand still stuck between your toes, reminders of your walk along a sunny California beach that morning with your husband. Your first thought is to get up and wash your feet so you don't get sand on the comforter, but then you realize that actually, you're enjoying the feel of those miniscule bits of seashore that you've inadvertently brought home with you, those tiny souvenirs of that lovely walk. So you decide to wait for a bit, to just let your mind drift back for a moment to the carefree morning, the salty ocean breeze, the way you held hands . . .

Yes, it can happen even then. The beginning of the event that changes your life forever.

* * *

I heard John calling me from downstairs—Melinda! Melinda!—a note of desperation in his voice, and I knew immediately what it was.

I dropped my book, sprung off the bed, and my feet barely touched the stairs as I ran down to find him trying to rise from the sofa where he had been watching a basketball game on TV.

"I've got to go to . . . ," he was saying, but the rest was unintelligible. His eyes were moving rapidly back and forth, and he was straining to rise, but he couldn't get leverage.

I knew immediately that this wasn't one of his focal episodes, which had become so common lately. Almost certainly, this was the onset of a major seizure, like the one he had endured almost exactly a year before.

It was too late to get his meds. Instead, I ran for the cordless phone in the kitchen. Out of the corner of my eye I saw him trying to rise again, then falling back.

"Melinda, I've got to . . ."

I realized the most important thing at the moment was to get someone to help me with him before the convulsions started. At over six feet tall and 220 pounds, John was far too big for me to handle alone once the seizure took full effect. I wouldn't be able to keep him from falling and hitting his head on the floor or the furniture. An image of what had happened last year skidded through my mind—when he had stood up on the bed and the ceiling fan had hit him in the skull, possibly creating more damage. He had to be protected.

With the phone still in my hand, I ran to the yard and saw my neighbors Carlos and Emily out on their patio with relatives who were visiting for Easter. Bill and Michelle, former neighbors, were there, too. "Carlos! Bill! John's having a seizure! Can you come help?"

I ran back inside to find John in the same position. His eyes were still oscillating and he was making a clicking noise in the back of his mouth, but he wasn't shaking yet. *We've still got time,* I thought, as I pulled the coffee table in front of the couch out of the way.

Carlos and Bill had gone around, and they came rushing through the open front door, Emily and Michelle right behind. "What can we do?" several voices said, almost in unison.

"Any minute he'll be in a full-convulsive seizure," I said to the men. "When it happens, try to protect his head, that's the most important thing, and make sure he has air." I felt I was talking twice as fast as normal. I hoped they could understand me.

I turned to John, who was still half reclining on the couch: "Babe," I said, "Carlos and Bill have come to help." I wasn't sure if he could hear.

"Hi Carlos," John said slowly, looking up but with eyes unfocused. He was trying to say something more, to get his tongue around some thought, but all that came out was a bizarre mixture of syllables and sounds.

As I dialed 911, I heard Carlos say, "Don't try to talk, John. We're here if you need us, buddy."

"What is your emergency?" a woman on the other end of the line asked.

I knew this by heart: "My husband is having a seizure. We need an ambulance right away." I gave her our address.

"Melinda!" I think it was Bill who said it. I turned to see that the full seizure, the grand mal, was there.

I cannot tell you. Really, I cannot tell you what it's like. I've seen it happen to my husband over half a dozen times now, and still, there's no way I can get my words around it.

It's the shaking that's the worst, the sudden violent shaking as if a million volts of electricity have suddenly surged into his body, causing every muscle, every sinew, joint, and piece of cartilage to cinch up, then erupt in random, hard jerks, jolt after jolt after incessant jolt. Or as if his brain is ordering him to go thirty directions at once, and his body has totally broken down under the overload of information, and it just lies rigid now, wildly vibrating, banging against anything in its way. Or as if some horrible invisible trickster has gained access to his brain, has pushed his will out of the way, and is now using his body as a tool to create the most appalling scene imaginable.

Within five seconds, John was on the floor on his back, his face a bright red rigid mask, eyes wide open, mouth locked shut, every muscle clenched like iron, his body listing to the left as convulsions exploded throughout his frame and his head hit the carpet repeatedly. From far back in his throat came a dreadful straining growl, as if he were begging, from the deepest part of his being, for this to stop, pleading with us to find some way to make this stop for him.

Oh, I would, I would, I would, John, if I only knew how! But I don't know how!

Carlos and Bill had pushed the couch back as soon as John fell, and they were trying to get cushions under his head, but he was moving too violently. The 911 operator was asking me if he was in full convulsions yet.

"Yes!"

"Has he done this before?"

"Many times! He's epileptic."

"Does he take medications?"

"Yes! He's not missed any!"

The operator must have heard the panic in my voice, because she was telling me to stay calm, while Carlos and Bill continued trying to force some protection under John's head. Emily and Michelle had come to stand by me, and I could feel their hands on my shoulders in support. I thought how terrible this must seem to the others and felt suddenly embarrassed—especially for John that his friends had to witness this. At the same time, I felt deep gratitude that they were there to help us.

But my main emotion was just an intense desire for the seizure to end *now,* and for the paramedics to get there. "Is the ambulance on its way?" I was practically shouting at the operator.

She assured me it would be there soon, and as she continued to talk with me, I watched Carlos and Bill kneeling by John, still trying to do something, anything, to help him. I felt their frustration as they realized there was nothing to do except try to keep him away from the furniture.

After a moment, Bill called to me, "Melinda, he's not getting any air. He's turning purple."

I took the few steps to where I could see John's face better, and it was true. His jaws were still rigid, and I could hear his raspy breaths as he tried to suck in air through a mouth clenched tightly shut and ringed now with foam.

"What should we do?" Carlos asked me.

"I don't know," I replied. There was no way the guys could pry John's mouth open while his body was gyrating so violently. And that might be dangerous, anyway. "Maybe if you turn him on his side, his mouth will clear of saliva and he'll be able to breathe better."

Then, to the operator: "He's asphyxiating! Please tell them to hurry, hurry!"

Be patient, I told myself. *They'll be here any minute now.* But then I remembered what had happened last year, when the paramedics had taken a wrong turn, which had delayed them by several minutes. "Do they have the right address?" I asked. "Do they know how to get here?"

"Yes, I'm sure they do," the operator replied. She continued talking to me, asking how John was doing, and I kept reporting to her that he was still in full seizure.

Emily and Michelle were saying something to me about shoes. I realized that I was in my bare feet and they wanted to help me get my things together for the trip to the emergency room. I quickly told them where my shoes and purse were and Emily went to get them.

The seconds were rushing by. Surely, it had been well over five minutes since I'd dialed 911. Where were the paramedics? I suddenly remembered that someone should be out in front to help guide them. "Michelle, will you talk to the operator?" I asked, and she took the phone from me as I ran out to the front yard barefoot, expecting to hear the siren and see the red lights rushing down the street. No sign.

I waited for a moment, then hurried back inside, hoping the seizure might have run its course by now, with John entering the post-ictal stage. But nothing had changed. His breathing was still labored and his face remained a vivid purple. He was soaked in sweat from the strain the convulsions were putting on his body. Red bubbles on his lips showed that he had probably bit into his tongue.

"How long has it been?" I asked Emily.

"About ten minutes, I think."

"They should be here!" I ran back out and tried to calm my breathing as I listened for the siren. Still nothing. Several neighbors from across the street had come out to see what was happening. One woman called over to ask me.

"My husband's having a seizure," I yelled back. "We're waiting for the ambulance. We need the ambulance!" After another minute I again ran inside to find John still convulsing as strongly as at the beginning.

"Where are they!? Where are they!?" I felt myself starting to cry. Dimly, I heard Michelle asking the operator what had happened to the ambulance. Emily was trying to calm me down.

"Melinda," Carlos said, "we have to do something. He's turning blue."

I looked at John and saw that all trace of blood had drained from his face. No longer with even the tinge of red that goes to make up purple, his skin had turned metallic blue. The only other color was a thin line of blood falling from the corner of his mouth. He was still alive, still shaking as violently as ever. But his face was a cold blue death mask.

"Oh my God, no!" I screamed.

It had never been like this before. Usually, the seizure was over by now, and John was up and trying to walk, acting belligerently, but on his way back to normalcy. And never before had he had such difficulty breathing, never had he turned blue like this. The rasps were still there, still loud, but seeming weaker, more desperate. Even If he was getting any air into his lungs, it couldn't be enough to sustain him much longer.

Breathe, John, breathe, breathe! I screamed in my mind, absurdly trying to will it to happen.

Suddenly it seemed clear to me: he was going to die. My husband, a mere thirty-seven years old, was going to die right there, on the floor, die this horrible death, with his friends wanting to help but powerless to do anything about it, and with his wife running in and out of the house like a madwoman, trying futilely to hurry along the only people who might be able to save him, people who were somewhere else, maybe at that very moment checking a map as they tried to find their way. Who knew where they might be? Close or far away, it didn't matter. The only important thing was that they weren't there, where they were supposed to be. And when they got there, my husband would be gone. All they would find would be a dead body on the floor.

Please, God! I prayed in desperation as I ran back out into the yard. *Don't let him die like this! Make it not too late. Make them come!* And I looked up the street and saw flashing red lights in the distance.

I started waving my arms wildly, and when the ambulance was safely in the driveway, I ran back into the house: "They're here! They're here!" A few seconds later, the paramedics were running in behind me, already opening their cases as Carlos and Bill stood back to give them access to John.

One of the men stopped beside me: "I'm sorry we were late. We lost contact with the tower and they had to radio us twice."

I looked at my watch and saw that it was a full fifteen minutes since I first called. But I was so glad they had finally arrived, I had no heart to complain. "You're here now," I said. "Just take care of him. That's all that's important."

The man led me to where I couldn't see very well what the other paramedics were doing with John, then started asking about the seizure and his medications. I knew I must be looking and acting like a wreck, with as much sweat dripping off of me as was pouring off John, and my voice still loud and shrill. I took a deep breath and tried to calm down so I could answer his questions as clearly as possible. At the same time, I kept trying to see what the others were doing to treat my husband.

Within a few minutes, they had him strapped onto a gurney and were taking him out.

"Would you prefer to go in the ambulance or follow in your car?" said the man.

"I'm going with him."

I watched them put John in the back and saw that he wasn't convulsing so violently now, though his arms and legs were still shaking despite the straps. I knew from prior experience that they had injected something to relax his muscles. Emily handed me my shoes and purse, and after I climbed into the passenger seat of the ambulance, I called a heartfelt "Thank you" to my friends. A moment later, we were on our way to Mission Hospital, siren blaring.

My view of John was obstructed when I looked behind me, but I could see the paramedics using some kind of air pump on him and could hear them asking him questions. *Maybe he's regained consciousness,* I thought. But I wasn't sure. His answers, insofar as I could hear them, were unintelligible.

In actuality, it didn't take long to get to the emergency room at Mission, but I remember thinking that the cars in front of us weren't making way for us quickly enough. *Move over, move over! Get out of our way!* I kept urging them in my head, upset that they didn't seem to understand the gravity of the situation.

At the ER, the paramedics rushed John in on the gurney, while I was taken to the reception desk through a waiting room filled with people in various forms of distress—mothers with babies, fathers with children, couples, entire families, an elderly man who appeared to be alone. *If these people are in an emergency situation, why are they just sitting here?* I wondered. The main ER was equally crowded. Patients, doctors, nurses everywhere, in every nook and cranny. *How can so many people get into so much trouble on Easter Sunday?* I thought. *On the most hopeful of holidays.* But I knew how. It just suddenly happens.

I filled out the forms they gave me as quickly as I could and answered more questions. I was then allowed to go to the small curtained cubicle where they had taken John.

I wasn't ready for what I saw. Somehow on the way to the hospital I had talked myself into believing that soon after we arrived, everything would be all right. After all, John's shaking had been greatly reduced before we left the house, the paramedics had been giving him oxygen on the way in, and they had apparently gotten enough response from him to be asking him questions. Not to mention the facts that the seizure was due to be over long ago and that he had already been in the ER for a quarter of an hour. I half expected to see him flash me a big smile and make some slightly risqué comment about the nurses.

But it wasn't so. He lay on the gurney, where four or five doctors and nurses were working on him. They seemed intent, their expressions worried as they talked quietly among themselves. John's eyes were shut and he was still sweating profusely as his arms and one leg shook. His face, though no longer blue, remained a vivid purple, and his breathing was still labored, as he continued to suck in air with those ragged, noisy breaths.

I didn't want to bother the people helping him, but I couldn't keep from asking, "Is he going to be all right?"

"He's still seizing," a man of about forty, whom I took to be a doctor, replied. "We're trying to stabilize him."

Still seizing. I tried to calculate how long it had been since the beginning of the convulsions and was shocked when I realized it had been over an hour.

"Do you think it will stop soon?"

"We can't say," he said.

I continued to watch the staff working over John as they hooked up and checked some monitor, occasionally conferring. I couldn't tell what their plan was, but it didn't make sense for me to be bothering them by asking more questions at this point. I needed to call back home to Missouri, anyway, to tell Mom and John's parents, Rock and Judy, what had happened. I hurried outside to use my cell phone.

There was no answer at home, so I left a message, then tried John's parents. When Judy answered, I told her that John had had a major seizure and was now in the ER, still convulsing. She was understandably very worried. We talked for a moment, and I said I would call again as soon as there was a change.

I then phoned my twin sister Melanie in St. Louis and my younger sister Amanda in Mississippi, and talked to each for a few minutes. I told them how scared I was. "I don't know what's going to happen," I said. "Please pray hard for John." They both said they would and encouraged me to stay strong.

When I got back inside, I discovered what the plan had been. A nurse stopped me before I got to John and told me they had hooked him up to a respirator and I should be prepared. I saw quickly what she meant. On one side of the gurney there now stood a new machine, out of which snaked a long white flexible tube that entered John's mouth and ended somewhere deep in his throat. I felt myself gag in sympathy, as if the tube were probing my own insides, and I cringed at the cavernous, metallic sound the machine made as it rhythmically pumped air into his lungs and then exhaled for him.

"It may look a little frightening," the nurse said, "but his color is better already." She was right. John's face was a bright red now. Despite my initial reaction to the machine, it was giving him the oxygen he needed, which was the important thing. *Thank you, Lord.*

But he was still seizing. His arms and legs continued to shake as several people hovered over him.

After a moment the nurse continued, in a somber voice, "You need to call his family." She motioned toward the desk. "You can use the phone here."

"All the family members are out of state," I said.

"It doesn't matter. Call them." She seemed adamant, as if John's being on the respirator was an especially ominous sign.

"Do you think he will be all right?" I asked her as we walked to the desk.

"The doctors will do their best, dear."

I dialed John's parents again. "Judy, they've attached him to a respirator to help him breathe. He's still seizing."

"Will it stop soon?"

"I don't know."

"Should we come out?"

"I don't know what to tell you. This isn't like any of his other seizures. I just don't know yet."

Judy said she would phone John's sister Jill and his younger brothers, Joe and Jimmy, to tell them what was happening.

I thought briefly about calling my twelve-year-old daughter Blake, who was spending the Easter holiday with her father in St. Louis. I decided that at this point there was no reason to worry her about her John-Daddy.

I wanted so badly to talk to Mom, but when I dialed home again, there was still no answer. "Mom," I said in my message, "it's me. Please call me as soon as you can."

Why aren't you home when I need you, Mom?

I went back to try to be as close as I could to John, while staying out of everyone's way. Several people were still working with him. It looked like they were doing some kind of test. Frightened and longing for someone to share the burden with, I decided to call Emily. I went outside again to use my cell phone.

"We're in the ER now at Mission," I told Emily. "John's still convulsing and they've put him on a respirator. It's really scaring me. I hate to ask you this, but could you possibly come down and stay with me for a while?"

Emily said that she and Michelle would be down right away.

I dreaded going back in, so I stood there for a few minutes in the cool evening. But I soon began feeling a chill out of proportion to the air. When I went back inside to John's cubicle, there was no change. It had now been two hours since the start of the seizure. I felt awkward just standing there, taking up space, while people on important missions were rushing by all around me. I didn't know what I was supposed to be doing. I could only watch helplessly as John lay unconscious and trembling, with that big tube going into his mouth. But where else did I belong?

I was relieved to see Emily and Michelle. After we hugged, we talked quietly, watching the people who were monitoring John. Michelle thought that at some level, he might be able to hear us, so she stood by the side of the gurney and tried to talk to him.

"John, if you can hear me, please know that everything's going to be all right," she said, her gentle voice contrasting with the mechanical breathing of the machine. "You're in a good hospital now. The doctors and nurses here will take excellent care of you. Don't give up, John. Never give up."

She turned to me: "Do you think he can hear me?"

"I don't think so, really," I said, honestly. I had asked John after other seizures what had been his last memory. Had he heard me calling 911, for example? His replies had always indicated that he remembered nothing that happened once the full seizure started, which seemed to show that he was totally unconscious during that time.

But one of the nurses offered, "Well, you never know for sure. It's possible. It doesn't hurt to try."

The woman's words encouraged Michelle, and she kept talking to John, telling him how everyone wanted so much for him to be well, listing the many people, including her kids and neighbors, who were rooting for him. There were tears in her eyes as she talked to him about how she and Bill missed the old neighborhood, including John and me, and how she knew that John was going to be all right and would be sleeping in his own bed soon.

It was touching to see this good friend trying to comfort my husband, and I wanted to believe that maybe the nurse was right, that at some level he could hear her. But when I saw Michelle's tears, I wondered at my own dry eyes, wondered why I wasn't the one talking to him.

Not that I wasn't caring for John. I stayed as close by his side as I could so I could hold his unsteady hand and reach out to rub his forehead or cheek, to assure him of my nearness and love. But even in doing so, I felt somehow numb, as if I wasn't fully occupying my body.

Just a couple of hours before I had been almost crazy with action, but now I felt emotionally separated from the reality before me. It was as if I was experiencing John and those caring for him through some strange filter that was protecting me from the brunt of what was happening.

Even my prayers seemed to be going through that filter. They were hurried, almost inarticulate, amounting to little more than my thinking *Please God, please help him.*

So I was thankful when a stylishly dressed young woman flowed into the scene, seemingly out of nowhere, to remind me that God was there with John and me.

"Are you a Christian?" the woman said, as she reached out to take my hand.

"Yes, I am." I looked at the cross hanging from her neck and felt for mine—my grandmother's cross with fourteen tiny diamonds—but it wasn't there. I couldn't believe it. I wore that cross almost constantly, and here, Easter Sunday, I had neglected to put it on. It was still back at the house in my jewelry box.

"You have such a lovely cross," I said. "And I'm embarrassed that I don't have mine on."

Immediately, the woman bowed her head and removed her chain. "Here," she said. "Wear this."

I tried to refuse, but she so graciously insisted that I took it. When I slipped it over my head, I felt heartened at once.

"Place your hands on your husband," she said. "We should pray." I did what she said. I took John's hand as I continued holding hers.

She bowed her head again: "God, this man is terribly ill," she said. "Please heal him. And please take care of this woman. Allow this couple to be together and to live a happy life. In your name we pray this, Lord Jesus. Amen."

I thanked the woman. Her generosity, grace, and simple prayer had managed to circumvent the filter, causing tears to well up in my eyes.

We spent a few minutes in conversation, and I learned that she had come there to see her father, who was having heart trouble. I asked her what church she belonged to, and when she said Saddleback, I was surprised. "That's my church, too," I said. I didn't remember seeing her there before, but the Saddleback congregation is very large. Still, she seemed so lovely and angelic that I wondered how I could have missed her.

A moment later, she said "goodbye" and was gone before I remembered that I was still wearing her cross.

Emily and Michelle stayed with me for another half-hour, then I told them I felt better and hoped they would go home to spend what little was left of Easter with their families. They had been a great comfort to me.

After they had gone, I located the father of the young woman with the cross in another part of the ER. Her mother was there, too, and she gave me her daughter's address so I could return the cross. Then I thought of Mom again. Surely, she would be home by now. After checking John and finding there was no change, I went outside to call.

"Mom, where are you? Please come to the phone! John's not doing well. He's still unconscious, still seizing. I need you to pray now, Mom. Please pray now."

I couldn't understand why she wasn't home. It was eight-thirty, over four hours after the seizure had begun, and ten-thirty back in Missouri. Where would she and Daddy be out so late on a Sunday night?

I stayed in the increasingly cool night air for ten minutes, dreading going back inside, thinking that the extra time would make it more likely that John would have stopped shaking when I got back.

It didn't work. A doctor who had previously identified himself as a neurologist was checking on John, and I asked him whether he had any idea when the convulsions would stop. He replied that he was sorry, but he didn't. They were doing everything they could, he said, but this was a most unusual case.

The presence of Emily and Michelle, and the woman who prayed with us, had dissipated my anxiety and fears for a while. But now they quickly returned. I had thought that over the years I had pretty much gotten my arms around the difficult business of John's epilepsy, but the length and severity of this attack showed me I had things to learn.

At some level, I was as horrified by what was happening now as I had been at the house. And in some ways, this was even worse. Back then, it had been easy to believe that getting medical help would solve the problem. But now it was clear that the doctors had no firm idea of how it would turn out: when John would wake, when he would be able to breathe on his own. They didn't even know when he would stop seizing.

With so many unanswered questions, the filter—that sense of numbness and distance—returned. It was probably a way of coping with my fear, but if so, it was far from perfect. I could feel the terror roiling around in me somewhere below the surface, threatening to break out at any moment into utter panic.

As I held John's hand, I thought about our morning together. It had been the most promising start to a day for us in a long time. For months, our marriage had been in trouble. We had argued and fought and cried, and at times it had seemed that our life together was almost certainly doomed. But then had come that morning, when we had decided to go to Laguna to have breakfast and take a stroll along the beach. In our several years in California, we had never, just the two of us, taken a walk by the ocean, and that Easter morning had turned out to be the perfect time. The shoreline was almost deserted, leaving us our own private beach, and it was a beautiful walk, with no arguments and no raised voices. We even held hands, as we often had during our early marriage. John took off his shoes and socks and rolled his pants legs up, and as we strolled along the wave-kissed sand, I saw him as a handsome beachcomber, a vital, confident man whom I had continued to love throughout our troubles.

And a very strong man. For twenty years now he had fought epilepsy, ever since it had developed after a baseball accident in high school when he and another player had both leapt for the same fly ball and their skulls had smashed together in a crack that everyone in the bleachers could hear. And despite several grand mal seizures, the many unpredictable five- or ten-second focal seizures that he experienced, the copious medications, and a sometimes misunderstanding society, he had managed to stay strong, vibrant, and positive, while rising to become a respected financial advisor.

Now look at him.

The questions jammed together in my mind. What was happening inside? When he woke would there be any permanent damage from this dreadful seizure? Or would he wake at all? Would he ever be able to hear me say the words "I love you" to him again?

It can't end this way. I thought. *It's not fair. He's fought too long. We've both fought too long and hard for this to happen. There's so much more to be done, to be accomplished by him, by us together. It just can't end here.*

You can't allow this to happen, God, I begged, almost angry. *Don't you understand? We've come too far, tried too hard. It isn't his time! Please God!*

The longer I stood there, facing the unknown, the more wrought up I became. I turned and went outside to try home again.

"Hello?"

"Mom! Finally! I've been trying to get you for hours!"

"Your father and I were at the movies and got home late. I just now played your messages, and every one sounded more desperate than the last. Is John all right? How is he?"

We talked for ten minutes, and I told her what I could. I hadn't fully realized how much I needed to hear her voice until she answered.

"Just pray, Melinda," she said at the end of the call. "Keep praying."

"I will, Mom. You too."

I took a deep breath, ready to face it again, then walked back inside. The neurologist and a nurse were standing over John. He had stopped shaking. For a moment, his stillness seemed odd, horrifying.

"Is he all right?"

"He's relatively stable now," the doctor said. "Just occasional movements of his arms and legs. He's quiet enough to enable us to do a CAT scan to determine if there is any skull damage. After that, we'll get him ready to transfer to intensive care."

Thank you, Jesus.

It was nine-fifteen, over five hours since the seizure had begun.

The CAT scan didn't take long. A few minutes later, several staff members were carefully wheeling John, along with the respirator, to ICU, as I followed behind. We had to traverse the waiting room that I had passed through when we first arrived. The faces had changed, but it was just as full as before.

As we slowly made our way, a man holding a wide-eyed little girl by the hand was arguing with a female receptionist. He seemed very angry. "What's going on here? Other people who came later have been getting in ahead of us!"

"Sir," the woman replied, "we are unusually busy tonight. And we have limited staff. We have to see the most serious emergencies first."

"We've been here for over an hour!" the man said. "Somebody needs to see her now!"

"Sir, I assure you that we will attend to your daughter as soon as we possibly can."

"It's because we're black, isn't it?" he said. "We have to go to the back of the bus, right?"

No, no, no! I thought. *That's not it! It has nothing to do with color. It's because they have to see those who are almost dying first. The ones whose hearts have stopped. The ones who turn blue because they can't breathe. The ones who can't stop shaking and shaking and shaking! Don't you understand? There are people on the edge of death in there!*

We left the man arguing with the receptionist as we turned into a hallway toward ICU. I stayed as close as I could to the gurney, worried that the orderly pushing the respirator wouldn't keep up and the tube would pull out of John's mouth.

Though the convulsions had finally ended, John still showed no signs of consciousness, and all of the most important questions remained unanswered.

As I followed him, I tried to appreciate the fact that the seizure had stopped, and not to think beyond that.

It was just as well. Not in my wildest dreams—or nightmares—could I have imagined what would occur over the next few days and weeks as I learned that what John had suffered was the rarest of seizures—*status epilepticus*—and as it gradually became clear to me what would be its aftermath.

Nor could I have imagined how, in the coming months, the effects of that long, hard day would play themselves out in the most bizarre, heartbreaking, and amazing ways. And how two bonafide heroes would emerge from those events—John and God.

CHAPTER TWO

THERE'S SOMETHING YOU SHOULD KNOW

With the respirator tube invading his mouth and his facial muscles slack from the ravages of the seizure, John was barely recognizable as we made our way to ICU. His pale, seemingly lifeless countenance contrasted starkly with that of the vigorous, animated man I had always known—successful financial advisor, proud father, skier, swimmer.

Oh yes, the swimmer. That handsome young swimmer . . .

Back in the early eighties, John swam for the Cape Girardeau high school swim team, while my twin sister Melanie and I swam for Sikeston. Because Cape and Sikeston are situated in the bootheel of Missouri, barely 30 miles apart, the two teams sometimes met in competition.

I know I must have seen John at several of the swim meets, because his parents and mine first got to know each other through those competitions. And years later, when he and I finally met, I immediately recognized his face. But I can't say for sure at which events I saw him, or the specific contexts. Somehow the memories got blurred during the intervening years.

I make up for it, though, by using my imagination to construct a scenario of what it may have been like the first time I saw John. In that way I re-create for myself the memory I might have had if the vicissitudes of youth had not eroded it. Here's what I see in my reconstruction:

I am sitting in the stands at some swim meet as I wait for my race to begin. I am watching one of the boys' events—after all, what else would I be doing at fourteen or fifteen? The event, let us say, is the men's one hundred-meter freestyle, and I notice one of the Cape Girardeau boys as he steps up on his starting platform. He looks to be about two years older than I am, and he's beautiful. Tall and lithe, with light brown hair and a golden tan, he has the classic broad shoulders of a swimmer. And I can see by the concentration on his face as he crouches slightly and focuses on his lane, that he's there to win.

The starting gun sounds, and the swimmers slice into the water. Being from Sikeston, I naturally want our boys to do well, and I cheer them on loudly. But at the same time, I pay close attention to the progress of the Cape boy I had noticed. At the flip and turn, he is a full length behind the leader, but halfway to the finish he is gaining ground. I see that he is swimming hard, with powerful strokes and kicks, stronger now than at the beginning. Near the end, he pulls even and, with his last stroke, stretches so far it seems he will throw his arm out of its socket, grazing the side of the pool with his fingers an instant ahead of the other boy.

The winner!

He glides up to the edge, turns, and tosses his head, causing drops of water to fly in a shining arc from his hair. And then, right there in the pool and the warm, wet air, amid smells of chlorine and the cheers and applause of the crowd—and I too am clapping loudly—he seems to look right at me and flashes a brilliant smile. As if to say, "I knew I could do it! Aren't you proud of me?"

Yes, I admit that the last little bit, the smile aimed right at me, may be a little fanciful. But erupting into a wide grin after a victory, or even after a good effort, is exactly the kind of thing that my John would have done. And as for looking my way—well, why wouldn't a good-looking Cape boy notice a not-so-shabby girl from Sikeston and want to show off to her a little?

However it may have happened that first time we had each other in sight, it wasn't until years later that we actually met. In the meantime, I had left home in Sikeston—where Daddy was a successful commercial farmer and Mom lovingly cared for me, Melanie, and our younger sister Amanda—to go to the University of Missouri to major in Interior and Structural Design. I graduated early in three years, started my career, married in 1988, returned to Sikeston, had my beautiful daughter Blake in 1990, and was separated, after much counseling and many tears, in 1996.

John, after graduation, had left his home in Cape Girardeau, where his father and mother both owned businesses, to attend Southern Methodist University in Dallas where, in 1988, he too graduated early with a degree in Business Administration. He also married that year, became father to his dear son Briggs in 1992, earned an MBA and his law degree in 1993 from Loyola University in New Orleans, and divorced in 1995. Afterward, he went to Denver and then to Dallas to work in the credit card processing field.

Our paths—John's and mine—had diverged considerably during those years. But because we were rooted in the same area of southeast Missouri, it wasn't all that incredible when they again intersected.

It was mid-August 1996, and I was at my parents' thirtieth wedding anniversary celebration, enjoying the festivities. But in the back of my mind I was probably wondering, as I often did in those days, what was next for me. My divorce would be final in January, and I had no clear idea of what I was going to do next with my life. I was residing in my hometown, supporting myself and Blake by doing freelance interior design work, but I didn't see myself living practically on my parents' doorstep for the rest of my days. Yet I had nowhere else to go. And though I was open to meeting someone new, I didn't expect that to happen in tiny Sikeston.

My irrepressible twin was at the party, too, and at one point I noticed her across the room talking to a lady who had been a childhood friend of my father's. As Melanie kept looking my way with a devious smile on her face, I wondered what she was up to. A few minutes later she walked over to me and casually asked if I remembered John Wilferth. I told her I knew who the Wilferths were—weren't there several boys, and a girl too?—but I wasn't sure which one was John.

"Well, I've met him," she said, "and trust me, he's something. Better than that, I was over there talking to Nancy, who knows the Wilferths well, and found out that he's available." She then told me about his divorce the previous year. "And best of all," she added, waving a piece of paper in my face, "I was able to finagle his number from her after I gave her a sob story about how you're dying to hear his voice."

"You didn't!"

"Don't worry. I only suggested that it might be a good idea if you two young people finally got to know each other. I think it was the phrase "young people" that did the trick. It sounds so respectable."

She went on to give me such glowing reports about this John Wilferth guy that finally, though somewhat dubious about my sister's matchmaking prowess, I took the paper from her.

"Don't just stick it in your purse where you'll forget about it," she said. "Call him! He's perfect for you! Have I ever steered you wrong before?"

I couldn't help but laugh as I remembered a few tiny childhood cliffs that I had been nudged off of by this nervy young woman who had been my womb-mate for nine months.

"Okay. I'll call him. If only to prove you wrong."

The next day, nervous and a little surprised at my forwardness, I got up my courage and dialed the Dallas number, half wishing its owner would be out. But a few seconds later I heard a confident, "Hello, John here."

I introduced myself a little apologetically, and he immediately made me feel comfortable: "I'm happy to meet you, Melinda. Nancy phoned to tell me you might be calling." He then told me that he knew who I was and what I looked like, while swearing he didn't have me mixed up with my twin.

Far from proving my sister wrong, the conversation that ensued showed her to be a possible matchmaking genius. The voice on the other end of the line was friendly and gracious, while at the same time there was unmistakable dynamism there. John was warm and funny, and his words seemed to flow on a current of smooth, joyful energy. He captivated me immediately.

Every night for nearly two weeks, and sometimes long into the night, we talked. And at the end of each conversation it was hard for me to get my head back on straight. Could I actually be falling in love with a man by phone? I had never even met the guy. Melanie had said that he was really something, but I had learned over the years that her "really something" was often quite different from mine. But as the conversations continued, I concluded that it didn't really much matter what he looked like. It was his personality, the person himself, that I found enchanting.

John, for his part, was apparently as taken by me as I by him. He never seemed to get enough of our conversations, hanging on my words as much as I wanted to hear his. As we continued to talk, we found ourselves agreeing on many important issues revolving around relationships—the way a couple should support each other, how to raise kids, creating a beautiful home, striving for the best.

Each night, after I had reluctantly put down the receiver and the glow had worn off a bit, I wondered if our seeming compatibility was another bubble that would soon burst. After tossing that around for a few minutes, I would tell myself just to wait: don't be too skeptical, or too hopeful, just wait.

That wasn't hard to do because I knew I wouldn't have to wait long. John had been planning for some time to come back home to go dove hunting, and the date happened to be the second weekend after our first conversation. We would soon be able to discover whether our mutual infatuation could stand the test of full-scale reality.

On a Saturday morning in late August, he arrived at my door to take me to his family's farm in Cape Girardeau. When I answered the bell, I not only immediately recalled his face, I saw that this time Melanie's "really something" very much agreed with my own ideas.

The first thing you notice about John is his huge smile, and as soon as I saw it, he captivated me all over again. As for the rest, picture that young man at the swimming pool, add a few years of seasoning out in the world—but keep a large measure of boyish charm—and you will have him.

I was able to meet most of John's immediate family at the farm. He introduced me to his parents Rock and Judy, his younger sister Jill and her husband August, and his younger brothers Jimmy, with his wife Chrisy, and Joe, with his fiancée Anna. The men spent part of the afternoon out playing man games, while we women held down the fort in style. Still, John and I managed to spend most of Saturday together.

Sunday was a continuation of our delightfully long first date, but by early afternoon it was time for John to drive me back to Sikeston and then continue on to Dallas. I expressed my appreciation to his family for their warm welcome, then climbed into John's small SUV. I had no idea that the brief trip I was embarking on would include John's saving my life.

The short dirt and gravel road that led to the highway passed through late summer woods that already showed a few hints of the coming fall. But the many oaks and maples were mostly arrayed in green robes, full and rich. It was a beautiful day, except the sky and the landscape kept jittering because of the road. I hardly noticed the rough ride, though, as John and I talked about the farm and the weekend that had gone by too soon.

Wanting to make sure my breath was fresh, I suppose, in case we were to pull over for a moment to observe some feature of the landscape and the opportunity for a kiss presented itself, I had just stuck a new stick of spearmint gum in my mouth. It never occurred to me that to chew gum while talking and riding over a bumpy road might be a bad idea. At least not until a particularly rough jolt and a sudden intake of breath left the wad of gum stuck at the top of my windpipe.

I tried to cough, but nothing happened. There was no air going out. I tried to say something, but again, with no air able to escape my lungs, not a sound, not even a whisper, resulted. And of course, there was no air going in, either.

John was focusing on the road and had no idea yet of the drama that had begun playing itself out beside him. For several seconds I continued trying to dislodge the gum by moving my neck or trying to force air out, unable to believe that such a tiny object could obstruct my entire airway. But still, not even a gagging sound came from my mouth.

In increasing panic, and finally realizing that this was a job I couldn't handle myself, I turned to John. Perhaps twenty seconds had elapsed since the gum had first gotten stuck, and it took me another few seconds to get John's attention, as he remained focused on his driving. He glanced at me with a puzzled expression, his eyes still half on the road.

"Are you all right?" he asked.

I motioned with my hands to my neck and shook my head hard: No!

A few minutes before, I had offered him a stick of gum, too, which he had refused, but he knew I had taken one for myself. He realized at once that I was choking on the gum I had been chewing.

He slammed on the brakes and at the same time pulled hard on the emergency brake. We stopped so fast that for an instant I thought the gum must surely fly forward out of my throat. But it didn't.

He undid his seat belt and was out of the SUV immediately. In the meantime, I continued my internal struggle to somehow dislodge the gum, or at least to change its position so that at least a little air would be able to get into my lungs. It wouldn't move.

By the time John was at my door, forty seconds must have gone by since the gum had gotten stuck. Maybe that wouldn't have been a particularly long time to go without air, but I had been talking, and therefore mostly exhaling, so there was little air in my lungs at the instant the gum got stuck. The evidence was in the fact that I was already feeling dizzy and weak.

John opened my door and began unbuckling my seat belt. *Hurry, hurry, hurry,* I was thinking in one part of my mind, while another was struck by the fact that I was just sitting there, doing nothing. *I should be helping him,* I thought, but I felt as if I were in a dream, with my will disconnected from my limbs.

I remember him pulling my shoulder harness away, taking me in his arms, and lifting me out of the vehicle. My head was somehow thrown back, and the trees above us seemed to be spinning. They also appeared to be losing the light. *It's too early for the sun to be setting,* I thought.

I vaguely felt John turning me until he was at my back, his arms around me. Everything was fading quickly now and my vision had turned almost black. Suddenly, I felt an enormous pressure in my solar plexus, accompanied by a tremendous exhalation, and at that instant felt something hit the back of my front teeth.

I was so near to passing out that I didn't realize the gum had flown from my mouth. But my body knew, and at once I began gulping in air. My lungs were so starved for oxygen, I couldn't seem to get enough of it.

Almost at once, the light started coming back, as quickly as it had gone. *Oh my God,* I thought, as I saw the trees returning. I had never seen anything more beautiful than the world in full light again.

I found my legs and John let me go. "Are you okay now?" he asked.

"I think so," I said between fits of coughing. "Thank you so much." Saliva had somehow gotten into my windpipe, and I bent over to try to get it out, my throat burning. Tears started forming in my eyes, not just from the pain in my throat but from my embarrassment as I pictured myself coughing and spitting on the ground. As I thought of my stupidity in allowing myself to choke on a piece of gum and my helplessness during the ordeal, I grew even more ashamed.

I think John must have sensed my mortification, because he started trying to make light of the incident. "It could have happened to anybody," he said. "I'm just glad I was able to do something."

"I sat there like a store mannequin," I said, straightening. "I didn't do a thing to help myself. Or you."

"What could you have done?" he asked. "You were totally limp in my arms. Almost passed out."

After a few more minutes of my coughing and sputtering, we climbed back into the SUV and proceeded to the highway and on to Sikeston. I didn't have much to say, but just sat quietly and processed what had occurred, still embarrassed. The incident kept playing through my mind, especially the way John had taken charge as soon as he understood what was happening. It seemed to me that no sooner had he opened his own door, than he was at mine. And every one of his movements afterward had been exactly right—pulling me out of the SUV, turning me, holding me, then immediately performing the Heimlich maneuver as he forcefully applied the right amount of pressure at the precise location. Every action had been perfectly executed.

At one point, he glanced at me and said, "Did you see the way that gum flew out?"

"I think I felt it against my teeth," I replied. "But by then I was as good as blind."

"Well, it shot out like a bullet," he said. "Too bad there were no doves flying by."

I started laughing and ended up in another coughing fit.

A little later, he walked me to my door. I still felt like a mess, but we had a brief goodbye kiss anyway. Through it, I tried to show him how I felt about what he had done for me. I had been the archetypal damsel in great distress, and he the proverbial hero. As far as I was concerned, he had saved my life.

As I waved goodbye, I realized that I had learned at least one important thing that weekend. I now knew that whenever I was in danger, I wanted John Wilferth to be right next to me.

With John back in Dallas and me in Sikeston, our nightly phone conversations continued over the next several weeks. Though we didn't talk explicitly about engagement or marriage, we seemed to be growing steadily closer. I wasn't sure of John's ultimate intentions, but for my part I was becoming increasingly certain that I wanted to be his wife.

One night about a week after our first date, he seemed a little withdrawn early in our talk, and I wondered if he was feeling under the weather. When I asked him, he said, "Melinda, there's something I should tell you."

The unaccustomed gravity in his voice suggested to me that this was probably not going to be a something I would like. "You know you can tell me anything," I said. "What is it?"

"There's a problem I've had since high school," he replied. He told me about the baseball accident in which he and the other boy had slammed into each other head-on. "The collision split my head open. There's a scar on the left side from my hairline to my crown."

"I never noticed it when you were here," I said. "But I don't see any problem. If you ever go bald, we'll just consider it to be a mark of distinction from your wild youth. Or we could tell people that I hit you over the head with a vase in a pique."

He laughed briefly, but his serious tone remained. "There's something else. Ever since the accident, I've had occasional seizures. You know, epileptic seizures. Not many, but once in a while I have them."

"Are they dangerous?"

"The biggest danger is of me hurting my head. But they're always over quickly. Then I'm fine."

"How often do they occur?" I asked. "Do you have any way to control them?"

"Yes. I take medications. They help. But it's not perfect control. I haven't had one for about two years, but it's always a possibility. It's just something I've learned to live with."

I was able to grasp the essence of what John was saying because, like most people, I had a vague understanding of epilepsy. And it wasn't a completely sanitized version, because I had seen a young man having a major convulsive attack on the University of Missouri campus. But what John was saying didn't overly concern me. He insisted that the episodes were rare and were over quickly, and that they didn't greatly impinge on his life.

Later, of course, as our relationship developed, I made it my business to learn more about epilepsy. I quickly discovered the difference between the small five- or ten-second focal (petit mal) seizures that the subject may not even realize he or she has had, and the full-generalized convulsive (grand mal) seizures that we tend to think of when we think of seizures at all. I learned to discern the signs of an impending attack, such as reports of an aura or of feeling dizzy, a clicking noise in the back of the throat, unfocused eyes, or difficulty in hand-eye coordination. And I learned a lot about the medications that are used to control epilepsy and about various seizure triggers, such as stress and alcohol.

I also discovered that there is much that remains a mystery about the condition. Though it is has long been known that seizures occur as a result of disruptive electrical activity in the brain, scientists still don't understand the precise mechanisms that bring on the disruption.

That air of mystery is probably one reason a stigma remains attached to epilepsy. I learned about that in time, too, the stigma. It may not be as strong as it was just a few decades ago, but still, when you tell people that your husband has epilepsy, their response is often subtly different than if you had told them he has arthritis or a broken leg. I think it's mostly because epilepsy still strikes many as a kind of mental illness because its focus is the brain and because of the unusual behavior that occurs during a seizure. But they're wrong. It isn't a mental illness. Yes, it's a disorder of the brain, but the brain is as much a physical organ as the heart or kidneys or gall bladder.

Though I knew few such details about the illness during that phone call, my attitude wouldn't have changed if I had known. It was clear to me that my proper role in the matter was simply to understand that this was a fact that came along with John and to support him totally. After all, by this time I was, without question, in love with the man.

After he had finished saying what he needed to say, I replied, "Okay. Well, thank you for telling me. But if you're trying to get rid of me, it didn't work. It doesn't change my feeling for you in any way. We'll deal with it together."

If anything, that brief conversation tightened our bond. I respected John for wanting to disclose his condition to me early in our relationship, and I know he appreciated my response of total acceptance.

Of course, it can sometimes be easy to "accept" something when it's not much more than an idea in your head. But would I be so accepting if I was present when John had a major attack? It had been two years since he had undergone a full-generalized convulsive seizure, and for all we knew at the time, it might be another two years, or more, before another one. As it turned out, however, we wouldn't have to wait that long. In fact, it would be only a few weeks before my words to John that night would be put to a severe test.

By mid-October it was time for our second real date, and John had suggested that we fly separately to New Orleans and meet for the weekend. He knew the city well from having attending graduate school there, and was eager to show me around.

We met at the New Orleans airport amid kisses, hugs, and avowals of love, and within an hour we were checked into a nice hotel where John had reserved a room. As we unpacked, I talked about how much I was looking forward to exploring the French Quarter that I had heard so much about.

"There's this great pub I know," John said as he hung up his shirts. "The best three-piece jazz ensemble in New Orleans plays there every night. We have to go there later. You will love it."

He continued telling me about other places he wanted to take me to, but then he grew quiet. When I looked at him, there was a strange, intense smile on his face. It was nothing like his normal smile, but more a grimace, as if he were frightened at something and using the smile to fight it off. At the same time, I heard a brief series of clicking noises that seemed to be coming from his throat.

"Are you feeling all right?" I asked. He shook his head, as if to say not to worry, but he said nothing.

I had grown up in a southern family in which food was always a chief tool for smoothing things over and keeping everyone happy, so that was my first thought, food. "You're probably hungry," I said. "I know I am. We've unpacked enough. Let's go find a restaurant and try some of that great New Orleans cuisine you keep crowing about."

"Yeah, let's do that," John replied. "I do need something."

As we took the elevator down, I chattered away, but John didn't say much. There were no more clicking noises, though.

When we stepped outside the hotel, we spotted a fried-food café directly across the street. It wasn't exactly the kind of eating establishment I had in mind for our first meal together in New Orleans, but John was already walking across to the restaurant, not even waiting for me. Very much unlike him.

"Hey, you!" I called, "Wait!" I hurried to catch up and managed to latch on to his arm as he made a beeline for the restaurant.

The place was a kind of diner, and a very busy one at that. "Your food must be good here," I commented to the host as he showed us to an empty booth.

John barely glanced at his menu before announcing that he had a craving for fried shrimp. I decided on something a bit lighter, and after ordering we sat back to wait. Though he appeared to be feeling better, John remained unusually quiet. I didn't have much to say either, as I continued observing him, trying to grasp what was happening. Despite the fact that the restaurant was so busy, our food came quickly, within five minutes.

"I'm starving," John said, lifting his fork. But when he tried to spear one of the shrimp, the tines of the utensil hit nothing but plate. Again and again he stabbed at the food, but was unable to make firm contact with even one of the creatures. Every time he brought up his fork, there was nothing but air on the end.

I couldn't understand why he was having such difficulty. Was he playing some trick on me? Or was he actually that uncoordinated? I watched him struggle for half a minute, then tried to make a joke: "Maybe those are the kind that prefer to be picked up by the fingers."

I glanced at his face to see if I had made him smile and saw at once that this was no laughing matter. His eyes were shaking back and forth faster than he could have possibly made them move by willpower. No wonder he couldn't coordinate the movement of his hand with his eyes. The shrimp plate must have looked to him as if it were on one of those paint-mixing machines that shake the can into a blur.

A thought that had crossed my mind back in the room was now confirmed: I realized I was probably observing the onset of that "something" I had learned about over the phone.

John's fork clattered against the plate, then fell to the floor as he lost his grip on it. I automatically bent down to retrieve it, thinking, *What do I do now?*

When I raised back up, John was facing me, saying nothing, apparently having given up all thought of food, his eyes still wildly vibrating and his head slightly shaking.

"John, look at me. Can you focus on me?"

He didn't reply, but it was obvious that the answer to my question was "No" as his eyes remained unsteady.

I turned to the people sitting at a table nearby. "Can someone help us here? I think my boyfriend may be having a seizure." The people glanced in our direction, but then looked away. I repeated my request to the customers in the booth behind me and received the same response.

I looked back to John. "Hon, can you hear me?" There was no answer.

I decided I had to get him out of there. For some reason I thought that if only I could get him outside to the sidewalk, into the fresh air, he might be better. And since no one was going to help me, I had to find a way to do that by myself.

I rose and stood by him. "John, can you get up? If we go outside, maybe you'll feel better." Still no answer.

I got a grip on his left upper arm and pulled: "Let's get out of here."

In reply, he slowly stood. But when I put one arm around him and tried to lead him out of the booth, he sat back down, hard. I tried to pull him up again, but he wouldn't budge.

Again I turned to the people in the tables and booths nearby: "Could someone please help us? My boyfriend may be having a seizure. He needs to go outside." People were staring at us now, but no one was responding to my pleas.

"I'll be right back," I said, then walked quickly to the host's podium at the front of the restaurant. It was becoming clear to me that John probably needed more than fresh air.

"I think my boyfriend is starting to have a seizure," I told the man. "He may need to go to the hospital, but I can't move him. Can you help us?"

The man accompanied me back to our booth. "Are you all right, Sir?" he asked John, but got no answer.

"We have to get him outside," I said, "and get a taxi to the hospital."

The man took John by his arm: "Sir, please rise."

"John, get up, get up," I urged. "We need to find a cab."

After some effort, the host managed to get John to his feet again. He then placed John's arm over his shoulders and led him out of the booth. I went to the other side and put his other arm over my own shoulders.

"Sir," the man said, "just walk with me outside."

"No!" John replied. His weight on my shoulder suddenly increased, as if he was about to collapse.

"Hon, it's okay," I said to him, "we're just going to find a taxi and take you to the hospital."

"No! Leave me alone!" he said loudly, but without trying to pull his arms away.

It took all my strength and that of the host, but we managed to move John a couple of steps. We stopped for a moment, then went forward again, slowly, slowly, weaving between tables toward the door. After we moved a staggering two or three steps, John would balk, telling us to stop, to let him be. He wasn't fighting us, but he wasn't helping us at all.

No one else was trying to help, either. The other customers remained seated at their tables, staring at us, talking among themselves. Maybe they thought John was drunk. Or on drugs. Whatever they thought, they didn't seem to approve of what was happening.

We don't approve either, people, I wanted to say. *But it's not what you think. It's not liquor or drugs. It's because he was in a baseball game and tried hard to catch a ball! It's an American thing!*

The progress of our clumsy trio was so painfully slow that it took over five minutes to reach the door. Once outside, we continued to laboriously make our way across the wide sidewalk to a taxi that had apparently been summoned by the restaurant management.

It probably took another five minutes to make it to the curb, with John still holding back. Occasionally he complained: "Stop! Leave me alone! I'm fine. I'm fine." But when I looked at his face, his eyes were still oscillating back and forth. Obviously he wasn't fine.

At several points I had to bend down, grasp one of his legs in two hands, and manually pick it up in order to move it forward. "Please take a step, John! Take a step, dammit!" I urged as I tried to force him to walk. At almost the same moment I would be praying: *Please God! Help me get this man to the car.*

When we finally made it to the taxi, it required another two or three minutes and the assistance of both the driver and the restaurant host to push John's head down and make him get into the back seat. When he was finally sitting, I thanked the host and told the driver that we needed to get to the nearest hospital.

"What's wrong with him?" the driver asked.

"I think he's having a seizure," I replied.

"Why didn't you call an ambulance?"

"I don't know," I said. "I didn't know what to do."

The driver shrugged. "I'll take you to Tulane University Hospital," he said as he got into the front.

The driver's question struck me as incredibly reasonable, and I've asked myself that same question many times since. Why didn't I just call an ambulance? The only answer I have is that I was a newbie at the matter of having a boyfriend with epilepsy. I wasn't even absolutely sure he was having a seizure. Or at least not sure that it was the onset of a grand mal attack.

He doesn't seem to be getting any worse, I thought as the driver sped away from the curb. *Maybe this is all there will be to it.*

That wasn't so hard to believe, because there was still no shaking. Though his eyes continued to vibrate, and he was making a kind of smacking noise with his mouth, it had been over fifteen minutes since the symptoms had begun, and they had basically stayed the same. *Maybe we should have just sat there in the restaurant,* I thought, *and let it run its course.*

There continued to be no change, for better or worse, during the ten minutes it took to get to the hospital. Once there, the driver pulled up to the emergency room, exited the taxi, and started trying to cajole John out.

I ran inside. "My boyfriend is out in the car," I said to the nurse at the counter. "I think he may be having a seizure. We can't get him out."

Inside of a minute, several medical technicians were running out to the taxi, pulling and pushing a gurney, with me following. Using the efficient movements of professionals, they quickly got John out of the car and onto the gurney. As I turned to the driver to pay him, I noticed that the men were pulling straps over John's midsection and buckling them down. I wondered why. It seemed inappropriate, given the fact that he wasn't shaking. The seizure just wasn't that bad.

I finished paying the driver, then went back inside to provide whatever information I could. A moment later the technicians were wheeling John through the door. *Thank goodness,* I thought. *We made it in time. And it isn't so bad as I had imagined. John said they don't usually last long, so he'll probably be over it soon.*

The technicians were pushing him past me. He couldn't have been more than ten feet away when I heard a low moan and the gurney seemed to jump. "He's going into it!" one of the technicians yelled.

What followed in the next moment, the severity of the convulsions, was shocking. I couldn't believe the power of John's sudden shaking. I started toward him, but the nurse I had been talking to took my arm: "Honey, calm down. He's having a grand mal seizure. They'll take care of him."

A few seconds later, the gurney disappeared through swinging doors. The nurse continued asking me questions, and I got the impression that they were at least partly to distract me as I kept hearing excited voices coming from the adjacent room.

"Good Lord!" I asked the nurse. "What's happening in there?"

"It's just the seizure," she replied. "He'll be all right once he's through it." She continued asking me questions—about his medical history, how he had behaved during previous attacks, his drugs. I had no good answers to any of them. Even if I had, I doubt that I could have concentrated on giving detailed information with the distressing commotion beyond the doors. At one point I heard someone yell, "Watch out! He's going into it again!"

About ten minutes after they had wheeled John into the next room, a young nurse came out, disheveled and sweating. "Your boyfriend is very, very strong," she said to me. "It's taking half the on-duty staff just to keep him down." She told me that he was going in and out of the grand mal seizure. She had left, she said, because he was swinging his arms so wildly that she was afraid he was going to strike her.

"I'm so sorry," I said, horrified.

"Don't worry," the older nurse said. "He doesn't know what he's doing. It's not his fault."

After a while, it got quieter in the other room. The older nurse told me that it sounded like he may have finally gone into the post-ictal stage that typically follows a seizure, and that he would probably be exhausted.

I called John's parents and told them what had happened. Rock expressed his gratitude that I had been with John, and I said I would make sure that the hospital took good care of him.

Finally, almost two hours after the full seizure had hit, they allowed me to go into the other room and talk with John. One of his arms was red from welts and scratches where the staff had tried to get an IV into him to inject calming drugs. He was very sleepy and kept nodding off as I held his hand. But he managed to tell me how sorry he was for what had happened.

"There's no need," I replied. "It doesn't mean I love you any less."

"What a trip this is turning out to be," he said, his eyes closed. "Let's get out of here and see some of New Orleans."

"Not at the moment, I'm afraid. They want you to stay overnight. And I concur. You obviously need the rest."

"Okay," he said. "But we'll hit it tomorrow."

That night I stayed in the ER, trying to sleep on the chairs and the floor. It wasn't easy, and I had a lot of time to think about what had transpired. I didn't know it then, but I had seen some things that day that I would see again and again in the future. I'm not referring just to the particular behaviors that signal the onset of one of John's seizures. I also saw, for the first time, the way he typically tries hard to deny that a seizure is coming, and even to fight it off somehow. That's what he had done all the way from the hotel room to the taxi as he kept saying that he was all right, when obviously he wasn't.

I had also seen, though only for a few seconds, what a full-generalized convulsive seizure was like for John. That brief glimpse, combined with the subsequent uproar from the other room and the harried nurse's report about John's strength and wildness, took away any last vestige of my innocence about his condition.

I decided that the experience had been a kind of test for me and that despite my ignorance, I had passed it reasonably well. Of course, I would do some things differently in the future. For one thing, I would dial 911, not a taxi. And I wouldn't wait, hoping against hope that the seizure wouldn't get any worse. I would call an ambulance right away.

But even with my mistakes, we had managed, just barely, to get to the hospital in time. Blunders and all, I had handled it.

Just as important, what I had told John was true. I loved him not one whit less for what had happened. Certainly, I understood better than ever that he had an unfortunate condition that had to be attended to. And I knew that if we were going to be together, I would have to make that my responsibility, too. But it made no difference to my feelings for him. He remained every bit as virile and attractive to me now as he had been before. He was the same man.

I prayed more than once that night, thanking God for allowing us to make the hospital in time and asking Him for John's full and quick recovery. I also wondered—as I have at other times since that day—at the fact that a major seizure occurred so soon after John and I had met. And that it had happened during one of the few times when we were actually together in those first months. Was God providing me a glimpse of what would be required of me if I were to stay with John? And was He, in that way, making it clear to me that I had better be prepared to love this man well?

At seven the next morning, John was wide-awake and ready to go. We still had an entire day and night in New Orleans, and he couldn't wait to get at it. Nor could I. I was eager to return to our room to shower and change, and then to learn what all the excitement about Bourbon Street was.

As John finished dressing, I talked to an early morning nurse outside his room. She asked me how John and I had met, and I filled her in on a few details of our relationship. She shook her head then and said, referring to the seizure, "You poor thing, having to go through this."

"Dear," I replied. "This is just the beginning. If I have my way, I'm going to marry that guy."

CHAPTER THREE

DARK CRESCENDO

John and I became engaged on Thanksgiving Day, 1996. We had both had big ceremonies in our previous marriages, so we decided to avoid all the rah-rah and instead to elope. We were married in Las Vegas at the New York, New York Hotel on my birthday in April 1997, after convincing a nice elderly lady who was playing the slot machines in the casino downstairs to act as our witness. A few days later, John and I set up housekeeping in Dallas.

The next six months felt like an extended honeymoon as we did practically everything together. To me, John was the perfect husband—thoughtful, kind, romantic, and with a thoroughly positive outlook on life. For my part, I tried to be the very supportive and attentive wife I knew he wanted me to be. But neither of us had to try hard to please the other, because we were in love and loved to show it. Our friends often laughed at us when we were out with them, telling us we should "get a room!" I was as happy as I had ever been in my life, having found this man who loved me as much as I loved him.

And it wasn't just to me that John was good. He strongly supported Blake, who was six at the time, signing on to be her soccer coach during the summer months. We were also able to spend many weekends with Briggs because John's former wife Charlotte lived in Dallas along with her new husband Patrick.

Briggs was four that summer, and we tried to do something special with him every weekend he stayed with us. John took rolls and rolls of pictures of his son on those outings, not knowing at the time how important the photographs would become to him a few years later.

But it wasn't all play back in those days. From the beginning, John was ambitious, always projecting himself into the future and wanting to better our lives as quickly as possible. He was fond of saying that he had never met a stranger, and he was prone to express his aspirations to anyone he saw, wherever he went. People seemed always willing to listen to him because of his ability to quickly ingratiate himself to practically anybody.

This skill made him into a wonderful natural salesman, and it wasn't long before he decided that his talents weren't being used to the maximum in the credit card processing field. He started looking for a job in the financial industry, and by the fall he had landed a position with a company selling high-level financial planning.

One drawback of the job was that John was required to do a lot of traveling, flying from state to state to talk with clients. This cut seriously into the togetherness we had come to enjoy, but by that time I had found a position as a representative for an interior design company, so I had my own work that allowed me to bring a second income into the household. And besides, we told ourselves that being apart occasionally was a price worth paying because it would enable us to more quickly make our dreams of a nice home come true.

By mid-1998, John's new position was beginning to pay off, with several lucrative deals almost ready to close, and all indications were that the company loved his performance. Then one day he arrived home from work in mid-morning.

"You're home early," I said. "Are you feeling all right?" My first thought was that he might have felt a seizure coming on.

"They let me go," he said, shaking his head. He looked dumbfounded.

"Who let you go?" I asked incredulously. "Let you go from what?"

"My job. I don't have a job any more."

"That's ridiculous! You've been doing wonderful work for them!"

"Not wonderful enough, I guess," he replied. "They dismissed me for lack of performance."

Neither of us could believe it. We *knew* he had worked very hard and had done an excellent job for the company. The firing made no sense whatsoever.

Later we came to understand that the real reason for John's being dismissed was that the person who had previously had his position wanted to return to the company. But it didn't matter what the reason—John felt betrayed after the fine start he had made. He wasn't one to sit around and mope, though, so he immediately started faxing and mailing out resumes. To help firm up our finances, I changed jobs from the rep position, which paid commissions, to one that offered me a steady paycheck.

Within a couple of months, John had found a position with another financial planning company. He felt he was back on the right track, but he was working even harder than before. It became increasingly clear that the almost idyllic early days of our marriage were gone. Those had been times in which hard work, combined with a relaxed and hopeful mental attitude, had carried us forward as if on a sea swell of good fortune. Now, because of being laid off from the previous job and his determination to excel at the new one, John's stress level had climbed, he was working longer hours, and our time together was less than it had been.

It was late 1998, a year and a half after we had gotten married, and during that time John had gone through two full-generalized convulsive seizures. Both of them had occurred in bed at night, but neither had lasted for more than fifteen seconds of shaking—not even enough time to call the paramedics. Immediately afterward, he had gone into a deep sleep, and in the morning had been fine. From this evidence, it appeared that the medications he was on were controlling his epilepsy.

But one night early 1999, just after we had gone to bed, he mentioned that he had a strange feeling in his stomach. "It's probably nothing," he said. "I just need some sleep."

But when I turned up the light, I could see that his eyes were oscillating. "I think you're going into a seizure," I said. "I'm going to call the paramedics." I reached for the phone, thankful that John had insisted on an apartment close to a fire station. Help was less than two hundred yards away.

He grabbed my arm. "I'm okay," he said, but his words were slurred. "There's no need to call." Then suddenly his body became rigid, and a second later he was shaking uncontrollably.

I called 911 while at the same time trying my best to prevent John from falling off the bed. After the operator had the information, I dropped the phone and put all my strength into trying to keep him near the middle of the mattress. Somehow I managed, though I'm not sure how long I could have held him, he was shaking so violently by that time. Thankfully, in only a matter of seconds I heard the siren, and I dared to leave him for a moment as I ran to the front door to make sure it was unlocked. Almost before I could get back to the bedroom, the paramedics were inside.

John stayed in the hospital that night and for part of the next day, but he was back at work the day after that, the incident apparently forgotten by him. But the seizure lingered in my own mind. It had been nearly on the scale of the one in New Orleans, and I wondered if the pressure he was putting on himself had helped bring it on.

For him, though, the episode was barely a hiccup in his busy schedule, and he continued driving himself as hard as ever, receiving several honors for exceeding company goals. After eight months, his efforts were about to pay off strongly as he began closing some of the deals he had put in motion. Then the company received a letter from the firm that had let him go, saying that John was under a three-year non-compete agreement and that his new company could be liable for having hired him. John protested this strenuously, pointing out how he had not violated the agreement in any way. But the letter apparently scared the management of his new firm, and they fired him the next day.

This turn of events was devastating to John. Most of the hard work he had put into the first job had failed to come to fruition when they fired him from out of the blue. Now much the same thing was happening again as the same people stuck their hands in and effectively turned the spigot off at his new company. I saw something change in my husband that day. It wasn't that he was naïve about business. He knew the business world could be tough. But now he was discovering that apparently, it could be virtually soulless, with people you had done a good job for hounding you into the ground to supposedly protect their bottom line. A new cynicism was born in John as he became more distrustful of others' motivations and friendly words.

Those feelings only grew as he looked for work. We hired an attorney to represent us, but no matter how much he pressed the first company, they would not release John from the three-year contract. And because he had been fired from the second firm, he found doors quickly closing in his face.

At the same time, he began having more frequent focal seizures. Over the last couple of years, I had witnessed several of these lapses in which he became unconscious for a few seconds. But now, instead of occurring two or three times a year, the petit mal episodes began happening about once a month. They were always frightening to observe because any one of them could be the onset of a larger event. I was always on the lookout for the flickering eyes or the telltale clicking in the back of his throat.

John, though, wasn't even aware of most of the focal seizures because he was unconscious at the time he was experiencing them, and they lasted only a few seconds. One day I walked into the kitchen and saw him standing near the refrigerator, staring at the wall. "What are you looking at?" I asked. He didn't answer. I walked up to him and saw a blank look in his eyes. "John, can you hear me?" Still no reaction.

I was about to turn and run for the phone, when he mumbled a few words.

"Can you hear me, Hon?" I asked again.

He slowly turned to me, blinking his eyes. "Did you say something?"

"I asked you several times whether you could hear me. You were out for a minute."

"Out where? What do you mean?"

"You had a focal seizure."

"No, I didn't."

"You weren't answering me. You were staring into nothing."

"I just did answer you," he said, then walked into the living room.

Most times he wasn't in that much denial about the focal seizures. He usually accepted my word if I told him he had just had one. But he never wanted to talk about their implications. When one occurred, he preferred to quickly dismiss it and move on. I understood why. At a time when he was having doubts about his career, he didn't want to be reminded of this other big problem that was always lingering in the background.

Later that summer, while John was still looking for a new position, he received a call from a close friend, Wain, whom he had worked with in credit card processing. Wain was now in Southern California, and he invited John to join him in a new venture there. John had misgivings about returning to the credit card processing field, and he also hated the idea of not being close to Briggs if we relocated to the West Coast. But after the serious setbacks he had suffered to his career, he badly needed some success, and Wain's offer seemed like a good opportunity. Another important consideration was the fact that he trusted Wain. Given recent experiences, that meant a lot to John. The net result was that after a few days of talking it over, we decided that it was time to load up the wagons and head for California.

The move was accomplished in two stages. John went out by himself in October to set up base camp in Las Flores, leaving Blake and me to wrap up our lives in Dallas and follow after the first of the year. The togetherness with which we had begun our marriage now reverted to something reminiscent of our first weeks together, when all we had was the phone. Except now, instead of hours-long conversations, we were usually limited to twenty or thirty minutes each evening because John was so busy helping to establish the new company.

When Blake and I finally arrived in Las Flores in January of 2000, the three difficult months of waiting for our family to be back together seemed more than worth it. I fell in love with Southern California immediately. Everything was clean and fresh, and the weather gorgeous. Living expenses seemed a little high, but John assured me that we could afford the area because the new business was doing so well.

"We're going to make a ton of money when we get this thing really going," he told me one morning as he got ready for work. There were bags under his eyes from the long hours he was putting in, but his eyes themselves were gleaming. "You see all these people working for dot-coms getting rich off their options when the stock skyrockets? Well, that's going to be us in another year or two. We'll be reading about ourselves in the *Wall Street Journal*."

Not only did the future sound exciting when John described it, he was already making more money than he had ever made before. We started looking for a house in the area, and within two months were in a new home in a beautiful section of Rancho Santa Margarita. We fit in right away, as if we had been born to the locale. Blake liked her new school there, John and I quickly made several friends in the neighborhood, and I set about putting my degree to work by decorating our new house as beautifully as I could. Finally, after so much trouble, we seemed well on our way to creating the fine home we had often talked about.

The only problem was that John was working such long hours. Typically, on weekdays he would leave at eight in the morning and not get home until nine or ten at night, and he was gone a good part of most Saturdays. For the first few months I put the problem on the back burner as I lost myself in the enjoyable task of decorating the house. Besides, the situation was only temporary, I thought. John kept telling me how the new company would soon achieve liftoff, and I convinced myself that once the operation was fully launched, it would settle down into a steady, successful orbit. Then John's hours would surely lessen. But as my decorating neared completion and his job continued to take up most of his life, I began wondering if that day would ever come.

One night after Blake had gone to bed, I sat watching television, waiting for John. I was looking forward to his coming home so I could show him a new lamp I had bought for our bedroom. But the clock passed ten, then ten-thirty, and there was still no sign of him. Finally, I turned off the television and just sat there, looking at the living room, at the new furniture, the rugs, the wall decorations—almost all of it chosen without John's help or input—and I wondered, *Who is this for? Blake is too young to really appreciate it. John is so lost in his work that the house is barely more than a bedroom for him. Is this just all for me?* I suddenly felt empty, thinking that all the effort I had put into the house was for no one else's real benefit but my own. After a while I fell asleep on the couch, and John woke me up at almost midnight. I don't think I even mentioned the new lamp when we went to bed.

As the months went by, I became increasingly lonely for John's company and for the family life we had enjoyed for a while in Dallas. But when I tried to talk to John about my feelings, he didn't want to hear.

"I've got to make a success of this thing, Melinda!" he said to me one day when I was able to corner him for a lunch date. "You know what happened in Texas. I've finally managed to put something together here. But I can't let up at this point or everything might fall apart."

"But I thought the company was doing very well," I said. "And if it's doing well, couldn't you lighten up just a little?"

"Look at me, Melinda," he replied. "Do I look healthy to you?"

"Of course you do."

"But I have a problem that usually doesn't show on the surface, right?"

"You mean epilepsy?"

"Yes," he said. "So you should know as well as anybody that not everything that looks healthy is as healthy as it looks."

"You mean there are some problems with the company?"

"Nothing for you to worry about," he replied. "Let's just say that everyone there needs to put in their best effort these days. Including me. If we do that, everything will be fine."

Though he would tell me no more, what he had said was enough to convince me that I had to be patient. The thought that he would again be stymied in his efforts to create the kind of career he wanted was worse than the idea of me waiting up for him late at night. It seemed clear to me that the best way I could support our family was to back my husband's efforts fully, even if that meant a very abbreviated home life for now.

What made that decision somewhat easier to take was the fact that I had found a nearby church that I liked. While in Dallas, I had attended church only a few times, but in Las Flores, a neighbor introduced me to nearby

Saddleback Church, with its huge congregation of over sixty thousand souls and numerous ministers. I asked John to start going with me, but he declined. I felt I needed to get back to church, though, so I started attending on my own or with one of my friends.

Despite Saddleback's size, I found the atmosphere warm and supportive, and I began going to women's support group meetings once a week. There I found other wives who seemed to understand my predicament of having a beautiful home but a husband who was never there. I also occasionally heard a friendly voice or two that challenged me by gently asking whether I was sure I had my priorities straight. If I had to choose between an expensive home and a husband who was able to be at home, what would I choose? What was most important?

I knew the answer to that question: I would choose my husband, of course. "But you don't have to make that choice," I would tell my questioner. "You can have both. It's just that it may take time to get there. And during that time you may have to make some sacrifices."

To me, that seemed a good reply. But still, the questions made me wonder whether John and I had perhaps put too much effort in creating a nice home in the physical sense and not enough in making sure we had ample time for family life.

The question became even more complicated a few months later, when John's company began floundering. I first learned about it one night when he arrived home after midnight with a bad headache. He threw his briefcase on a table, went into the bathroom for a couple of pain relievers, then came back in and sat down heavily on the couch. "The bubble's almost ready to burst," he said, shaking his head.

"What do you mean?"

He proceeded to tell me that for some time, company expenditures had been far outrunning income and that new sources of revenue had not materialized as quickly as expected. "We've been trying everything," he said. "We probably should have moved our offices three months ago to a lower rent location and all of us should have gone on half salary. As it is, the others want me to start selling credit card services directly in order to drum up more business. Can you imagine that? Me back on the street, selling door-to-door. I hate the idea."

He did it, though, at least for a while, but the business plan couldn't be saved. In October 2000, almost exactly one year after he had begun, John was again out of a job as the company declared bankruptcy.

For us, it was back to square one. Do not collect two hundred dollars or anything else—and even worse, possibly forfeit everything we had earned. The substantial income we had ridden into a new house and nice furniture was suddenly gone, without any residuals, and we didn't even have a supplementary salary from me to act as a buffer.

There was nothing to do except to tighten our belts and look for some silver lining to this new trouble. We decided that one bright edge lay in the fact that John might now be able to get back into the financial planning field, which was where he had wanted to be all along. That idea was somewhat heartening to him as he got to work freshening his resume for the arduous task of finding a new job.

Another advantage was that we were finally able to spend more time together. That was something I luxuriated in for a couple of weeks. But then the silence of would-be employers and headhunters in response to John's letters and resumes became deafening, and the inaudible roar started taking its toll on both of us.

John became increasingly irritable and volatile as the weeks went by and the most promising companies showed no interest in his skills. It was at the height of the dot-com bust, and the job market for white-collar workers was glutted with prospects. We also discovered that companies that would otherwise be interested in John were wary of hiring him because he was still under the three-year non-compete contract, an albatross that continued to weigh him down. Soon there was hardly anyone left in the area to send his resume to. Both of us spent all of Sunday mornings perusing the papers trying to spot any new openings that might fit John's skills as soon as they were posted. If there was anything that looked promising, the rest of Sunday might be passed in relative peace and harmony. Otherwise, it tended to be a gloomy household.

I again found strength by turning to my church group. At the weekly get-togethers, I sometimes talked about how our problem at home had changed from John's never being there to his being there too much. I explained how the latter was actually worse than the former because the worries centering on John's finding a job and of our being able to stay in our new house were constantly there.

Occasionally, one friend or other at the meetings would suggest to me that my constant anxiety might be part of the problem. A typical conversation:

"But how can we not worry?" I asked. "These are real problems. We can't just lay them on a shelf as if they don't exist."

"Of course you should work on them," the friend replied. "But at the same time, try to put the problems more into God's hands. Let Him take on the main burden, while you and John do your best to follow His wishes."

"But how do I find out what God wants? And how do you work on solving a problem without worrying about it?"

Though my friends were emotionally supportive, I couldn't quite grasp what they were advising me to do. Finally, after several months passed with our financial situation steadily worsening, I decided to talk to one of the spiritual counselors at the church. Maybe one of the ministers could help me understand how better to deal with a home life that was devolving into constant worry and bickering.

I explained our situation carefully to the counselor, including some of the things I was doing to try to make things better. "I help John search for good job prospects," I said, "manage the finances so we spend as little as possible, and do everything else I can think of to keep us afloat. But I still feel we're heading for disaster. What I don't understand is why God seems to have just abandoned us."

"You're doing your part, right?" the minister replied. "And your question is, why isn't God doing His?"

"I wouldn't put it quite like that," I said. "But I don't understand why we keep on having these troubles, especially when John works so hard at every job and I do my best to support him."

"Could part of the problem be," he asked, "that you and John are trying too hard to control everything?"

He then started saying the same kinds of things my friends had—that I needed to give my problems to God and trust more in His wisdom. As he talked, I repeated several times that I did trust in God, but that it didn't seem to be helping us much.

At the end of our session, the minister said, "Melinda, I believe you when you say you have faith in God. But your faith is immature. You need to pray to Him for guidance about how to put yourself more fully in His hands."

Immature, I thought. *What a thing to say to somebody who has shared their troubles in the hope of spiritual guidance.* I walked out of the minister's office a little angry with him. But his words stuck in my mind, and on the way home I kept wondering if there might be some truth in them. Maybe he was right. Maybe I wasn't trusting God in the way I should. The conversation had stirred my thinking, but it would be some time before I began to understand what the minister and my friends were trying to tell me.

In the meantime, with our financial situation deteriorating, I started looking for work myself and found a part-time position as a rep at a nearby design center. It wasn't much, but it helped to stave off the wolves for a while. Then, in March of 2001, John was offered a position with a company selling employee benefits to other companies. It was a new kind of responsibility for him, but he immediately seized the opportunity.

This was definitely progress, but it didn't solve our financial problems immediately because John's income stayed small while he learned the ropes of the new position. At the same time, our large house payment continued to seriously drain us each month. As a result, we decided to sell our house and buy a smaller one. It was heart rending to see our beautiful home go to someone else that summer, but the decision made good sense financially. We quickly bought a smaller home in a nearby area and proceeded to make new friends there. With the modest proceeds of the house exchange, we managed to gain breathing room as John established himself in his new job.

I also started earning some extra money from my hobby of creating small pendants that I called "she-she things." Soon after we moved to the new house, I set up a Web site from which to sell the pendants, and I also marketed them by word of mouth and through small parties I held in our home and at those of friends. I didn't see myself as a budding jewelry tycoon, but my pendants did bring in several hundred dollars a month.

Though John was working again, there was little change in his moodiness and hot temper. He often came home from work agitated, and I seldom got the sense that he felt confident in his future at the new job. His last three positions had all looked promising soon after they began, and he had worked very hard at all of them. But in each case, the apparent opportunity had abruptly disappeared. Why should this time be any different? I knew that's what he sometimes thought, and there was nothing I could say to counteract the evidence of recent history.

I prayed hard every day that John would find lasting success at his new position. Not mainly for the money, but so his mind would be more at ease and he would be happier at home. Many of my prayers took the form of entries in a journal I kept. Journaling is something I had begun as a teenager, and now it became almost a daily thing as I asked God to help John face the future with hope, and to help us both create a more peaceful home. As I wrote, I often remembered what the minister and my friends had told me about giving my problems to God, and I tried my best to do that. But I continued to worry incessantly.

One of the things I was anxious about was John's epilepsy. He was still having focal seizures at the rate of one every few weeks, and I worried that he might have another full-scale attack at any time. And what if one occurred while he was away from me? His office mates knew about his epilepsy, and he wore medical I.D. dog tags indicating his condition and the drugs he was taking. But having gone through four full-generalized convulsive seizures with him, two light and two very substantial, I felt I knew best what he needed during such an attack, especially in the way of protection. Still, 2001 passed and we were into 2002, and he had not had a major seizure for three full years. Again I started to tentatively think that maybe his epilepsy was finally under control.

Then came April, which, according to a famous line by the poet T.S. Eliot, is the cruelest month.

In early April of 2002, John was even more harried at work than usual as he prepared software documents and Web site information for an important out-of-town presentation. The night before he was to leave, he stayed up late and then was up early to catch his plane. After being on the go for the next two days, he arrived home late at night, and when he rose the next morning, he said he didn't feel well. He went to work anyway, but decided at around eleven to come home for a nap. After he went up to sleep, I left to run a few errands.

I came back not more than an hour later to a horrible banging noise erupting from our bedroom. I ran up the stairs to find John lying on the floor by the bed, in the midst of convulsions as severe as any I had before witnessed. I don't know how long he had been there, but at the beginning he had apparently been trying to call either 911 or me, because the phone was off the hook.

His head was lodged between the bed and the nightstand and was banging against both. I grabbed a pillow off the bed and tried to put it behind his head, but the space was so cramped and he was shaking so violently that it took ten or fifteen seconds before I could situate it to give him at least partial protection. I then grabbed the phone, called 911, gave them the information, and turned to work with John.

I struggled with him, trying to get him away from the nightstand, but he was so heavy and strong I found it impossible to move him. I couldn't even hold on to his legs. The bedroom window just above us was open, and I started screaming for help. The houses in the neighborhood were close together, and I thought that surely, someone would hear me.

I kept trying to hold John steady while I continued yelling, stopping periodically to listen for anyone at the door downstairs, or for the siren that would indicate the paramedics were on the way. But after five minutes, no one had come. Then John started trying to rise.

"John, you need to get onto the bed," I said to him as he managed to sit up. I didn't know if he could hear me. His body was still trembling and his movements were uncoordinated, but he was trying to say something through the foam that had gathered on his lips. At first I couldn't understand what it was, then I realized he was saying that he needed to urinate.

He started trying to get to his feet, pulling himself up by the edge of the nightstand. I was afraid of him going into the bathroom because it was so small. And with its tile floor and hard surfaces everywhere, it would be the worst possible place for him to be if he were to fall. But when he made it to his feet, still trembling, he immediately climbed onto the bed.

At first I thought he was going to lie down, but he started to stand, still mumbling something unintelligible. This was even more frightening than his going into the bathroom, because the ceiling fan was on, and I saw that it would strike him if he stood. Wringing with sweat myself by that time, I pleaded with him and tried to pull him down. But there was no stopping him, and as soon as he rose up all the way, the blades of the fan hit him in the head, knocking him over. He fell against the heavy footboard, jarring his back, then went the rest of the way off the bed, landing on his head.

He was up immediately, like some unstoppable bionic man that you might see in the movies, and he was stumbling toward the bathroom. I ran around the bed, grabbed a planter that stood on the floor, pulled out the silk tulips, and clutched his arm with one hand as I held the planter out with the other: "John, go in this!" He stopped and again seemed to be trying to say something, but I still couldn't understand. At that moment I heard the paramedics at the door downstairs.

"We're up here! The door's unlocked! We're upstairs!" I yelled at the top of my voice, thanking God they had made it before John hurt himself any further. He became belligerent when they got to him, fighting against them. In the end, it took four men to get him tied to a stretcher and down to the ambulance.

Two days later, he was home, with many scrapes, cuts, and bruises on his head and other parts of his body. The day after that, he was back at work.

Not only had this been John's most violent seizure since the one in New Orleans, it was the most disconcerting because I hadn't been able to protect him. Again and again I went over the event in my mind, trying to understand what I could have done differently. But I always concluded that I had done the best I could given the fact that physically, I was no match for my husband. I tried to tell myself that in the end, it had turned out all right, with the cuts and bruises healing quickly. But still there was the problem of him being struck by the ceiling fan and hitting his head. I knew that neither could have done him any good.

Over the next few months, in fact, I wondered if some of John's behavior might be due to his having suffered brain damage during the incident. Not only did his irascibility become even more pronounced, but there was also a noticeable change in his judgments about work and about friends and acquaintances. Often, he was very distrustful, seeming almost paranoid. Our own relationship also continued to suffer. He seemed constantly on edge at home, and though I was sometimes cowed by his volatility, at other times it only raised my own ire.

I don't know whether his erratic behavior displayed itself at work. If so, it didn't appear to affect the bottom line, because by that time he was enjoying considerable success on the job. At one point during the summer, however, John's boss, who knew he still had a hankering to get back into the financial services field, suggested that he contact a friend of his who was a senior manager in a company called Capital Management Strategies, which sold financial plans. "That's the natural place for you," his boss said. "That's where you can shine the brightest."

John did talk to the people at CMS, and they were interested in him. After becoming assured that the three-year no-compete clause had elapsed, in the fall of 2002 they offered him a position selling high-end financial strategy packages. He eagerly snapped the offer up, and almost immediately he established himself in the new position and began contributing to the firm.

It was clear that John felt the new company was where he belonged, and I was sure that would mean a happier John and a changed attitude at home. But it didn't happen. He still seemed to half expect the rug to be pulled out from under him, and he was still often infuriated with the world in general and with me or Blake in particular. Instead of life being calmer and closer at home, our relationship continued to deteriorate.

I was becoming desperately concerned about the survival of our marriage. The harmony with which we had begun had gradually dissipated into a cacophony of yelling, arguments, and hurt feelings. There was no longer any order to our marriage. The only pattern was in the fact that the chaos was getting worse. The discord was intensifying, building into a dark, dissonant crescendo that I feared would not reach its culmination until John and I had been torn apart.

Yet I couldn't really accept that our marriage was doomed. We had begun so well, with so much love at the beginning. More important, I was still in love with John, and I was sure he still loved me. I couldn't believe that God wanted our marriage to end, and I prayed to Him fervently every day in my journal, asking Him to show us how to return to what we once had.

Finally, in January, the turmoil at home became almost unbearable, and I begged John to see a counselor. He said he would if I would do the same, and I agreed. After a couple of weeks, it seemed to be helping a little. I didn't know if it was turning us around, but at least we didn't seem to be rushing quite so rapidly to the apex of disaster.

Still, whatever was troubling John didn't let up. He was now having as many as three focal seizures a week while with me, and I was sure that he must also be having them at work sometimes. If so, he was probably aware of that fact from the reactions of his partners, which could only add to the pressure he felt.

It had been a year since his last grand mal episode, and I was convinced that if he didn't slow down, he would have another. I tried to discuss it with him, but he wouldn't listen. "I don't want to talk about it," he said. "Not even think about it."

"It's as if you think it makes you less of a man," I said. "But it's a disease, like any other. The people at work should be able to understand if you need to slow down a little to make sure you don't have another seizure."

"This is the business world we're talking about, Melinda! And in the business world, having epilepsy is a weakness! You don't go around asking people for easier duties because you're worried about freaking out on them. Now just drop it!"

So I did drop it. For me to keep trying to press my point would have likely created even greater stress. And that was one thing neither John nor our marriage needed.

When I woke on Easter morning, 2003, I didn't know quite where we were. Though life was still a bit calmer at home, everything seemed unresolved. But John had the day off, and that was something to be thankful for. I would have liked to go to church, but I knew he wouldn't accompany me, and I thought God would understand if we took advantage of our opportunity to spend some time together.

"It's a beautiful morning," I said when we got up. "And Easter Sunday. Why don't we go out to breakfast and maybe go to the beach this morning?"

I was happily surprised when he said yes.

I was even happier when, during our drive to the beach and our breakfast at a small inn, there wasn't a cross word between us. It was just pleasant conversation about how beautiful the day was, how good the food tasted, and why we hadn't done this before.

Then we went for our walk along the beach, which was the most romantic thing we had done in the over three years we had been in California. I kept asking John to hold my hand, and when he did and I saw his smile, I could easily believe that our troubles were over and our pathway together was now as clear and easy as the wide sandy beach along which we walked.

Even the fact that John had a focal seizure as I drove us back home couldn't erase my sense that today was some kind of watershed. After we arrived, he lay down on the couch to rest and watch the basketball game, and I went upstairs to read for a while, feeling happier than I had been for a long time. I picked up a book that I had been reading about Mary Magdalene, a woman whom I admired greatly, and lay on the bed to read a few pages.

But my mind wouldn't stay on the words. I kept thinking that God had heard my pleas and had shown us, through our Easter Sunday walk, that a new beginning was possible for us, as it had been for Jesus on that holy day. I kept thinking that he was showing us that our marriage, too, could be resurrected.

After a few minutes, I became conscious of the sand between my toes, and I was back there again, walking the beach with John, feeling him holding my hand.

And suddenly there was his voice, calling me from downstairs: "Melinda! Melinda!"

Chapter Four

WHERE'S MY HUSBAND?

It was past ten Sunday night by the time the Mission Hospital staff got John settled into the intensive care unit. Six hours after the seizure's onset.

I was thankful they were able to put him into an actual room instead of one of the small curtained cubicles that made up most of ICU. The room had a glassed-in front, which allowed the nurses to see him at all times, and there was plenty of space for all of his equipment—respirator, heart rate monitor, IV stand—and for me.

I pulled a chair up to his bed and took his right hand, which was still strapped down at the wrist, as were his ankles and his other hand. I wanted to say something to comfort him: "John, don't worry, Babe. You're going to be fine." But I knew he couldn't hear me. They had given him sedatives, and I told myself he was just in a very deep sleep. I wouldn't allow myself to even think the word "coma."

Instead, I focused on the fact that his color was normal and thanked God that he wasn't shaking any longer. That was definitely progress. *We're out of the ER,* I thought. *The worst is surely over now. He's only sleeping. It's been a rough day and he needs his sleep. In the morning he'll wake and want to know what happened. I'll have a lot to tell him.*

I tried my best to keep that positive attitude while I sat there, but whenever I focused on the big tube entering his mouth, my confidence dissolved. The nurse who kept looking in on him could probably see the uncertainty in my eyes; at one point she said, reassuringly, "Don't worry. The plan is to get him off the respirator tomorrow morning. Then he'll look much better."

That helped some: *More progress, just around the corner.* But then I remembered how purple his face had been, even blue for several minutes, and the way he had been gasping for air in the ER, breath after breath after breath. *How can he have been starved for oxygen that long and not be seriously affected?* And there had been the shaking—it had seemed to go on forever, so different from all the other times. It was hard not to imagine that something terrible had been going on inside.

I thought again about our morning walk on the beach. It felt like it had happened a year ago, in a different world. *Maybe that special walk is God's final gift to me from my husband,* I thought, despondent. Five seconds later, I was deciding that as soon as he woke, we should make a date for another special stroll by the sea.

My thoughts and emotions kept vacillating that way until I realized how pointless it was to speculate about positive or negative outcomes. The truth was, neither I nor anyone else knew if any permanent damage had resulted from the seizure—so there was no good reason for either optimism or pessimism at this stage. The only thing that made any sense was to do whatever I could to help: hold his hand, watch him for any sign that he might start seizing again, figure out how to get a little sleep myself so I could make good decisions.

That's what I'm here for, I realized. *Not to fret or cry or try to figure out what only a trained neurologist could possibly determine, but to listen to what the doctors and nurses say, keep a clear head, and make the best decisions I can, based on what develops and whatever information I can gather.*

At that point, I managed to steady myself a bit emotionally. The near panic I had felt during the seizure and that had been barely submerged in the ER was gone. In this new, post-ER reality, it was time to set my mind for what might turn out to be a long, difficult journey. And to do that, it was important to keep my emotions at bay.

Does that mean I wasn't afraid? Oh, absolutely not. At some deep level I was brimming with fear about what had been happening that day, what was happening inside John right now, what was going to happen tomorrow. But I had to push it into the back of my mind. I couldn't permit myself to dwell on it, or it might petrify me. *Just do whatever you can to help, Melinda. Do it as well as you can. Let God take care of the rest.*

I sat there for several hours, taking only a few breaks to go to the bathroom or to step outside for a moment. At one point, I went out to call the house to see if there were any messages on our answering machine and got John's recorded greeting: "This is the Wilferths. We can't come to the phone now, but . . ." It was surreal to hear his normal voice again after all that had happened. I wanted to jump into the phone and crawl through the line to find him there at the other end, waiting for me with open arms and his welcoming smile—strong, confident, healthy. Instead, I set my teeth as I listened to the few messages, then returned to the bitter reality of ICU.

At about two a.m., I asked the nurse if there was a place to lie down for a while. She directed me to a kind of waiting room that included a few chairs that could be made into beds. An older and a younger couple who were obviously together sat in one area of the room, talking quietly among themselves. I arranged my simple bed off to one corner and was just lying down, when a doctor entered and said to the others, "I'm sorry, she's gone." When I heard the sobs of the two women, I suddenly pictured myself listening to a similar announcement somewhere down the line. I quickly banished the disturbing image from my mind, but it left me wide-awake.

I lay there feeling awkward while the drama of the couples' personal tragedy continued to play itself out as they tried to comfort each other. After a few minutes, I rose and went to check on John. No change. I walked outside and stood for moment in the chilly April night. Then inside to lie down again. Fifteen minutes later I was back in ICU.

This back and forth went on until four a.m., when I decided that it was imperative to get some sleep before the day began. I grabbed my things, checked John once more, and told the nurse I was going home for a quick nap.

Ten minutes later I was there. I took off my clothes, washed up, put my hair in a ponytail, lay down, and tried to pray. I still felt like I was just going through the motions in my prayers. What was happening was too big. I couldn't get my thoughts, my words, my arms around it. All that came out is, "Please God help John, please God help John, please God . . ." Again I tried to sleep, but my mind was racing. The bed felt odd—there was no comfort there with John in that other bed.

Within thirty minutes I was up. I threw on my sweats and sat down at my desk to make a list of what I had to do. *Call Judy early. See if they're coming out.*

Did she contact Jill and John's brothers? Call John's work. Call Mom. Be sure to be there when they take the tube out. I looked at the list. So short. *Is that it? Is that all I'm able to do? Unbelievable.* I went to the kitchen, grabbed something out of the toaster, and was back at the hospital before six.

When I arrived, I learned that Rock and Judy had called the nurse's station and were coming in that night. John was still in a deep sleep. I sat with him and held his hand for a while, then went outside to make a couple of calls. I thought again about Blake, out in St. Louis visiting her father, and debated with myself whether to tell her yet about what had happened to her stepdad. I decided to hold off until he showed some change. I called John's work, then phoned a few people who knew what had happened yesterday to keep them updated. The calls were good therapy for me, helping me to stay in the present and not speculate about what might happen next.

John was scheduled to be taken off the respirator at ten. At 9:45, the nurses started getting him ready. I waited outside as they backed him off his oxygen to see if he could breathe on his own. He couldn't. They would have to try again later.

For the rest of the day I kept waiting for any sign that John was starting to come out of it. I talked to the main neurologist who was working on his case and met another neurologist who had been sent by John's general practitioner and would be consulting with the first one. Neither was sure when John would wake.

At three p.m., the nurses gave him an EEG, an electroencephalogram. The results showed a great deal of activity still occurring in his brain despite the anticonvulsant drug mix he was being given. The main neurologist interpreted this activity as his brain still seizing. It was appalling to learn that though John had seemingly been resting quietly since the previous evening, the seizure was still going on inside. The doctor decided to add phenobarbital to the mix, and to slowly increase the doses of the anticonvulsants to therapy levels over the next few days.

Through the afternoon, John lay virtually motionless. As I sat with him, the word "coma," with all of its troublesome connotations, kept entering my mind, but I still fought against it. *Don't try to predict the future, Melinda. Just do your job.* I then busied myself with working through my mental checklist of things to do. At the same time, I occasionally had the feeling—one that would recur many times during the next few days—that I was actually standing two or three feet behind my chair, a mere shadow looking on at myself as I went through the activities of holding John's hand, checking his heart rate monitor, ticking off in my mind who to call: insurance people, Nancy, Mom again. It was probably a kind of dissociation, maybe connected to my efforts not to get emotionally wrought up.

At six I went home to wash up and get something to eat. I was back at the hospital by 7:30. In the meantime, the staff had made another unsuccessful attempt to get John off the respirator. This was becoming a matter of concern for the doctors, because the longer John stayed on the respirator, the weaker his breathing muscles would become.

John's parents arrived at nine. After they had seen John and we had talked, Judy seemed convinced that once he got off the respirator, he would be okay. I hoped she was right, but given that this seizure had not been at all like the others, I wasn't convinced.

Rock and Judy's arrival meant they would be able to stay with John that night, which allowed me to think about getting some real sleep for the first time since this had started. I was thankful for that, but it was difficult to leave him. I finally convinced myself that I absolutely had to get some rest if I was going to be able to make good decisions about his care. "Promise to call me immediately if he should wake up before I get back tomorrow morning," I told Rock and Judy just before I left. "I'll be back here in a flash. I want to be able to see him right away."

At 10:30 I arrived home and dropped into bed, but at midnight I woke, realizing I hadn't called Charlotte. *God forbid, what if John should die suddenly?* I needed to inform Charlotte of what had happened, so she could tell Briggs if she felt he should know. I called and left a message, and half an hour later Charlotte called back. She was very concerned, and wonderfully supportive. Her husband Patrick, a cardiologist, also spoke with me. He asked questions to try to understand the situation as well as possible and provided encouragement. It was comforting to speak with someone in the medical profession who had a personal connection with our family. When I hung up, I was able finally to fall into a sound sleep.

I woke at nine a.m. There had been no phone call. I immediately called the nurse's station in ICU and was told, "He's been awake for a while. He recognized his parents."

I rushed to the hospital as fast as I could. Maybe it was selfish, but on the way I thought about how much I had wanted to be there when John woke—or at least immediately after—but I hadn't had that opportunity. Still, all that really mattered was that he was awake, and for that I was very grateful. *Thank you, God.*

When I got to ICU, I saw that yes, his eyes really were open! I leaned over him: "I'm here, Honey. You had a seizure. I love you." He recognized me and lifted his head a little as if for a kiss. When I bent down to kiss his forehead, he started trying to say something past the tube, but only succeeded in making muffled sounds. "It's okay, John," I said. "You don't need to talk." He tried to move his hands, but they were still strapped down, as were his feet. He started jerking at the straps with his hands and wrists, then began kicking. I tried to calm him. "Babe, take it easy. You'll hurt yourself." After a moment he gave up and closed his eyes to sleep.

After Rock and Judy left to get some rest, I sat with John. As the day progressed, he alternately slept for a while, and was then awake for fifteen or twenty minutes, spending much of that time fighting against his straps. It was difficult to watch him in such distress, but the staff felt the restraints were necessary in case he started seizing outwardly again.

While awake, he often looked at me plaintively, as if begging me to release him from his captivity. "Hon, I can't. The doctors say you can't be unstrapped quite yet." He would then start fighting like an enraged tiger in a cage, contorting his body, sometimes making a twisting lunge at his catheter. A few times, he succeeded in maneuvering his body so he could get a partial grip on the breathing tube that snaked across his chest. Alarmed, I would grab his hand: "John! That's your airway! You have to leave it there so you can get oxygen." If he didn't let go, it would take all my strength to pry his fingers away.

Such prolonged combative behavior following a seizure was something new for John. After his previous grand mal episodes, there had always been the post-ictal stage in which he had acted belligerently and required restraints. But before, he had always gone to sleep after five or ten minutes, and when he woke he would be feeling normal. Now he fought against his restraints for much of almost every waking period. Sometimes my voice could calm him, while at other times he looked at me as if I were betraying him and struggled all the harder. After the nurse gave him Atavan to calm him, he would sleep for a while, but when he woke the cycle started again. Soon, his wrists and ankles were red and raw from working against the straps. It was heartbreaking. I didn't understand what was happening to him.

They did another EEG that afternoon despite the fact that his twisting and turning made it difficult to attach the machine's leads. His brain activity still showed spikes, though they were somewhat diminished. Again, the doctors saw them as indicating ongoing seizure activity. It seemed incredible to me that his brain could still be seizing 48 hours after the initial attack.

The doctors were still puzzled about the underlying cause of the initial seizure and the prolonged abnormal activity. The neurologist treating John announced to us that he was arranging an MRI to examine the brain tissue for a possible tumor, and a lumbar puncture of his spine to test for meningitis and other infections. They had already determined that the CAT scan they had done before he got to ICU on Sunday night showed no skull damage.

Rock and Judy returned in the evening, now rested, and again took the night shift while I went home to sleep. I was back early Wednesday.

At 9:30 that morning, the staff managed to get John off the respirator. *Finally,* I thought, *he won't have to put up with that huge tube invading his body. He'll be able to talk.* He was breathing oxygen through nose tubes now, with an oxygen concentration indicator attached to one of his toes. It was a big improvement, though he still looked like he'd been through a disaster—which, of course, he had.

He slept until noon, then woke intermittently through the day. I had been expecting him to be much calmer now that the tube was out, but it didn't happen. Whenever he was conscious, he was very emotional—crying, laughing, lifting his head to be kissed, and still often fighting against the straps. When he tried to talk, his voice was weak and hoarse from his throat having been scraped by the tube, and he could barely utter the word "Hi" in a rough whisper.

You could see how miserable he was, tied down and having to lie continually on his back. I started asking the nurses if they could unstrap at least one hand when he was quiet, and a few times they agreed. "John," I would say, "If you're calm, they'll unstrap your arm. Just take it nice and easy, Hon." He would seem to be listening, but once he realized his arm was free he would start slinging it around. One time he knocked over a tray by his bed. Another nurse would have to come in to help the first get him strapped back down. Then more Atavan to calm him.

And now that the tube was gone, there was something else: he seemed to be having hallucinations. At times, he would look up and jerk his head quickly to one side as if something were coming toward him. As he regained some of his vocal strength, he sometimes yelled, in a gravelly voice, "They're coming for me!"

That afternoon, Rock and Judy accompanied John to another building for the MRI. When they returned, Judy reported that it had taken over half a dozen nurses and technicians to control him during the test, and that at one point John had grabbed her wrist as she was trying to calm him and had almost broken it. Though the MRI showed some visual artifacts caused by John's movements, the staff seemed to think it was acceptably accurate. It showed no tumors.

On Thursday, John's volatile behavior continued. He was so tenaciously difficult to control that only male nurses were dealing with him by that time. In his kicking and fighting he often dislodged either the oxygen tubes or the indicator attached to his toe. As a result, someone had to be with him virtually every moment.

At one point they were going to give him another EEG, and as before, I tried to make a deal with him: "John, if you stay calm, they'll take the straps off." He seemed to be listening, but when they freed him, he grabbed my ponytail and yanked hard. The two male nurses there managed to quickly free me, but it hurt—not so much physically as emotionally. "He doesn't really hate me," I said to the nurses, a little embarrassed for both John and myself. Inside I was wondering, *Where's my husband?*

That afternoon, as a nurse was preparing to take John to a different room for the lumbar puncture, he added something to the IV. When I asked what it was, he replied that it was to calm John for the procedure. "He won't remember any of this," he said. "We call it the 'mind-eraser.'" I felt a chill at those words. *Erase his mind?* I thought. *That can't be right.* In hindsight, the incident seems like a premonition of what was to come.

The lumbar puncture results indicated that there were no infections in John's nervous system. So far, skull fracture, tumor, and infection had been ruled out as possible causes of his seizure and subsequent behavior. The case remained a mystery to the doctors.

I wondered about all the Atavan he was ingesting. It seemed like every time he got unruly, a nurse gave him more of it. Was the drug somehow affecting him when he was awake? Perhaps causing his hallucinations? Or could the increases in the dosage of the anticonvulsants somehow be related to his behavior? I wondered whether John was possibly in a catch-22 situation, where treatment of his condition was actually exacerbating some of the symptoms. I didn't know. All I knew was that now that he was awake and off the respirator, I just wanted to be able to give him a hug, to tell him I loved him, and to hear him say he loved me.

It was harder now to keep the fear down than it had been on Sunday night and Monday. Back then, it had been possible to envision John opening his eyes and feeling normal again, with us then going home to resume our lives. But now that he was displaying such bizarre behavior, the picture had become much more complex.

While I had many questions, the doctors had few answers, and there was no one nearby to discuss my concerns with in real depth. Judy had her partner—her Rock—to talk with about any anxieties she might have; but my partner—my rock—was lying in bed, still very ill and seemingly getting no better. How I wanted to be able to crawl in with him so we could cuddle and talk: *How do you feel now, Babe? You were really a wild man there for a while. You're so strong. You were throwing everybody around. But everything's going to be okay, Hon. I was scared before, but now that I can lie here next to you, I know everything will be fine.*

But that was only a fantasy for now.

It's not that I didn't have support. John's parents being there was a tremendous help. And I often spoke to Charlotte and Patrick during those days. Charlotte continued to be a great source of strength, while Patrick helped me understand the rationale behind some of procedures being used with John. I was very thankful for his clear explanations and kind words.

There were also friends who often came by to say "Hi" and express their concerns. I usually met them outside, they gave me a welcome hug or two, and we visited for a few minutes. "How do you manage to stay so stoic under all the pressure?" they sometimes asked. That always surprised me a little because I didn't feel very stoic. "I'm just doing the same as you would in my shoes," I replied. "Just trying to stay clear-headed and to focus on whatever I might be able to do to help."

And that was true. That was still my plan: just take one thing at a time. But the plan was getting a little shaky. And so was I.

Though my rock was terribly incapacitated at the time, I thankfully had three other strong supports to steady me. First there was Jesus, and certainly my father concerning strategic and financial consultation, and then there was my mom. I called her several times a day to update her on the situation and to share with her my worries and frustrations. She phoned me, too. These calls were an enormous help to me in dealing with the situation emotionally. But when John's volatile behavior continued, I decided that I really needed to have her right there with me, at least for a little while. So on Wednesday night I called her: "Mom, could you possibly come out to stay with me for a couple of days? Could you talk to Daddy about that?" She was soon making plans to fly out Friday evening.

My other special support—and of course the greatest of all rocks in Himself—was God. Over the last several days, He had been my main source of strength. Now, with John's condition failing to improve and my doubts and fears welling to the surface, He must have decided that it was time to take me into his loving embrace even more securely.

Let me explain:

Ever since Sunday evening, I had wondered at my inability to really concentrate when I prayed for God's help. I was raised to believe that in prayer, it's most desirable to be on our knees and to talk clearly and fervently to God. Yet over the past few days I had never felt I had the time to do that. I was saying all my prayers on my feet or where I sat, and they seemed to lack focus—as if, instead of plumbing the depths of our Lord's endless waters, they were just skimming the surface. I knew that God forgave me for this. And I knew He could hear me. In fact, I often felt Him right there with me. But still, I wasn't communicating with Him quite in the way I wanted to.

I understand now why that was happening: it was because my mind was constantly racing a mile a second. Every waking moment I was thinking about medical tests, what's John's behavior meant, how to calm him, possible drug effects, who I had or hadn't called, insurance issues, and on and on. As a result, there wasn't a free second available in which I could talk to God calmly, clearly, and with the kind of focus that He deserves. There was always some thought waiting to crowd in and hurry my prayer along.

But this changed at some point on Thursday evening, at least for a few moments. And it was a change that made an increasingly important difference as the repercussions of John's seizure played themselves out in the coming months.

At the time, I was sitting alone with John while he slept, and I was trying not to think about those two glaring facts: that there had been no apparent improvement in his situation for the past couple of days, and that the doctors seemed to have no clear idea of how to get him back to normal.

As usual, my modus operandi was to stay busy busy busy by going through my mental checklist of things to do that I dimly felt would somehow contribute to fixing the situation. But then, for the first time, it suddenly dawned on me: none of those activities—trying to calm John, asking the nurses to release one of his straps, checking on messages, making phone calls, or any of the others—was fixing anything. That's not to say that some of those things weren't helpful; they were. But in relation to the only issue that really mattered at the time—that of my dear husband getting well—they weren't getting anything done at all.

At that moment I realized the simple, obvious fact that whether John got better or not wasn't up to me in the slightest. It was out of my hands. And that was the instant when I was able to do what I had never been able to do before. The moment when I finally managed to accomplish what the counselor who said that my faith was immature had advised me to do—give it to God.

And that's what I did. I just handed it to him. All of it.

When I think back on that moment, I see what happened as being a kind of action, a spiritual action, one that involved no words. At least none that I can specifically recall. Instead, I simply experienced a profound sense of acceptance and release. But I also think of it as a kind of wordless prayer. And, unlike the quick prayers I had been uttering over the last several days, this voiceless communication with God was one of the deepest I had ever prayed. If there had been words to it, they would have been similar to these:

> "Dear Lord, I give this to you—this terrible burden that John has been bearing and that I've been trying to bear. I understand now that it's not up to me what happens here, but only to You. Please take us—John, me, his doctors, all of us—into Your loving, all-encompassing arms, and lead us where you will. Thank you, Merciful Father."

At that instant of releasing my burden to God, a beautiful peace came over me for the first time since the terrible trouble had begun on Sunday. I have to confess that the sense of tranquility lasted only a short while before my loquacious mind began chattering away again about what I should be doing to help: make a call, talk to the nurse about John's medication, ask the doctors about this or that. But for a moment I understood something—how to lay a problem completely in God's hands—that I had never really comprehended before. And in the future, it would be easier for me to again perform that spiritual action, that deepest of prayers.

It was about then that my shadow self, the one who so often had stood behind my body observing it go through the checklist of things to do, began appearing less. The two parts of me, observer and doer, were starting to come together. Thanks to God.

On Friday, there was little change in John. But that night was a watershed because it was time for Rock and Judy to return to Cape Girardeau, at least for a while, and because Mom arrived just as they were leaving. Also, and most important, the doctors had determined that there was nothing more that they could do for John at Mission, and the nurses had started trying to get a bed for him at the University of California at Irvine Medical Center. They were concerned, however, that it might take as long as one or two weeks to do so.

Mom and I sat with John for several hours. He was awake for a little of that time, and he seemed to recognize Mom, but we weren't sure. Sometime around eleven we went home. A nurse would stay close to John until morning. Before we left, we told the nurse at the main station to call us any time of the night if there was even a whiff of a bed being available for John at UCI. We would come back to Mission right away, or go to UCI, or do whatever we had to do.

At home, Mom and I got into our jammies and lay down. Mom started talking about John and how he had looked, and about my own exhaustion and mental state. I told her that for much of the past few days, I had felt somewhat separated from myself, and she said that that was understandable because I had surely been in shock since Sunday.

Then she began crying. "We have to pray, Melinda," she said as she hugged me. She started praying out loud, and I joined her as fervently as I could. I still couldn't dive in completely, because the lesson I had learned about giving it to God had not sunk in nearly as far as it eventually would. But for the first time since the beginning of all of this, I really cried. I cried for John, for us, and I guess for me too.

I cried with my Mom.

CHAPTER FIVE

HOLES

The phone rang at three a.m.

"We have a bed for your husband at UCI," the nurse on the other end of the line said. "We would like to transport him as soon as possible, but we need your signature."

We were at Mission Hospital within half an hour. After I signed the papers, I went to see John, who was awake. "They're transferring you to UCI Med Center, Hon. It's a great hospital, a university hospital. I know they'll take good care of you. You'll be home in no time."

His only reply was to look at me suspiciously and start fighting against the straps.

A nurse took me aside. "He's still very combative, so he'll need to be sedated before we move him. We also have to transport his ICU and some monitoring equipment, so there won't be much room in the ambulance. It's best if you go home and get some sleep. You can visit him in the morning after he's settled in."

I didn't like the idea of him going without me, but the nurse was adamant.

"Okay, here's the plan," I told Mom. "We'll go close our eyes for another couple of hours. Then we'll shower and go to UCI and just stay there for I don't know how long."

In bed, I managed to doze on and off. Several times I got up and went to another room to call the new hospital, first to make sure John had arrived all right and later to find out how he was doing.

Soon after we got up at seven, I received a call from Judy saying they had arrived back in Missouri and that John's brothers, Jimmy and Joe, were planning on flying out. They would arrive on Sunday. "That's great," I told her. "They'll be good medicine for him."

By eight-thirty, Mom and I were at UCI. John was in the neurological intensive care unit, a room about twenty by sixty feet with six or seven cubicles and a nurse's station. His area, set off from the others by curtains, contained his bed and equipment, a small television on a wall bracket, a chair for a visitor, and enough standing room for one other person to squeeze in.

I was happily surprised when I saw him. He had looked a mess just a few hours before. During his entire stay at Mission, he hadn't had a thorough wash, probably because he had been so difficult to control. But the staff at UCI had taken advantage of his being sedated for the transfer and had given him at least a sponge bath. They had also shaved his face and combed his hair. He looked fresh, neat, and clean except for the green and blue bruises that lined his arms where he had fought against his straps.

He was asleep when we arrived, his face thin from weight he had lost, but pink and peaceful, with not the slightest hint of the belligerency that I had so often witnessed over the past week. I wondered what now lay behind that innocent, almost cherubic expression.

I began finding out half an hour later, when he woke. As soon as he saw me, he started trying to rise, but then he realized he was strapped down.

I leaned over to give him a big hug and a kiss. "Mmm, you smell good now," I said.

Mom came up and stood by me. "Hi, John. It's Janet."

"Hi Janet." His voice was still a little hoarse from the scraping it had taken from the respirator tube. "What's happening? Where am I?"

"You're at UCI," I said. "You were just transferred here this morning. They gave you a bath. You look great."

For a moment he looked at me as if confused, then he smiled. "About time you realized it."

This reply, so typical of him, made me laugh in delight. *My John is coming back.*

That seemed to be confirmed as we visited throughout the morning. Not only was his appearance improved, there was a big change in his behavior. He seemed resigned to the straps now, and little of his former truculence remained. His hallucinations also appeared to be gone. No longer was he sometimes reacting as if he were seeing something flying at him from above.

The weekend neurologist came by an hour or two after we arrived, and I learned that he had changed John's drug regimen immediately after admission. For one thing, he was no longer being given Atavan. I wondered if that might have something to do with his calmer demeanor.

Still, he was far from being back to normal. At one point early in the afternoon, he asked me to turn on the television, and I clicked through the channels until I found a basketball game. As I sat on his bed watching the game with him, he began insisting that one of the players had been on his high school team.

"He couldn't have been," I said. "That man's at least fifteen years younger than you."

"I know that's him! Bet you a million dollars."

Another unhappy sign was his continuing distrust of the hospital staff, which was something he had sometimes vociferously expressed at Mission. Several times when no one else was within earshot, he confided in me that he was suspicious of the doctors. "Don't tell them anything," he said. "I don't trust them. I think they're going to experiment on me."

I repeatedly assured him that the doctors and nurses were there only to help him get better and that no one was about to do any experimenting on him. But when I tried to reassure him, he narrowed his eyes and regarded me as if I were somehow in on the conspiracy that he believed surrounded him.

He was also having difficulty with his memory. At one point Mom left for a little while, and when she returned he seemed surprised, saying, "When did you get here, Janet?" as if she had just arrived from Missouri. Several times, he asked me why he was in the hospital, and I reminded him of the seizure and his stay at Mission. Each time, he accepted the explanation with surprising equanimity, as if he had simply forgotten for a moment, but it was clear from his comments that he had no recollection of the past week.

That afternoon I again spoke with the neurologist. I wanted to report what I had observed and get whatever information I could. "He seems better,"

I said, "but he's having memory lapses. That never happened before after a seizure. It's only temporary, I hope."

It was too early to tell, the doctor replied. The results of an EEG they had done that morning indicated that John's brain activity was still abnormal. The doctor couldn't say whether the memory problem and the misidentifications might straighten themselves out as John's brain normalized. He didn't even have a good idea of when that might happen.

After the conversation, I took a moment to remove my frown and put on my most positive face for John. "Everything's going to be fine," I said as I went into his cubicle, though the words were probably more for me than for him.

"I know it is," he replied, but there was worry in his expression. His eyes searched mine, as if appealing to me for answers I didn't have. I suddenly felt tears starting to well up. Thankfully, Mom was there and saw what was happening. She quickly took my hand and led me out beyond the curtains.

"I'm worried about you," she said. "You should take a break and go get some fresh air. And something to eat. You need to keep up your strength or you'll have to be admitted to the hospital, too. I can stay here."

She was right. I told John I was going to go get a snack, then located the cafeteria and bought coffee and a roll. Sitting there, I tried to put some kind of face on what was happening. I was tired of hearing the words "abnormal activity" and "it's too early to tell." I was tired of hearing John say odd things and ask questions he should know the answers to. At times it seemed my husband was coming back. But in some ways he still seemed far away.

I caught myself then. *Get a grip, Melinda,* I thought. *You just want what you want. The person who's doing the real suffering is back there lying on a bed, understanding even less about what's going on than you do. Stop feeling sorry for yourself.*

I remembered what Mom had said the night before about praying for strength. Two nights ago I had found new fortitude by at least momentarily putting my burden in God's hands. I tried to do the same now: *Jesus, please be with me,* I prayed. *I feel unsure about everything. Show me the way to be strong for John. And most of all, please help him. He needs You now more than ever. We both need You more than ever.*

I was still wobbly when I got up. But I knew the Lord was nearby and had been listening. *Well, it's up to You,* I thought as I re-entered neuro ICU. And with that little amen, my mind relaxed a bit.

"Hi, Hon," I said, this time with a real smile on my face. "You're a great sight to see for these sore eyes." And he was, he was.

Mom and I stayed with him through the evening, though we each took a break for some dinner. The nurses began untying his straps for short periods, and for the most part that went well. Once, they had to rush back in to restrap his wrists when he started trying to get up. But by the end of the day, the restraints were off his arms much of the time, and the ones securing his ankles had been loosened, enabling him to move his legs with greater freedom. He still had to have a urinary catheter attached, though.

He dozed off and on during the afternoon and evening. Sometimes when awake he seemed fearful and confused, but for the most part his mood was positive and calm. He was sleeping peacefully when we left at about ten.

It was important for Charlotte to know how John was doing, for the sake of Briggs, so I called her. I also talked to Patrick, who seemed pleased by John's now being at UCI Medical Center.

"It's a teaching and research hospital," he said. "It will be on the cutting edge of neurological medicine. It's exactly where John needs to be right now."

Those words helped me sleep better. Next morning, Sunday, a week after the seizure, Mom and I were up and back at the hospital by eight.

John's memory difficulties remained obvious. As we talked, I realized that not only was he having problems with his short-term memory, there were also gaps in his recollection of events and people before the seizure. Some periods of his life, especially his youth, he recalled normally. But much of his long-term memory was like Swiss cheese, shot through with seemingly random holes. Though he remembered the fact that he worked as a financial planner, he didn't remember the names of his partners at CMS. He also had only a spotty recollection of key events in our lives together. As for his memory of events since the seizure, that seemed like a black hole into which everything kept disappearing.

The staff gave him another EEG that morning, and I learned later that the results were similar to the previous day's. When the neurologist came by, I asked him outside the cubicle if that meant John was still seizing, but he declined to put that interpretation on it. He would only reiterate the importance of letting him rest and keeping him under observation. Maybe then answers to other questions would become clearer.

Joe and Jimmy arrived early that afternoon, and John was overjoyed to see them. He started joking with them right away, which included informing them about which nurses he thought were the best looking.

"You had better watch your mouth, big brother," one of them told John. "Melinda is right here and can hear everything you're saying. You'll have more reason to be in the hospital than some little seizure."

The truth was, I was happy to see John so animated with his brothers. Again, this was the old John coming back, the guy who loved life and had a big smile on his face that brought one to your own.

There wasn't room for all of us to stay with him, so Mom suggested that we leave him to visit with his brothers for a couple of hours. "Let's get out of here!" she said. "Let's go do something fun! Why don't we do some antiquing?"

I knew what she was thinking. She wasn't really interested in antiques. She just thought that going out to the stores for a while might get my mind off what had been happening.

"All right," I replied. "I know a great area in Orange for antiques. It's just a few minutes from here." Maybe she was right. I knew I was leaving John in good hands, and I always loved to shop for antiques with Mom. Maybe it would help me relax a bit.

But it didn't. I tried to focus on what we were doing and get John's condition out of my thoughts for a few minutes, but I wasn't very successful. Though over the past week it had often been hard to be with John at the hospital, it was harder to be away. I kept going into a corner of whatever store we were in to call the hospital and ask if he was awake and okay, making a nuisance of myself.

Finally, at around four, no more than two hours into our excursion, we returned to the hospital. Thinking that after being with his brothers, his mental state might have improved even more, I was looking forward to talking with John. But he was asleep when we got back.

Mom and I talked with Joe and Jimmy for a while. They said that John had continued to be in a happy mood, but they, too, had noticed that his memory wasn't working well. And some of his comments had struck them as a bizarre.

Mom was scheduled to return to Missouri, so we all decided that Joe and Jimmy would stay at the hospital that night. John woke long enough for Mom to say goodbye to him, and I kissed him and told him I would see him first thing in the morning. After I saw Mom off at the airport, I drove home, called the hospital once to make sure John was okay, then went to bed and slept on and off through a lonely night.

Early the next morning I relieved Joe and Jimmy. They had arranged to stay with a cousin of Joe's wife Anna, and they wanted to take some time to visit Anna's grandfather, who was in another area hospital. They would be back late that afternoon to spend more time with John.

Before they left, they mentioned that at one point the previous night John had gotten angry after some minor factual disagreement. It had taken some time to calm him down. They also said that at one point, he had reached down and tried to rip out the urinary catheter that was still attached, saying that it was hurting him. They had immediately called in a nurse, who had had to recatheterize him.

This news was disturbing. I had been hoping that being around his brothers would do more than anything else to bring John back to himself. But even their presence didn't seem to have the power to fully counteract whatever injury the seizure had caused to his brain.

It was a new day, though, and John seemed not to have a care in the world. I found him in great spirits, just finishing his breakfast. After the tray was taken away, he told me he had decided to make some paper roses to thank the nurses for being so kind. This was something he had first done for me when we were in New Orleans, the day after his seizure there. I wasn't jealous that he was making them now in order to flirt with the nurses. I knew his flirtations were innocent, and it was good for him to have a project to work on.

As he lay there twisting papers around in order to create his flowery gifts, he looked so bright and healthy that I decided to be bold and lie down with him for a minute. "Move over, you," I said. "That bed looks too inviting to resist."

"What, are you going to seduce me here in the hospital?" he asked.

"I can't let those nurses get the jump on me."

"Then hop in," he said, "and we'll make our escape plans."

It was wonderful to be able to lie down with my husband again, even if I was on top of the covers and he underneath. We may have been surrounded by nurses and doctors, but I didn't care. At that moment, despite the memory problems and what Joe and Jimmy had told me about the previous night, it was easy for me to again believe that John was almost back to normal. He was looking increasingly healthy, and for the most part acting rationally. Though at times he might still be a little hot-tempered, he wasn't constantly fighting everyone or accusing me of betraying him. And overall, he was in a better mood than he had been for most of the last several years—cracking jokes, making gifts for the nurses, selling John Wilferth as the likeable guy he had always been. Surely, I thought, he and I would soon be walking out of the hospital hand in hand, a little wiser about the vagaries of epilepsy, a bit more battle hardened, but glad to put these days behind us and open a new chapter in our lives.

But as we lay there talking, he occasionally made some bizarre comment that would shock me back to reality. At one point, he mentioned that he would be glad when he got out of the hospital so he could see his mom and dad. When I said that his parents were in Missouri, so he might not be able to see them right away, he turned to me with a questioning look.

"But we're in Missouri, too, aren't we?"

"No, we live in California."

Those two aspects of his condition—the memory problems and the fact that he still misidentified times, places, and even some people—didn't seem to be improving. But if he didn't get any better in those ways, what would it mean for him? For us?

The only person who might have some answers was the weekday neurologist who was now overseeing John's case. He stopped by that morning with a group of four or five others who appeared to be medical students, to observe John.

After the doctor had introduced himself to John and me, John said, "How am I doing, Doc? Am I still in as good shape as I was in high school?"

The doctor laughed. "I can't say, John. I didn't know you in high school."

"Sure you did. Don't you remember?"

"I'm afraid not. By the way, can you tell me where you are right now?"

"Sure, the hospital."

"And where is the hospital located?"

"Cape Girardeau."

"I see. And do you know what year it is?"

"2004."

"Thank you, John. Now, I want you to remember three words for me: green, five, and parrot. I'm going to ask you what those words are in a few minutes. Green, five, parrot."

After a brief discussion with a nurse, the doctor turned to the group and made a few remarks about John's case. I hung on his every word, trying to locate something that would tell me what to expect, but most of what he said was beyond me. I think it was then that I first heard the term *"status epilepticus."*

The neurologist turned back to his patient. "John, can you tell me the three words that I asked you to remember?"

John appeared to search his mind, then made several stabs at the words. He got one of them right.

Before the doctor left, I was able to corner him for a moment where John couldn't hear. "I have so many questions. Why does the EEG keep showing abnormal activity? Can you tell if the memory problem is getting any better? Have you been able to draw any conclusions at all so far?"

He sounded much like the weekend neurologist in his initial reply, saying that John's brain had had a severe shock and that they were continuing to try to stabilize him. But he added something new, which was the fact that an MRI they had taken showed slowing in John's temporal lobe, which he said accounted for his memory difficulties.

"Do you think his memory will start returning if he has a few more days of rest?"

"It's impossible to say at this point, Mrs. Wilferth," he replied. "We can only wait and see." He then gathered his group together and led them to the next patient.

Whoever said that no news is good news?

It turned out to be a day for meeting doctors and trying to sort through the meager information that I could glean from them. Later that morning, John's primary physician came to visit him, and he seemed to carry a more positive message than the neurologist had. He emphasized the importance of getting John back home as soon as possible and seemed to be hopeful about his recovery.

I also met Dr. Kim, an epileptologist associated with the hospital, for the first time. That meeting, too, made me feel a little better. At least for a short while. Like the other doctors, he emphasized the importance of getting John stabilized and then home. But he also added, "and back to work." I immediately seized on those words as indicating that he thought John's memory function would improve enough for him to return to his job. But when I asked him whether he believed that was likely, he only replied that it was too early to tell.

I heard the term "*status epilepticus*" for the second time when Dr. Kim told me that he wouldn't be sure until further testing whether that's what John had suffered. He said that it was true, however, that a hallmark of a *status* seizure was its inordinate length.

"How long is a long time for a seizure?" I asked.

"Fifteen minutes is considered to be a lengthy seizure," he replied. My heart sank. *Then what does that make a seizure that lasts over five hours?*

I was left with even more questions after meeting yet another doctor that morning. The man introduced himself to John and said a few words, then asked if he could speak with me outside the cubicle. He told me about a conference of neurological specialists that was currently being held in conjunction with the university and the hospital. They had learned about John's case and would like my permission to devote a special forum to him on Wednesday, with John appearing before the specialists so they could ask him questions.

The invitation immediately brought to my mind John's plea not to let the doctors experiment on him. I wondered, what good could come of such a meeting? John's emotional tone, while improved, still seemed precarious at times, with Jimmy and Joe having witnessed the outbreak of anger the previous night. Also, John was already mistrustful of doctors. Could his being grilled by a group of neurologists cause him to become frustrated and fly off in a rage? And might that, in turn, bring on another seizure?

"I don't think that would be a good idea," I said to the doctor.

"It would be a carefully controlled situation."

"I'm afraid it would upset him," I replied.

The man was obviously unhappy with my response. "Please think it over, Mrs. Wilferth. I'll come by again tomorrow morning and perhaps we can further discuss the possibility then."

After he had gone, I mulled over my decision. In declining the invitation, was I really acting in John's best interest? Wasn't this a great opportunity to have him looked at by an entire group of specialists? Perhaps the doctors could learn something at the session that would benefit him. On the other hand, maybe they just wanted to have a good look at the latest medical anomaly. Maybe it would be a kind of scientific "freak" show. After all, if these specialists wanted to talk with John so badly, his case must be rare.

Then the thought struck me that if his malady was rare, maybe it was also incurable. What did these doctors know that I didn't? Was I losing everything here? Had John already lost everything? Maybe to a group of specialists, he was an interesting specimen. To me, he was my life. And I wanted to hold on to my husband, my life. But for all I knew, they might be slipping away from me.

I suddenly felt exhausted. This was just one more important decision to make, and I never seemed to have enough information to be sure I was making the right one.

On the other hand, I thought, if I didn't make the decisions, who would? The responsibility was squarely on my shoulders. And the truth was, that's exactly where I wanted it. I was the one who lived with this man. After he was out of the hospital, he would be going home with me. Others cared about his health and wanted his best interests, but he was my husband and my charge above all. And even if I didn't have all the information, I knew him best and felt I was the best equipped to make the right choices.

This wasn't the first time I had realized, over the past eight days, that while making the decisions about John's well-being frightened me, it was also a responsibility that I fully embraced. Now, that realization buoyed me up. *I need more information,* I thought. *I'll ask that doctor more about the forum of specialists. And I'll get some feedback from Joe and Jimmy. I'll just put together all the information I can find, then make the best decision I can. That's my job.*

Please Lord, help me do it well.

When Joe and Jimmy arrived that afternoon, I told them about the invitation to the forum and asked for their opinion. They both saw the same kinds of pros and cons that I did and confirmed that it was my decision to make. They also pointed out that they were not leaving until Wednesday afternoon, so they would be there on Wednesday morning to help me with John if I agreed to the forum.

The next day the doctor showed up again, as promised. I was better prepared this time and had a list of questions about how the forum would proceed if John were to go. Where would it be held? Who would do the questioning? What kinds of questions? What would happen if he started becoming upset?

The doctor answered my questions straightforwardly, while emphasizing that this was an opportunity to understand John's condition better. Some of the best neurological minds in the country would be there, and every precaution would be taken to ensure that John was made comfortable.

"Okay," I finally said. "We'll do it. But his brothers will have to be there, too, to help reassure him."

He agreed, and we proceeded to work out the logistics of getting to the forum room the next day. After the doctor had left, I went back into John's cubicle. I considered telling him what had just transpired, but decided that it might only upset him and that he would probably forget about it within a few minutes anyway.

Is this what it's going to be like? I asked myself. *Making decisions about my husband's welfare behind his back and then not even informing him of the decision that was made?* I hated the thought, but that's exactly what I was doing. Still, what other choice did I have?

"Sorry to take so long, Babe," I said. "I missed you." It was true. And it was a relief just to be able to hang out with my husband for a while and forget about making decisions.

The next morning, the staff had washed and shaved John by the time I arrived at eight. I had brought pants and a shirt for him, and when he put them on—the first time he had worn street clothes since the seizure—he looked handsome, though a little gaunt. A nurse inserted a stent into his left wrist in case he needed a quick injection of medicine during the forum. He was unsteady on his feet after being in bed for a week and a half, so Joe, Jimmy, and I pushed him in a wheelchair to the meeting room, which was in another building.

I had told John when I first came in that we would be attending a special forum at which neurological specialists would ask him some questions. But on the way over he asked me several times where we were going: "What's this all about, again?"

I repeated what I had said before.

"Do these guys have a lot of money? Will I need to take notes?"

He seemed to be confusing the meeting with one in which he would be trying to interest prospects in financial planning strategies. "No, it's not that kind of meeting," I said. "They just want to talk to you about the seizure and your medical condition."

When we got to the forum room, we found several dozen people—doctors, nurses, and a few medical students—enjoying a buffet of rolls and coffee in a reception area. John's weekday neurologist greeted us, along with the doctor who had given the invitation. We declined the offer of food and sat for a few minutes, taking the opportunity to prep John again about where he was and what the meeting was about. He was apprehensive, still asking whether he needed to take notes.

"No, this is just for your health," I said.

"Okay," he replied. And then, "Will it be recorded?" He was still distrustful.

"No. And don't worry. You can't say anything wrong. Just be yourself."

A few minutes later, we were all invited into an adjoining lecture room with about forty seats. Joe and Jimmy wheeled John to the front, where two doctors whom I had not met before seated themselves, facing John. One, a thin man of medium height, was dressed in a sport jacket. The other, somewhat plump and lighter complexioned, was in a white lab coat. It quickly became clear that these two would be asking the questions. I took a seat in a folding chair in the first row, about a dozen feet from where John was sitting at a forty-five degree angle from me.

The forum began with someone introducing the four of us and the two doctors. The thin doctor then rose and said, "With your permission, Mrs.

Wilferth, we will ask John a few questions." I nodded "Yes," and the man proceeded.

"John, do you know where you are right now?"

"No."

"Do you know what day of the week this is?"

"No."

"Do you know what year this is?"

"2004."

"And the month?"

John looked around the room as if searching for a calendar. "February, I think."

As he tried to answer these first simple questions, I felt increasingly dismayed. Without realizing it, I had been looking at the questions, maybe even at the entire forum, as a kind of test—one that I hoped John would somehow pass with flying colors as an indication that he was getting better. So far, though, he was getting everything wrong.

Then the doctor asked him if he was aware of the war that was going on at the time.

"The Iraq War," John replied.

The fact that he had correctly answered a question that was more difficult than the previous ones seemed to impress the two men at the front. As for me, I felt like clapping. *See?* I wanted to shout out. *It's not as bad as you people may think. My husband is a smart man.*

"Do you know who that is?" the doctor asked, pointing to me.

"My wife."

"And who are these men up here with you?"

"My brothers."

"What do you do for a living, John?"

"I'm a lawyer, an MBA guy."

The doctor looked at me for confirmation, and I nodded because what John had said was true. But he hadn't really told them what he did for a living, which was financial planning.

"What kind of law do you practice?"

"Personal injury."

This time when the man looked toward me, I had to shake my head. John had not practiced personal injury law since before I met him.

When the doctor again asked about his work, John's demeanor started changing. So far, he had been sitting back in the wheelchair with an air of being somewhat removed from the interrogation. He now leaned forward and informed the doctor that he worked with individuals who had a high net worth. He started asking questions of the man, suggesting that he might be able to help him to develop effective financial strategies.

The room seemed to be getting hotter with each passing moment. I felt myself starting to cry. A nurse tapped me on the arm and handed me a box of tissues.

The doctor interrupted John, I thought rudely, as he tried to regain control of the questioning. "Do you know why your wife is crying?" he asked.

"Oh, she always cries," John replied.

No, no! I almost never cry! I wanted to say. *It's just that this is going all wrong.*

The tenor of the questioning then changed: "Have you ever beaten anybody up, John?"

"Not really."

"What would you do if someone was hurting your wife?"

"If I needed to, I'd beat him up."

"Have you ever needed to do that?"

"No."

"But you could hold your own, though, right?"

"I had a couple of run-ins in high school. I did all right."

This line of questioning was even more upsetting. The doctor seemed to be goading John, trying to get him to say things that indicated he was an angry, aggressive man. I shook my head firmly, indicating to the doctor that my husband was not aggressive in that way.

John was still leaning forward, still apparently waiting for an opportunity to interest the doctor in a financial strategy package. Maybe the man took this as a sign of aggressiveness. But if so, he was wrong. Talking to groups in a positive way was something that John did with CMS all the time, including giving presentations to doctors.

Despite the tissues, my tears were still leaking out. Part of it was anger at the doctor for his questions and part embarrassment for John. Most of his answers had been so wrong, and he was almost delusional about thinking he was talking to a group about financial planning. I felt mortified, as if I were up there with him. And why shouldn't I feel embarrassed? It was a matter of pride, both his and mine, all the more so because I felt that in some deep way we were one person.

The second doctor finally rose, saying he wanted to ask a few questions. Maybe he sensed that the session was getting nonproductive. His manner seemed calmer and less provocative than the other man's.

"Are you angry now, John?" he asked.

"No."

"Are you upset right now with your wife and brothers?"

"No."

"Are you upset with your doctors?"

"No."

The man calmly questioned John about his emotions for several minutes. His attitude seemed conciliatory. I started thinking that the two doctors might be playing Good Cop, Bad Cop. If so, the first doctor had the role of goading John to some degree in order to see his reactions, while the second was taking a gentler approach.

Finally, over half an hour after the session had begun, the first doctor rose and said, "John, thank you. Would you like to stay and listen to my evaluation of you?"

"Sure."

The doctor looked at me, and I nodded. Then he asked John's neurologist if it would be all right if John stayed, and he agreed.

After making several comments to everyone in the room about John's replies, the doctor concluded, "This man obviously has a right frontal lobe disorder. The good news is that the condition is treatable. Right frontal lobe disorder is treatable. We need to treat this man." He then went on to say that John was suffering from short- to mid-term memory loss and suggested that he have neuropsychological testing done to determine the extent.

The other doctor seemed to concur with the evaluation. He said that John was obviously very strong and well educated. He agreed with the diagnosis of right frontal lobe disorder.

With that, the meeting was over. The two doctors shook John's hand and thanked him, his brothers, and me. I had stopped crying, but I felt a little bewildered, trying to take in what had just happened.

Joe and Jimmy were due to fly out in a few hours, so they gave John a big hug and left almost immediately after the forum.

"How did I do?" John asked as I pushed him back to the other building. "Did I answer the questions okay?"

"You did fine," I said.

"Did I get good information from these doctors? Did they understand what we can do for them?"

"It really wasn't that kind of meeting," I replied.

I continued trying to digest the forum. I didn't know just what I had been expecting from it, but I didn't feel like we had gotten much. At least John hadn't become belligerent, I thought, when the first doctor had seemed to be challenging him. That was one good result. And at the end, the doctor had said that John's disorder was treatable. That certainly was encouraging. But treatable how? And what kind of recovery could John reasonably expect from the treatment? The evaluation of John as having a right frontal lobe disorder didn't seem to answer the most pressing questions.

As soon as we got back, John was taken out of neuro ICU and assigned a new room nearby that he would share with three other patients. That seemed to be a good sign. At least he had improved enough that he didn't need intensive care now.

Throughout the past few days, I had been staying in touch with Rock and Judy, and they had decided to fly back out to help care for John. They would be there that afternoon. In the meantime, I stayed with John, taking every opportunity to lie with him on his bed. At one point he dropped off into a nap and I took out the book I had been reading when the seizure occurred, a book on Mary Magdalene. Here was a woman who had borne a very great burden. Maybe I could learn something from her, I thought. But it was hard to concentrate as I listened to John breathing beside me. And it was also hard to understand what I would have to do to bear the burden if I didn't even know what burden it was that John and I would have to bear.

At one point, the weekday neurologist came by. He announced that John could probably be released the next day.

Tomorrow? I thought. *Isn't there anything else they are able to do for him?*

I caught the doctor outside the room. "What steps should we take once John's out of the hospital?" I asked.

The neuropsychological testing that the doctor at the forum had mentioned should be done, he said. And telemetry, which was a kind of ongoing EEG to locate the focal point of John's seizures, should probably be done at some point.

"But what about his memory?" I asked. "What can we reasonably expect?"

"At this stage, it's not clear how much of his memory function can be restored," he said.

"Do you mean this might just continue? How will I be able to deal with that?"

"It depends on how long you're willing to deal with it," he said. "At some point, you might want to consider institutionalizing him."

"Institutionalize him?" My own brain seemed almost to go into shock when I heard those words. *What is this man talking about? John has some memory problems. And he's been misidentifying people. So what? Are those supposed to be reasons for putting someone into an institution? Not my husband.*

"In no event will I ever, ever institutionalize him," I said, feeling like the man had said something almost obscene. I thanked him for his time and went back into the cubicle.

John was awake.

"Hey, sailor," I said. "Got any room in that lifeboat?"

"Hop in, matey," he replied. "Have to warn you, though. I've got no idea where we're going."

"That makes two of us, Babe. But wherever it is, there's no way we're not gonna get there. Scoot over."

Chapter Six

LEARNING TO LIVE IN FRACTURED TIME

John was released from the hospital the next afternoon. As we prepared to leave, a nurse presented me with his discharge papers—or I should say *paper*. It was a single page saying that John had been diagnosed with neuropsychosis. It gave instructions about medicine and provided a phone number to call for neuropsych testing, along with some numbers at the hospital. That was about it.

It was frightening to be totally on our own with only minimal guidance. *Still,* I thought, *we made it!* After almost two weeks in which hospitals had been home for me as much as for John, maybe now we could return to some semblance of normality.

At least that was my cautiously hopeful thought as we pulled into our driveway. But my naiveté became immediately clear when the first thing John said as we entered the house was a disbelieving, "We live here?"

"We've been in this house for over a year now," I replied.

"Is this Missouri? I thought we were going home."

"We're in California. Your mom and dad are out here for a few days, but this is your home."

He proceeded to investigate the house thoroughly, then went outside to explore the yard. After a few minutes, he came back in and stood staring at me.

"Sit down, ants-in-your-pants," I said. "We're home! You can relax now."

"Where were we?" he asked.

"In the hospital. Two different ones. You had a terrible seizure on Easter and were hospitalized for twelve days. We just got home from there."

He shook his head: "Really? I don't remember any of that."

"That's because the seizure played havoc with your memory," I said.

"Is that why everything looks so strange?"

"Don't you remember the house at all?"

"I'm not sure," he replied. "It looks odd."

"Maybe it's because you've been away so long."

"Was I away?"

"Yes, silly goose. That's what I just said. You were in the hospital."

"How long was I there?"

And so it went. Far from easing us back into a sense of normalcy, our return home emphasized, all the more starkly, the severity of John's memory dysfunction. And it made clear that what was to be normal now in the Wilferth household was a far cry from what had been standard operating procedure just a few weeks before.

John's early confusion about his surroundings included more than his not recognizing the house. Even more disconcerting was the fact that he continued to misidentify people on television, as he had at UCI, sometimes claiming to know them from his childhood. The incidents were bizarre. On the second or third day back, he was looking at a young woman being interviewed on television and remarked, "That's Madonna."

"Who is?"

He pointed to the screen: "That woman there. It's Madonna, the singer."

"Madonna is white," I said. "That woman's black."

"I'm sure it's Madonna," he said. "Bet you a million dollars."

The woman was clearly African American and didn't have the remotest resemblance to the pop star Madonna, but no matter what I said, I couldn't convince him otherwise.

Such incidents were very disturbing. For a while John seemed caught between reality and some world being manufactured by his mind. I was afraid it might continue indefinitely—and if it got worse, what then? But after a few days, the misidentifications faded away and then stopped altogether.

Whatever cross-wiring in his brain was causing the behavior somehow straightened itself out.

But the memory problems remained. During the first week back, we discovered that there were still many holes in John's long-term memory, the part relating to events more than a few days old. Though he had no special difficulty recalling scenes from his boyhood and his days in college, numerous gaps remained from the years just prior to and after our marriage.

Thankfully, though, some of the lost memories started returning. Occasionally, when I brought up some past incident in conversation, his face brightened as he recalled something he had previously been unable to remember. This was a hopeful development, and I was eager to help him fill in as many of his long-term memory gaps as possible. I often took him back to our life together before the *status* seizure, trying to spark memories. I talked about family, friends, his job, things we had done, and places we had been to together—anything that occurred to me. Whenever he showed a glimmer of recognition, I tried to reinforce it by helping him focus in on and expand the memory.

It was like trying to rebuild a brick wall that had suffered a terrible barrage and was now shot through with huge holes. We laid down one brick at a time and tried to cement it in firmly. Our problem was to find the bricks. By the end of May, many large gaps still remained. Over half of the wall that was the memory of his life over the seven or eight years prior to the *status* seizure was still missing.

Even more troublesome was the damage to his short-term memory. This was something we had not been able to get a clear picture of at UCI, but the extent of the problem became evident at home. He forgot most new information within minutes. Occasionally, he could retain a vague partial memory for a few hours, but not in any detail. And a night's sleep erased all new input. Each morning he woke with no recollection of what had occurred the day before.

He couldn't even remember why he couldn't remember. During the first couple of weeks, he often expressed wonderment at his difficulty in retaining new information, and I had to repeatedly remind him of the seizure and how it had affected him. The tone and substance of the conversations were predictable:

"How bad is the problem?" A puzzled expression on his face.

"The doctors say there was damage to the part of your brain that controls your short-term memories."

"Will I get better?" His eyes narrowing.

"They don't know yet. You're supposed to have neuropsych testing in a couple of months. That should tell us a lot."

Shaking his head: "I guess I have to believe you. All I know is that everything keeps slipping away from me. Far too fast. And I can't find a way to keep it from happening."

His short-term memory impairment affected almost every aspect of our family's life. Blake had returned from Missouri the first weekend we were back home, and we were both kept on our toes by having to serve as John's memory. Though he didn't forget to perform basic activities such as to eat, shower, or dress, he had to be reminded daily of many other things—to take his medicines, to return perishables to the refrigerator if he made himself a sandwich, or the fact that his socks were in a certain drawer.

Even something so simple as watching television together took on an entirely new character. John and I had always enjoyed an occasional TV drama, but now when we watched a dramatic show, he repeatedly lost the plot line, especially during commercials, and had to keep asking what had gone before in the story. When the show was over, he typically complained that the ending made no sense to him. We soon discovered that about the only television programs he could truly enjoy were stand-up and impromptu comedy shows, and sporting events.

His ability to perform simple household chores was also affected by his memory difficulties. If I asked him to take out the garbage, he invariably returned with the bag of trash, complaining that the pick-up receptacles were not in the garage where they were supposed to be. I then explained to him—again—that we had never kept them in the garage and told him where he could find them outside. Or if he took a short break from a task such as fertilizing the lawn, he forgot that he had been doing the job. It remained only partly done until I reminded him or he accidentally stumbled onto the fertilizer spreader, which might or might not trigger his memory of what he had been doing.

"I think you've found the perfect way to avoid doing anything around the house," I said to him one day after finding a box that he had promised to sort through sitting on the garage floor, the job half finished. He was now ensconced on the couch, watching a golf game on TV.

"What's that?"

"You've discovered a great way to avoid any household chores. You just forget what you were doing and move on to something more enjoyable."

"Yeah," he said, his eyes still on the television, "that's a pretty good ploy, isn't it? Maybe I should write a book: *How to Forget Your Way into a Soft Life.*

I'm sure there are a lot of husbands who would pay good money for that." He then turned to me and raised his eyebrows in a look of innocence. "Okay, tell me. What am I supposed to be doing?"

I broke out laughing.

With that little joke, which was typical of John, he demonstrated two qualities that softened the blow of his memory dysfunction and showed that he was far from being defined by his limitations. The first was his ability to occasionally laugh at his situation. The second was the fact that after the confusion of the first few days was over, he was often very sharp in the moment.

He was so sharp, in fact, that sometimes friends and others could barely believe that he harbored any dysfunction when they talked with him. As long as the sense of what was being said did not rely much on what had been talked about five or ten minutes earlier, he often carried on a conversation with no obvious impediment. At those times, the personality that had made him the life of many gatherings was able to shine through as brightly as ever.

Even if you knew John had a memory problem, his ability to carry on a seamless conversation could lead you to overestimate his cognitive capabilities. Melanie, who came to stay with us in early May to help out for several weeks, made this mistake. One day she had a small run-in with John because she kept telling him that he could remember something he had forgotten. Later she said to me, "I don't understand it, Melinda. When we talk, he seems just as intelligent as he ever was. It's hard to believe that he can't focus in on what he needs to remember and just do it."

I made the same mistake myself a few times. One day about a week after we were back home, I was giving John an impromptu short-term memory test. I kept asking him about his specific recollections from a few minutes before, fifteen minutes before, an hour before, while he tried his best to articulate what, if anything, he recalled. At one point I could tell that he was getting a little frustrated, so I said, "Try hard, John! Take your time and think about it. You can do it!" I then asked him another question.

He sat for a moment trying to remember, then suddenly rose: "No more of this!" he said. "You don't understand—I can't remember these things!" He strode angrily out of the room.

I quickly realized that my words, which were meant to be encouraging, had suggested to him that the memories were within his grasp but that he wasn't trying hard enough to retrieve them. By that time, I should have known better. In reality, the memories simply weren't available, and my insisting that he could remember only succeeded in making him more frustrated.

Melanie and I weren't the only ones to make this misjudgment. Other of our family and friends fell prey to what I called the *You Can Do It John* syndrome. But that was just the thing—he *couldn't* do it. To understand why, it helps to draw a comparison. Imagine that someone asked you to remember what you were specifically doing a month ago Tuesday between ten and eleven a.m. If something very significant had occurred in your life at that time, you might find the task easy. Otherwise, it would probably be impossible to recall your specific actions during that particular hour. And if so, no amount of urging by someone saying, "You can do it, you can do it!" would help you retrieve the memory. Why? Because whatever brain traces might be left of that period would either be gone or be so meager as to make the memory inaccessible.

That's what it was like for John. Except instead of the memory being of something that happened a month ago, it was typically of events that had occurred within the past hour. The memory traces laid down in his brain were just like anyone else's except for one crucial fact—they didn't last nearly as long. And, just as with everyone else, when they were gone, they were gone irretrievably.

Gradually, John became accustomed to his dysfunction in the sense of not being surprised that he couldn't remember. He came to understand it as a continuing fact of his mental life. But while he accepted it cognitively, he fought against it emotionally, becoming increasingly frustrated and irascible. Visitors seldom saw this side of John—the sullen, withdrawn, uncommunicative man who could abruptly lash out in an angry tantrum if he felt his peace was being disturbed.

The Lord knows he had ample reason to feel frustrated. For one thing, his freedom of movement was restricted by the fact that he was no longer allowed to drive. The law in California was that after a major seizure, an individual couldn't drive for a year, and then only with a physician's approval. So he had to rely on me to take him everywhere.

He had mixed feelings about that. On the one hand, he was thankful for my help. His cognitive map of the area we lived in had been one of the long-term memory casualties, and he was unable to develop a new one because of his impaired short-term memory. As a result, he had no clear sense of how to get back home when we were out, and he was frequently apprehensive, asking me how far we were from the house and in which direction it was. So even if he had been allowed to drive, he wouldn't have been able to go far without getting lost. He understood this and often remarked that he was glad I was at the wheel.

On the other hand, being unable to drive weighed heavily on him. He had always been very self-reliant, and having to depend on me to take him everywhere was a bitter and somewhat emasculating pill for him to take. He sometimes mentioned how much he missed being able to drive, and how not being able to made him feel powerless. "What freedom that would be," he said one day. "To be able to drive somewhere to have lunch on my own, or even just go to the market by myself—that would be fantastic. To feel like I'm not trapped in my own house."

But it wasn't just his not being able to drive that made him feel confined. He was trapped not only spatially, but also mentally. Even a man in a prison cell who has lost most of his freedom of movement can still feel free in his mind as long as his memory is functioning. He can fly into the past at will. He can write a letter to a loved one and recount what he read in some book the night before and how it helped him in planning for the future. But for John, the vital connections that the rest of us, including the man in prison, can ordinarily make between past, present, and future were severed.

As a result, his most basic way of feeling trapped was his sense of being imprisoned in the moment, unable to think much beyond what was right here, right now. And that meant he couldn't soar in his mind in the way that was normal for him. From my first conversation with him over the phone years before, it had been clear that he wanted to accomplish many things in his life. He was always dreaming, planning, and trying to cut out a pathway of achievement by using the present as a stepping stone to the future. Now he was finding out that to be useful for the future, the present has to be tied closely to the past. But for him, that tight connection had been lost. And without it, the present couldn't serve as a firm foundation to help him achieve—or even formulate—new goals. He was no longer able to make and then act on plans for tomorrow for the simple reason that any such plans quickly fell through the holes in his memory.

He often sat quietly for long periods, his eyes closed. Though sometimes he was only dozing, at other times he was trying to focus his mind on what had happened earlier that day, looking for a way to force his memory to do his bidding. But the exercises accomplished little, if anything, and left him feeling even more thwarted. He would then rise and pace around the house like a caged animal separated from its natural environment. Or, more accurately, like a man separated from his most natural self. A man lost in the here.

Blake and I started walking on eggshells, never sure of his mood. If one of us made some comment to him or asked a question, he might respond vehemently, telling us he needed it to be quiet.

One day Blake was talking to one of her friends on the hall phone while John sat watching television in the living room. Twelve-year-old girls are full of life, and even from where I was upstairs, I could hear that she was getting a little loud. Momentarily, I heard John's voice: "Blake, keep it down! I'm trying to watch TV!"

The noise level abated for a few minutes, but Blake's voice and laughter grew gradually louder. As I came down the stairs, I saw John rise and start toward her. "For God's sake," he roared, "I told you to be quiet! How do you expect anyone to be able to put two thoughts together with all that racket? Give me that phone! You are grounded young lady!"

Blake dropped the phone and rushed past me and up the stairs.

"You didn't have to yell at her like that," I said to John, angry myself now.

"I told her to keep it down! I need it quiet so I can think!"

"You were only watching television."

"Dammit, Melinda, I have to think just to watch TV."

"Well, that doesn't justify you shouting at the top of your voice," I said.

He turned and walked back to the couch. "You don't understand," he said. "You just don't understand anything."

I went up to talk to Blake. I saw she had been crying, but when I sat down and reached for her to comfort her, she looked up at me and said, "Mom, it was my fault. John-Daddy told me to be quieter, but I forgot."

"There was no need to yell at you," I said.

"But it's hard for him now with the memory problem. I know he gets frustrated. I have to try harder not to be too loud."

I was so proud of my daughter at that moment. She was taking responsibility for her actions, while at the same time reminding me that my own angry response to John had been inappropriate. It could only make him feel more frustrated.

We talked for a while longer, then I went back down and sat with John on the couch. "Do you have a minute?" I asked.

"What's up?" he replied, his manner serious but calm.

"I just talked with Blake upstairs and she apologizes for being too loud."

"When was she too loud?" he said.

I reminded him of what had happened no more than twenty minutes before, but he had no recollection of it. When I told him that he had yelled at her, he was very apologetic. "I don't remember it, Melinda. But I'm sorry if I did. Sometimes I feel crazy inside."

I saw that our conversation was starting to get him down, and I wondered if it wouldn't have been better if I had just dropped it. I leaned over and kissed him. "I know, Hon," I said. "I know. And I'm sorry for yelling at you, too. All we can do—you, me, Blake—is the best we can. And that's just what we'll do."

"Deal," he said.

But my immediate thought was that he would probably forget the deal in a few minutes. I prayed to God, though, that he wouldn't—and that I wouldn't, either.

Further complicating John's life were the side effects of the drugs he was taking. At the time, he was on three anticonvulsants, and they often tended to leave him tired and listless. This, added to his growing frustration and his sense that he had little useful to do, started making him increasingly inactive. After the first couple of weeks back, he spent more and more time in front of the television and sometimes even sleeping during the day.

I hated to see this. He was withdrawing from life, which seemed to me the worst thing he could do. If there was to be any hope of improvement, it was crucial for him to keep exercising his mind and seeking ways to effectively cope with his decreased memory function. He had to keep trying.

I prayed about this every night and often wrote about it in my journal. I asked God to make John well, but in the meantime to keep me strong and to help me understand how I could best help him stay active and hopeful. The prayers kept me focused on the question of what I could do to make a difference. They also helped me become increasingly clear that my job now was to empower John in any way I could.

Empowerment meant helping him feel stronger in himself. Short-term memory, I was learning, was such a vital part of cognitive functioning that John's deficit left him severely weakened both in his abilities to perform simple tasks and in his sense of who he was. My job was to find ways to help him do as much as possible on his own and not feel weak and frustrated at every turn.

One day Blake and I came up with an idea that we thought would help John become more self-reliant: we would leave sticky notes for him in prominent places, such as the bathroom mirror, where he would be bound to read them. The notes would remind him of what he needed to do that day and of where things were. That way, he wouldn't have to rely on us constantly reminding him of what he should be doing.

We tried the idea for a couple of days, but it failed miserably. John read the notes, but he followed through on few of them. In talking to him about it, I discovered that he forgot their content almost as quickly as he read them. Or he would get confused, wondering if he had already done what the piece of paper instructed. I realized then that if he did what a note said but forgot to take the note down, he might read it again later and repeat the action—which could be disastrous if it instructed him to take some medication.

Our next effort was to make lists for John. We reasoned that if each morning we created a list of things for him to remember to do that day, he could simply check off the items on the list as they were done. It seemed like a simple, workable idea in its conception. The problem was, John took the list in the morning but forgot to consult it. He had to be reminded repeatedly about its existence, and often we would find that he had misplaced it.

We eventually realized that there was no good substitute for just being nearby and serving as John's memory. The job couldn't be given over to pieces of paper.

Some other ways of trying to help John feel stronger were more successful. One of those was for me to change my way of talking to him so as not emphasize his memory problem. I had been in the habit of often asking him whether he remembered this or that occurrence that had happened earlier in the day, hoping his answer would prove that he was getting better. But his reply was almost always "no," and the questioning only served to remind him that he had a memory problem—which was the one thing for which he needed no reminder.

I decided that if I wanted to discuss with him something that had happened earlier that day, I would talk to him as if he remembered it, while giving him the information that would enable us to discuss the occurrence. An example: The old way would be for me to start a conversation by asking him if he remembered that his friend Jack had called earlier. Then, when he almost certainly said he didn't remember, I would explain what the call had been about. The new, better way was to start the conversation by saying something like, "It was nice for Jack to call you this morning and invite you to the race track tomorrow." This might or might not remind John of the call and the invitation—and it probably wouldn't—but it would at least ease him into the conversation by providing information about what the call had been about. And it was far preferable to the blunt "Do you remember the call?" which inviting a negative answer that would only remind him of his limitations.

Blake and I often discussed how to talk to John in more empowering ways. What we should aim for, I explained to her, was to view the world from his perspective as much as possible and always to talk to him with that perspective in mind. He was living in the present, restricted to the here, much more than most people. Instead of trying to make him live in our expanded time, we should meet him where he was, in the moment. That way, he would feel more engaged with the world and with us.

And that was really our main objective—to create an environment in which he could stay mentally and emotionally engaged. To help do that, I always asked him to go with me whenever I went to the store or on some errand. Even if he initially declined, I would gently badger him until he agreed, telling him how important it was to get out into the world often, even if only for a few minutes.

At home, we found that playing simple card games such as Spades and Gin Rummy, games that require little in the way of short-term memory, was a good way to keep John engaged and interested. Many afternoons and evenings found John and me, and sometimes Blake, in the kitchen or the living room, playing cards. That may seem like an inconsequential activity, but actually those gatherings were much more than just games. As we dealt and played the hands, we were able to continually interact—talk, make jokes, just put our troubles aside for a while and be together. And the games brought out John's competitive nature, which was good to see. In between the laughs and the chitchat, he was always determined to beat the pants off me. And he often did.

One day he and I had a marathon session of Spades that began in the early afternoon. I forged ahead quickly and stayed there, so he kept wanting to extend the number of points required for someone to be declared the winner. I kept agreeing, and the game continued through a dinner of sandwiches. Finally, at ten, we decided to go for two more hands, with the one ahead after that to be declared the winner of our Spades Marathon. Of course, John was dealt two super final hands and pulled ahead of me at the last minute—just as he had nosed ahead of his closest competitor in that imaginary swim meet in Sikeston. And just as back then, he flashed me a big victory smile.

"Da winna!" he said, as I showed him the point totals. "When did we begin this game anyway?"

"I'll give you a hint. You didn't need a shave back then like you do now."

"That long, huh? Well, I hope you don't mind my big smirk. I have to enjoy my victory while I can. I'll probably forget all about it in half an hour."

"Good," I said. "Then I'll be able to tell you that I'm the one who won the big card game."

"What big card game?" he said, looking around as if he had lost something.

Every night I thanked God for the opportunity to help John, even if my efforts sometimes went awry. Being in that position was something new for me. Before the *status* seizure, he had seemed to need me very little—a fact that may have had something to do with our pre-*status* problems. Just about everyone who is married wants to feel needed by his or her spouse, but I seldom felt that way back in those days. That had changed radically since the seizure, and I embraced the responsibilities that had been placed in my care—though I would have given them up in a second for John's getting better.

Of course, responsibilities always come with a price to pay, which was certainly true in this case. I often felt uncertain of what I was doing, and afraid. I leaned hard on God every day, praying for the strength and intelligence to do what was best for John and our family.

What scared me most was that he might have another major seizure. The doctors still didn't fully understand what had brought on the *status* event, and it seemed very possible for him to have another horrendous attack at any time. If so, would it cause further brain damage? Would he even survive it? These questions were often gnawing at the back of my mind. I didn't discuss them with John because it would have made him worry. The one thing the doctors had identified as a partial cause of the *status* seizure was stress, and John was already under plenty of pressure from his memory problems; he didn't need to be told of my fears.

At the time, John had up to three doctor's appointments per week, seeing his general practitioner, a neurologist, a neuropsychological specialist, and the epileptologist, Dr. Kim, who had dealt with him at UCI. Doctor Kim seemed cautiously optimistic about John's regaining some of his short-term memory function, but he was less hopeful about his not having another major seizure. He thought it would be a good idea to subject John to telemetry to determine the focus of his epilepsy for possible removal, but not until he further recovered from the *status* attack. In the meantime, I would just have to make sure that he took his medications, try to keep him as unstressed as possible, and look for any signs of an impending seizure.

One bright light on the medical front was the fact that the focal seizures John had often suffered just prior to the *status* attack had stopped occurring. He remained completely seizure free through May. This, added to the fact that some of his long-term memory gaps were being filled, suggested that his brain was gradually getting healthier.

But in late May a new medical problem erupted that seemed to threaten any progress he was making. The problem arose from the fact that while fighting to get out of his straps at Mission Hospital, he had repeatedly torn away his urinary catheter, and this had caused internal damage to his waterworks that the doctors had not been aware of at the time. The problem showed up at home when going to the bathroom became increasingly difficult for John. A visit to a urologist showed why. Urinary tract stricture had developed due to scar tissue and was growing worse. The only way to correct it was with an operation.

But the operation required John to go under anesthesia, and my immediate question was what the anesthetic might do to his brain. Could it cause him to lose further memory function, either long—or short-term? Would he come out of the operation with the kind of psychosis he had had in the hospital? Might it even trigger a seizure? John's neurologist, who had to give permission for the operation, didn't think that the anesthetic would have any adverse effects. But he couldn't guarantee it. The urologist, though, could guarantee that without the operation, John's waterworks problem would only get worse. So we had no choice.

I was worried sick about the operation, probably partly because I was still shell-shocked from what we had gone through the last time John had been in the hospital. Whatever the reason, I was so anxious that I asked Mom to fly out and stay with us for a few days to hold my hand while I held John's.

She arrived the day before the operation, and the next afternoon we were with John at UCI while they prepped him. I had the bright idea of giving him something simple to remember beforehand, thinking that if he was able to recall it afterward, that would be proof that the anesthetic had not damaged him. So, just before they were to take him into the operating room, I grabbed his hand and said, "Babe, I know you're going to be just fine. But I want you to remember three things for me: one, two, blue. Will you try?"

"One, two, blue," he said, giving me a thumbs up. "I'll remember."

Mom and I waited anxiously, alternately praying together and reassuring each other that John was strong and everything would go well. We also took turns reminding one another that at least he wouldn't have to be under the anesthetic for long, because the doctor had said the procedure should take less than an hour.

But that hour passed, and then another, and no one had emerged to announce that the operation was over. I started envisioning all sorts of things that could have gone wrong. One of the worst was the possibility that he had had a seizure in the middle of the operation and was at that moment strapped down, shaking violently. The image was almost unbearable, and Mom and I redoubled our prayers.

Another hour went by.

"Mom!" I yelled at one point. "It's been way too long. Something has gone wrong!"

"Melinda, it doesn't help to assume the worst. We have to have faith in the Lord. We have to. Now let's pray together again."

Finally, three and one-half hours after the operation had begun, the surgeon came through the doors with what I interpreted as a grim look on his face. Before he could open his mouth, I was begging him to tell me whether John was all right.

"Yes, he is," the doctor said. "The operation took longer than we had thought because we ran into some complications. But in the end, it went reasonably well. He should be able to go home later tonight, but we'll need to do a couple of follow-ups over the next few weeks."

Fifteen minutes later we were able to go into the post-op area where John, not even groggy, greeted us with a smile.

"The surgeon said you survived it," I said, giving him a kiss.

"Well, the main thing is that they didn't cut off anything important."

"Okay, wise guy," I said. "Now here's my question: Do you remember what I told you just before they rolled you away?"

"Hmmm, let me think," he said. "What I remember is this: one, two, blue. Is that it?"

"That's it!" I turned to Mom and we gave each other high-fives. "That's perfect! And that was over four hours ago!"

I was overjoyed that he had remembered those three simple words, and Mom was just as happy. For the next few minutes, we held a veritable party.

"Maybe that's the answer," John chimed in to the celebration. "Just keep me under the anesthesia, and I'll be able to remember everything."

"Now there's a brilliant idea," I said, hugging him. "We'll keep you asleep. I'll only wake you when I want you to remind me of something I told you."

I couldn't get over how happy I was about this small accomplishment that seemed so big to me. *Thank you Lord,* I kept saying under my breath, *thank you, thank you, thank you. And thank you for Mom, too.*

Aside from the possibility of John suffering another major seizure, and how best to empower him, probably my main worry at the time was our finances. With neither of us working, our financial situation was increasingly precarious.

The biggest part of the worry centered on health insurance. Fortunately, John had been covered in his job at CMS when the *status* seizure hit. Without that, we would have been facing horrendous medical bills. He remained covered for the time being, but if he couldn't continue at his job, the coverage would lapse and COBRA, the government program, would kick in. But the premiums for that would be astronomical, far from what we could afford. And without insurance, another major seizure could devastate us financially.

We had three options. John could go back to work at CMS, enabling his insurance there to continue; I could find a job that included reasonable health insurance for our family; or both. In late May we started talking about what we should do. I always began the conversations by laying out our financial situation, which John would have forgotten since our last discussion. But once reminded, he quickly understood the options, including the first one, because over the past few weeks he had begun recalling more about his job and his coworkers at CMS. And the more he remembered, the more eager he was to return to work.

"The solution is obvious," he said in one of our first conversations about the matter. "It's for me to go back to CMS as soon as possible. That's the answer to lots of things—not only money and insurance, but to my getting out of this house and back into the world."

"But are you sure you could handle it?"

"What all did I do there?"

"A big part of your job was to set appointments over the phone with potential clients. You would set the appointments for both you and your partners. You used to say that you were the one 'in charge of the charge'."

"So I talked to potential clients over the phone about the products we offered, right? And then I made appointments for them to talk to someone in the office who could close the deal?"

"Yes."

"What can be so difficult about that? How much memory does that require?"

"I guess not much," I replied, knowing that the client information that he needed would be on his computer.

"Then I should be able to do it. And I'll never know if I don't try. The question is, will they want me back?"

"I think they already do," I said. I reminded him that most of his coworkers had spoken to him over the phone several times since his return home and had been continually supportive. And Rich and Julian, the major partners in the firm, had both indicated that they hoped he would be able to return to work.

"Good. Then that's our answer."

I wanted to believe he was right, but I was worried whether he would really be able to handle the job. And how stressful would it be? On the one hand, there seemed no better way of empowering John than to support his going back to work. Not to mention the financial benefits. But on the other hand, would his return cause so much stress that it might bring on another major seizure?

The bottom line was whether it was advisable medically, so we talked to Dr. Kim about it. His view was that the only way to find out what John was capable of was for him to test himself out in the world. If the stress became too much, he could always withdraw. On the other hand, necessity is the mother of invention, so the need to perform might help his brain create new pathways to restore some of his lost memory function. And though there was danger that the stress would prove too much, maybe he would actually be under greater stress if he remained at home, feeling frustrated and powerless.

With Dr. Kim's medical opinion in hand, the next step was to find out for sure how John's partners felt about him returning to work. So we invited Rich, Julian, and several of the others to come to our house for coffee.

On the scheduled afternoon, John and I spent an hour beforehand talking about what the visit was for and going over details of CMS and his job. He was a little nervous, so I kept telling him that he would be all right because he was so good at thinking on his feet. I was actually pretty nervous myself, but after his co-workers arrived, John proceeded to amaze me by being very much on top of the event. He gave few indications of his memory difficulty, and when the subject did come up, it was because he took it on directly:

"I just want to make one thing clear," he said to everyone near the end of the get-together. "I do have this small memory problem, so sometimes I might ask something that you think I should already know. But just bear with me. Melinda tells me I do well in the moment, and I think that's the main quality for the job."

His partners liked John, and it was obvious that they wanted to believe in him. As they left, they all mentioned again that they were looking forward to John's returning to work as soon as he felt able to.

"You did it!" I said after I had closed the door. "You won them over!"

"I did?"

"It's that boyish charm again. But you know what that means, don't you?"

"What's that?"

"Now you have to go to work and support me in the style to which I would like to become accustomed."

"I knew there was a catch."

I called John's work the following Monday, and we arranged for him to begin in mid-June. He would start on part days, and we would see how it went.

On Monday, June 16, I drove John to the CMS offices in Newport and we went in together. Everyone shook his hand and welcomed him back. They showed him to his old desk, and I helped him locate some of his main files on his computer. Half an hour later I left.

As I rode down in the elevator and walked out to the car, I felt more anxious than a mother leaving her child—one with very special needs—at his first day of school. There were countless questions going through my mind. How would his body and mind react to the new challenges he would be facing? How would others react to him? Would he still be able to hold his own in a competitive environment? How much stress would he put on himself trying to make a successful return to the business world?

Yes, I knew very well that John was no child. He was my husband, and every bit a man. And he was a brave one at that, determined never to act the invalid and willing to venture out and try his hardest in a world where he often felt lost. I realized that he was scared when I left him. I could see it in his eyes, even as he told me he was going be fine. And I realized why he was frightened. Because at a time in his life when he was being tested severely at every turn, he knew that this might be his hardest test of all.

I knew it, too, and as I drove away I was as scared as he was.

Chapter Seven

HEROIC, BUT FLAWED PASTICHE

They say you can get used to anything, but I don't think it's true. Watching John disappear into his office building on the mornings I took him to work never got any easier.

He often woke on those mornings knowing he had something important to do, but not remembering what it was. At other times, he surprised me by somehow remembering that it was a workday. Much of the forty-five minute commute was spent in a pep talk, as I did my best to build his confidence. While we sped toward Newport, I assured him that I would call him within the next few hours; that I would be there to pick him up at some prearranged time; and that I was sure he would have a successful day.

Arriving at his building, I pulled into the parking lot. From there, he knew the way to his office. "Hon, please don't be hesitant today about asking questions of the other guys. They're on your side one hundred percent. I'll call you soon to see how you're doing."

"Do you have my number?"

"Yes, of course I do."

"When will you be back?"

"You have an appointment at three with your neuropsychologist. I'll be here at two. If you need me before then, my number's on your cell phone list and in your Rolodex."

A hesitant smile, but his voice strong: "I feel like I'm going to get a lot done today. I want to get totally organized."

"That's exactly the right attitude. I know you'll do fine."

A kiss, then he was out of the car and walking toward the building. A brief turn, a questioning look, then through the doors and gone.

As my heart fell.

It wasn't that I saw him going off unprotected into a den of wolves—at least not one consisting of other people who might take advantage of him. After all, what I told him about his partners' support was true. But there were wolves, of a kind—they were the hopes and expectations he put on himself each morning. My fear was always that if he wasn't able to live up to those expectations as he moved through his day, they would turn on him, gnaw on his spirit, and bring him down.

That's why I tried to build him up on the way to work—so he would be better able to meet the challenges he set for himself. In a way, though, I was also feeding the wolves by reinforcing his expectations.

Maybe my encouragement only amounted to one more version of the You Can Do It John Syndrome. I don't know. Many times, I wished I could just turn the car around and drive us home, where the demands were fewer, the wolves more controllable. But that's not what he wanted. Though I could see the uncertainty in his eyes when we entered the parking lot, the only thought of turning around was in my mind, not his.

As I drove back home, I tried to picture what he was doing at that moment. Was he getting a good start to his day? Perhaps organizing his files or calling a client on the phone? I knew from talking with him after work that he was finding it difficult to perform his main job functions. His entire career had been based on interacting with people: meeting them, winning their confidence, accessing their needs. In doing so, he had always relied on his ability to manage his calendar and juggle times, which was something that had been second nature to him prior to the *status* seizure. But now it was hard for him to keep times and appointments straight in his mind.

He also found it more difficult to exercise one of the main skills necessary for someone in his position—discerning and keeping focused on the needs of prospective clients, whether he was talking with them face-to-face or over the phone. He often worried that the other person would detect his memory problem, see it as a weakness, and respect him less. He told me more than once that his anxiety so crippled him at times that it was hard to force himself to get on the phone.

To me he was a hero. I couldn't imagine doing what he was trying to do. How do you resume your role as a financial advisor when one of your most important cognitive faculties, your memory, repeatedly leaves you grasping for thoughts that are no longer there? But his will to succeed was so great that I couldn't believe he wouldn't find a way to do it. Maybe my pep talks helped. But mostly it was just him, fighting hard to get back some of what he had lost.

He was not only brave, but also right, to go back to work. It was the only way he could discover what he was capable of now. Would his memory function improve by being put to the test? Would fresh neural pathways develop that could take over for those that had been destroyed during the seizure? None of his doctors knew the answers, but from the beginning, Dr. Kim had emphasized the value of getting him back to work. If nothing else, it was a return to some normalcy, and that's what John needed more than anything. I wondered, though, if it ever really felt normal to him to be back in his office, with his memory constantly disappearing.

I tried not to call him immediately after I arrived home, but around eleven I almost always picked up the phone to see how he was doing. I was always longing to hear a clear, definitive rendition of what he had accomplished over the past few hours, but I seldom got one. The recounting of his morning would usually be vague or confused as he attempted to explain to me what he had been up to. I listened carefully to what he said, gauging the tone of his voice, and trying to pick up his spirits if he seemed down.

Two hours later we were on the phone together again, and then again before I left to pick him up, or on my way. As we returned home, he would try once more to explain his day, but usually all he remembered were events of the last hour. Sometimes he consulted notes he had made to try to clarify for me—and himself—what he had done, whom he had talked to, and what progress he had made. He might or might not remember enough to understand what the notes referred to.

There were some high points, enough to keep us both hoping that gradually, over time, he would find a way to re-deploy the organizational and people skills that we were sure remained somewhere deep inside. Once in a while he would report what he considered to be an especially good conversation with some prospective client. And once, soon after he returned to work, I called him late one morning and found him excited about a discovery he had made.

"It was incredible!" he said. "I was getting ready to start putting together a file of potential clients, and I found an extensive database already on my computer—names, occupations, addresses, phone numbers. I couldn't believe it! All that work!"

"That's great, Hon!"

"You didn't by any chance have something to do with that, did you?" he asked.

"As a matter of fact, I think I know what database you're talking about," I replied. "I helped you put it together at home before the *status* seizure. It has about six thousand entries—contacts across the western states."

"Six thousand! That'll keep me busy for the next year."

Later, when I picked him up, there wasn't a word about the database. And when I mentioned it, he didn't remember our earlier conversation.

He was always exhausted by the time we got home, an effect not just of work but also of his medicines, which still tended to make him lethargic. Dinner was at five-thirty or so, after which he typically watched a little television, then fell asleep. I woke him at nine to take his medicine. We then visited for a while or watched television together, but he would again be asleep within an hour or two.

While John was resting early in the evening, I often wrote in my journal. I told God about what had happened that day—as if He didn't know already—asked Him to bring John full recovery, and prayed for strength for myself:

> *God, You are in control. Don't let me lose my joy. I have been feeling so low. Keep John and me close. I accept my husband for who he is. John is wonderful just the way you made him. I love him and I am so thankful that he loves me. Please use this heartache for your good—I want you to be proud of me during such a hard time. Give me wisdom and strength to do the best for my husband and Blake. Be with us. I love you. Amen.*

The strength always came right away, just from talking with God, sharing my worries and thoughts with Him. I was always sure that He was very close, listening and loving all of us.

I also continued to find fortitude and understanding at Saddleback Church. I paid close attention to the sermons, seeking messages that I could apply at home. One Sunday, Pastor Rick told us that when we prayed we should not ask for the same thing over and over because God hears us the first time. He pointed out that Our Heavenly Father does not get nearly the credit He deserves. He blesses us with the food we eat, a roof over our heads, people to love who love us, and much more. We should spend more of our prayer time praising rather than asking. This was another lesson on the way to understanding more fully how to lay a problem on God's shoulders, and I took it to heart. I stopped asking, in every journal entry and prayer, for God to make John better. He already knew what I longed for. He would answer my prayers in His own time in His own way. It was for me to accept His answer.

I was beginning to understand that God was already giving us unexpected blessings that stemmed from John's condition. For one thing, we both had a changed attitude toward material possessions. Only a few months before, too much of our lives had revolved around clothes, cars, and furniture. Plopping down a credit card or a check for some new item had become a way of telling ourselves that everything was just fine, that our marriage wasn't heading for disaster. Now that disaster had actually struck—though in a form we had never expected—we understood much better what is truly important in life. Health, making the best of what we have, and standing together in the face of adversity—that's where the real action is, I realized. Not in things.

Another blessing was that for the first time, John sometimes prayed with me, something that was very unexpected. Though he was a believer, he had never taken much interest in religion or prayer during our marriage. Once, before the *status* seizure, we had gotten into a discussion about an upcoming work meeting, and I had suggested that he pray about it. His reply had been, "God is great for everyday problems, but this is business." It had amazed me how he could parcel his faith out so that he viewed prayer as something suited for Sundays and holidays, but not for work.

That had changed. No longer did he believe he was in control of everything in his life. Like me, he had come to realize that control is a relative thing. Yes, we can control some aspects of our lives, but many of the most important elements are gifts that we cannot give ourselves.

Our shared acceptance of this idea brought us closer. And the fact that John now sometimes prayed with me made me love him more than ever. It also reminded me of a memorable event that had occurred when I was a child, and led me to hope for something I had never before had much reason to think would happen.

The event had involved my paternal grandmother and grandfather. My grandmother, who was very religious, had lived with and loved my grandfather for many years, but she had always gone to church alone because he was not a believer, or at least not a practicing one. One of my grandmother's great wishes was that her husband would someday be baptized and start attending church with her. But she never begged him to go or used her longing as a lever to try to get him to convert. She simply lived a good, honest, loving life and allowed her deeds to speak for her faith.

In time, that apparently turned out to be the secret that opened my grandfather's heart to God. He was in his sixties, and they had been married for almost forty years, when he started taking a greater interest in my grandmother's church activities. Then one day he announced to her that he wanted to be baptized. Not long after, I stood in the church along with my mother and father and witnessed the event. I asked my mom about the tears I saw that day. Why was Granddad crying? Was he sad? Oh, not at all, she told me. He was very very happy.

The fact that John now prayed with me once in a while brought back that beautiful memory. It also led me to dream that someday he would start attending church with me on a regular basis.

What I dreamed about and prayed for most, though—John's improvement—was getting no closer to being realized. Every time I took him to one of his doctors in the early summer, I hoped to hear some positive words about his prospects for recovery. But there were none. It wasn't that his physicians were totally negative. Doctor Kim kept a wait-and-see attitude about what would eventually come of John's return to work, and none of the doctors ruled out the possibility that his epilepsy, his memory, or both would improve. But they were hesitant to make any predictions due to their lack of hard data.

That was about to change, though. Soon they would have some data on which they might be able to base a conclusion. John had begun seeing a neuropsych specialist who had arranged for him to take a battery of tests at UCLA—the University of California at Los Angeles. These were the tests that some of the doctors at UCI had suggested he undergo after recuperating at home. The tests would focus on several functions related to the frontal lobe of John's brain, including memory, emotion, and logic. He had been having difficulties in all of those areas, though the problems were most obvious for memory. The battery of tests consisted of John orally answering a series of questions posed by someone. His answers would give the doctors a clearer idea of specific deficiencies in each of the areas and a stronger foundation from which to make predictions.

He took the tests over a two-day period in late July. He was also given an MRI—magnetic resonance imaging—procedure, a kind of brain scan. The results of that would be compared to the results of an MRI he had been given at UCI. This would help the doctors determine if any of the injured portions of John's brain had healed.

At the end of the two days, John felt that he had done reasonably well on the tests and was hopeful about the results. But it would be a week and a half before we could find out.

In the meantime, our lack of a steady income was becoming a major concern for me. John had not yet found a way to marshal his efforts to become truly productive, and though his partners continued to back him, he had not brought any new accounts into the business. As for me, I had redone my resume, sent it out to a number of design firms, and posted it on the Internet. But though I had gone to a couple of interviews, nothing had come of them. I still got an occasional contract interior design job by word-of-mouth, and I continued to sell a few she-she things, but we were far in the red every month.

I had not shared my financial worries with John, trying to spare him the stress. But one evening soon after the neuropsych testing had been completed, he caught me at my desk shaking my head and in a grim mood. I had been looking over the bills that were coming due—house, car, insurance—and wondering how we could possibly hold on for more than another month or two. It was clear that if John wasn't able to start functioning more effectively at CMS soon, I had to find a job. But if I did, I didn't know how I would be able to handle it while being John's chauffeur, supporting him emotionally, and staying home with him on days he didn't go to work. Not to mention mothering my daughter and keeping up a house.

John asked me what was wrong, and I broke down and told him. "I don't know what to do. I want to work, but who's going to hire me on a constantly changing schedule that's geared to yours?"

When I saw the look on his face, I quickly added, "Babe, it's not your fault. We're in this together. I want to do everything I can to help you get back on the right track at your work. It's just that I can't see right now how we're going to do this."

I wasn't expecting John to suddenly come up with some wonderful solution; I just needed to share with him what I was feeling. But that turned out to be the right thing to do. As we talked, we came to a couple of conclusions. First, I would become even more proactive in seeking a good job with a flexible schedule. Second, we would allow God to guide our finances and lead me in my job search. The fact that John acknowledged the importance of trusting in God picked up my spirits enormously.

I redoubled my efforts to find a position and was heartened when I received a call one day from an administrator at a design school in Anaheim. He liked what he saw on my resume and wanted to talk with me in person and view my portfolio.

This seemed a wonderful turn of events! I didn't know how I would be able to manage the considerable distances and time that would be required in going back and forth between home, Newport, and Anaheim if I landed the position. But I figured that God was well aware of that problem, and if He wanted me to have the job, He would make it possible for me to deal with the various commutes.

I was proud of my portfolio, which contained fifteen years worth of design, art, and engineering drawings, along with photographs of my work, and I was sure it would impress the administrator. How could he not hire me? I couldn't wait to prove to him how right I was for the job. But I never got the chance. The day before my interview, I was at home copying my resume and gathering my notes, and I ran out to get my portfolio from my car, where I remembered having left it after showing it to a potential client for my contract design work. It wasn't there. I checked under the seat, between the seats, in the trunk. No portfolio. I decided that I must have taken it inside. I went back in and turned my office, the rest of the house, and the garage upside down looking for it. I enlisted John's help. Still no portfolio. Crazily, I found myself looking in places where it could not have possibly been—sugar jars and tiny drawers in tables. It was nowhere.

Had I inadvertently left it at someone's house or at a previous job interview? Had I knocked it off the seat and out of the car somewhere when I got in or out? Racking my memory gave me no clue about what had happened to the portfolio or where it might now be. *How ironic,* I thought, as I realized that the kind of frustration I was experiencing—a frustration that visits all of us now and then—was something John had to face practically every day on the many occasions when he forgot where he put something. Except in his case it was even worse, because if he misplaced an item and started looking for it, he would often forget what he was looking for. He would then find himself no longer searching for the item, but searching for some hint of what it was he was supposed to be searching for.

Finally, I gave up. The only thing left was to rebuild the portfolio as best I could from loose drawings and photographs. I might be able to put something presentable together, but it couldn't be done overnight. I called the administrator at the design school and told him of my plight: "Would it be possible to reschedule the interview for next week to allow me to replace my portfolio?"

He told me that the interview couldn't be put off because he had to make a hiring decision quickly. He apologized and wished me well in my job search. And that was that.

I felt myself getting angry. At whom or what, I didn't know. Myself maybe, or the situation, or maybe even God. Here I was, trying my best to get a job to help support our family, and now this. The single promising opportunity that had opened up for me lately was ruined. It didn't make any sense to me. I walked out on the porch to get some air, and a minute later the tears started coming.

I heard John behind me: "What's wrong?"

Through swollen eyes, I reminded him about the lost portfolio and explained that I wasn't going to be able to interview for the job in Anaheim. He looked at me for a moment, then said, "Melinda, God must not want this for us. This just isn't it."

That's right! I realized immediately. *He's absolutely right.* How could I forget that I had asked God to show us the way? That's exactly what He had done—and John had been the one to remember and to realize what it meant. The missing portfolio was the answer to my prayer. For whatever reason, God had decided that the opportunity with the design school wasn't even worth the time spent in an interview. John and I agreed that there couldn't have been a clearer answer.

We were back to the starting gate financially, but I was more certain than ever that God had his eyes on us and would show me the way to the right job—the one He wanted me to have.

I didn't have to wait long. In early August, I learned about an insurance agency located in Newport that was seeking new agents. I had never before sold insurance or anything similar, but living with John I had picked up a little knowledge over the years about selling financial instruments. Why couldn't I do something similar? The agency offered training, and there was the prospect of making a substantial income quickly. It also struck me that the insurance sales training might somehow enable me to help John in his work. And the best part was that the agency's offices were only a block from John's workplace and the hours would be flexible, which all but solved the main problem of my taking a job. In all of those important ways, the opportunity seemed almost perfectly designed for me.

I interviewed with several people at the agency, and they quickly offered me a position as an agent in training. I snapped it up. It would be a month or more of classes and hard study before I could actually take the insurance exam and start selling insurance, but it seemed clear to me that this was an opportunity that God had led me to.

The news was not so happy on our other major front. Two weeks after the neuropsych tests, Dr. Kim gave us the results. John had done poorly on the tests, and the MRI had shown no substantial healing. Given that it had been over three months since the *status* seizure, Dr. Kim wasn't encouraged about further recovery of John's memory function. It wasn't impossible, he said, but he thought it unlikely that John would get significantly better.

The news was hard for both of us to take, and especially John. Though he could no longer remember taking the tests, he understood very well his cognitive limitations. It was bitter for him to hear from his epileptologist that those limitations were probably always going to be there.

Doctor Kim did offer us one ray of hope, though, something he had previously mentioned several times—a possible treatment for John's epilepsy. If it worked, it would be a tremendous blessing. My greatest fear continued to be that John might suffer another major seizure that did further damage to his brain. If the epilepsy could be healed, an ominous hammer would be lifted from over his head.

The treatment involved using surgery to remove the part of John's brain that was the source of his seizures. First, to identify the source, John would have to go through telemetry, a procedure in which he would be taken off his medications so that seizures could occur. Dr. Kim admitted that the procedure was a little dangerous, but he assured us that the seizures could be controlled. John had stabilized enough, he said, to undergo the procedure in the near future. He asked us to talk it over and let him know whether we wanted to go ahead with telemetry. If so, he would make the arrangements for it to be done that fall.

Even in regard to John's memory problems, we weren't ready to give up entirely. A friend mentioned to me a naturopath she knew of, a Dr. Steenblock. His methods were somewhat unorthodox, she said, but he had apparently enjoyed some success in treating individuals with cognitive dysfunctions. I ignored the feeling that I was clutching at straws and called him almost immediately to make an appointment for John.

As a naturopath, Dr. Steenblock emphasized the importance of stimulating the body's own healing mechanisms and achieving optimum balances of nutrients, minerals, and other bodily elements. He ran some tests and discovered that John was seriously out of physiological balance in several ways, especially in the amount of iron in his blood stream. He mentioned the possible use of hyperbaric oxygen as a treatment for rejuvenating brain cells destroyed during the *status* seizure, but he said it would be necessary to get John into better physiological balance before it could be seriously considered.

John and I decided that we would need a lot more information about the possible efficacy of the hyperbaric oxygen treatment before thinking seriously about it. But in the meantime, Dr. Steenblock's emphasis on balance and natural healing seemed reasonable, and we asked him to set John on a dietary and exercise regimen that would be compatible with his anticonvulsive medications.

Whether God had directed us to Dr. Steenblock or not, we didn't know. But his words helped keep alive our hope that eventually we would find some way for John to regain his memory. We now found that what had been so maddening while John was at UCI—the fact that so little is known about the brain—had a positive side. With no one knowing for sure what was possible, we were free to believe that healing could somehow occur. When that was added to our belief that with God, all things are possible, it wasn't hard for our hopes to keep burning.

My insurance training went well. I had to study long hours to prepare myself as quickly as possible, but our neighbor Carlos, who also worked in Newport, graciously volunteered to take John to and from work whenever we needed, which helped free up time for my studies. On September 2, I took and passed my insurance exam. Within two weeks, I had already made several sales.

John continued going into his office at least three days a week, and I kept hoping that one day soon he would announce to me that he had made a sale of his own. His accounts of his day were still typically vague, but I reminded myself that like an armless man who learns to drive proficiently using his feet, he might be able to relearn his old skills by using parts of his brain not injured in the seizure.

The most positive sign that he was making progress was the fact that his partners continued to back him in his efforts. I reasoned that they must be seeing some improvement in his ability to contribute to the company, or else the realities of business would lead them to withdraw their support.

Then one evening in late September while John was asleep, I received a call from Rich asking if John and I could meet with him and several of the other partners after work the next day. A chill went through me as I agreed. This, I thought, would not be good.

The meeting was attended by four of John's partners, and it didn't take long for me to find out that my intuition was right. CMS had two divisions in the same building: the smaller one marketed and sold high-end financial planning packages, while the other, considerably larger, focused on selling insurance. John had been vice president of marketing for the first division. His partners now explained that they thought he would be more effective if he switched to the insurance sales division.

"It would actually be a move in your favor, John," one of the partners said. "You would get excellent training, and there would be more people around to help you out whenever you needed it."

No, not in his favor, I thought. It was clear that the main reason for the suggested move was that John had not shown enough progress. For that to be acknowledged and out in the open was a huge blow. Even worse was the fact that his partners were, effectively, suggesting that he be demoted.

John's eyes were immediately flashing anger: "You're saying you don't have faith in me to do the job, right?"

"It's just difficult, John," the partner continued. "We're all hoping for a full recovery, but right now you need a lot of support, and unfortunately we don't have the time or personnel to give you the assistance you deserve. You would have more resources available on the insurance side."

I couldn't be angry with John's partners. They had gone out of their way to support him, displaying a decency that had been especially welcome after the way he had been treated by a couple of companies earlier in his career. And even now, they were trying to find a place for him in the organization. Still, I hated what was happening because I saw that being forced to leave his current job would devastate John.

"Please don't transfer him over there," I said. "It won't work. John knows this job. The skills are still inside him somewhere. And he knows you guys. He trusts you. If he's to continue getting better, right here is his best chance to do it."

John and I argued his case as best we could, but his partners, though regretful, seemed to have made up their minds. Nothing we said was swaying them. Then I had an idea—something I had thought about a few times before but had never considered to be realistic.

"What if I came in to help John at his present job?" I asked. "I have my insurance license now, and I'm not entirely ignorant of the kind of work he does. I even helped him put his database of potential contacts together. I could come in with him and do the job that you guys don't have time for—answer questions, help him stay organized—until he gets up to speed."

I turned to John: "Why couldn't we do that? I would be your short-term memory when you need it."

John didn't take my suggestion particularly well. I understood why. His pride had been deeply hurt, and here was his wife rushing in, offering to help him do something that he wanted to be able to do himself. But to me, the idea of assisting him made sense, and because nothing else was working to get the others to reconsider, I continued to press it.

For the next ten or fifteen minutes the six of us talked the possibility over. What would it involve? What were the logistics? John's partners weren't entirely convinced by the end of the meeting, but they seemed to be reasonably accepting of the proposition and promised to consider it further. As John and I got into the car at about 6:30, I felt a tentative sense of relief, thinking that for at least the time being we had escaped what I saw as a veritable tragedy.

But John was not happy. As we drove toward home, he showed just how upset he was at what had gone on at the meeting.

"The bottom line is that they're trying to fire me!" he said.

"No, they're not," I replied. "They're offering you a position on the insurance side."

"It's the same thing. They want to fire me from my old job, and send me out to the street to sell."

"Not necessarily. They seemed very interested in my idea to come in and help you."

"They're not going to go for that! They want to get rid of me, not keep me! And anyway, the thought of you coming in to work with me is ridiculous. How would that help anything?"

Nothing I said would pacify him, as he became increasingly irate. We were on the tollway heading toward home when he unhooked his seatbelt and started reaching into the back of the SUV.

"What are you trying to do?"

"I need my briefcases," he replied.

"Why do you need them?"

"I can't reach them. Pull over so I can get out and get my damn briefcases!"

"You want me to pull over right here on the tollway?"

"Just pull over. There's hardly any traffic."

It was getting dark, and there was little light on the highway, but I did as he said. He got out and opened the rear of the SUV. Then, two briefcases in hand, he marched directly away from the vehicle and started toward the grassy embankment to the right.

"Where are you going?" I yelled from inside the SUV.

He didn't turn.

I got out. "John? Where are you going?"

He said something I couldn't decipher as he started up the embankment. It was an anomalous sight—a man in a suit, two briefcases swinging from his hands, climbing rapidly up a steep, grassy hill as if late for a business appointment being held at its top.

"John, what are you doing? Stop!"

"Leave me alone!" he called back.

In the suit and heels I had worn for the meeting, and no doubt appearing no less odd than John, I started up after him, still yelling, as he reached the crest of the embankment and went out of sight.

A couple of awkward minutes later, I too reached the top of the hill, where I found a two-lane road paralleling the tollway. In the dusk I could barely make out John, already a hundred yards down the road, hurrying away from me.

"John!" I screamed "Come back here! Where are you going? You need to get home to take your medicine!" As far as I could tell, he didn't even turn around.

To catch up with him on foot was out of the question, so I decided to return to the car, get off at the next exit, and come back around to meet him from the other direction. I slowly made my way down the hill in the dark and five minutes later was back on the highway, looking for the next exit. As I drove, I dialed his cell number several times, but there was no answer.

The exit was farther than I had hoped, but once off the tollway, I managed to find the road John had been walking along and started back to intercept him. He was nowhere to be seen. For the next half hour I drove up and down the road, getting out many times to call for him and trying, unsuccessfully, his cell number. He had disappeared.

At that point, my panic really set in. The first thing I thought of was that he might go into a major seizure. He had been extremely upset in the car, and he didn't have his medicine. Was he at that very moment having a seizure somewhere out there in the night? Was I repeatedly driving by him while he lay in the dark just off the road, with no one there to help him or even see him?

Another possibility was that during the fifteen minutes or so it had taken me to get back to where I thought he should have been, he had been the target of foul play. With the suit on and the briefcases, he would look to a potential robber like someone with money, credit cards, an expensive watch. And also someone on foot, out of his element, and vulnerable. Should I be calling the police?

Not yet. I decided that he could have easily started walking down some street that connected to the roadway. Or maybe he had decided to hitch or had even called a taxi with his cell phone. I realized that the likely reason he wasn't answering my calls was that he could see it was me calling. If someone else called him, he might answer. I rushed home, and by eight o'clock I was on the phone to Mom, his parents, and his brother-in-law Augie. "Try him on his cell phone," I said to all of them. "If he answers, find out where he is."

Not knowing what else to do, I started calling the hospitals in the area to see if he had been admitted. In between calls, I kept trying his cell phone. Still nothing.

It was almost nine when I got a call from Judy: "Augie got hold of him. He's in a hotel. He won't say where."

Thank God he was safe. But for how long? Without his medicine he had a greatly increased chance of going into a full seizure.

I immediately got the phone book and started calling every hotel in the area to ask if a John Wilferth was there. I must have made fifty calls over the next two hours, with no success. Finally, sometime after eleven, on the second call to one of the hotels, I located him in Irvine, ten or fifteen miles from where I had last seen him. The clerk patched me through to his room.

"John, this is Melinda. Please don't hang up. You have to have your medicine. I can bring it to you. Just tell me which room you're in and I'll drop it off. Then you can stay there all night if you want."

Once he told me his room number, I grabbed his medicine and took off for the hotel. When I arrived, he was sitting outside on the edge of the walkway.

I got out of the car in a hodgepodge of emotions including relief at seeing him, anger, and fear that he would jump up and run away from me into the night. "What are you doing out here?" I asked, trying to be nonchalant.

"I came out for some air and couldn't remember which room I was in." At another time, he might have smiled as he said that, but this time he wasn't smiling.

"Please come home with me."

Silence.

"How did you get here?" I asked.

"I think I got a ride with a Mexican guy. Nice guy."

"You can stay if you want," I said. "But you need to take your medicine. I have it with me."

For a moment he seemed to be considering, then he said, "No. There's nothing here for me. Let's go home."

We found his room and retrieved his briefcases. On the way back, he apologized. "I don't even remember why I left, Melinda."

"Let's not talk about it now," I said. "But please, please, please, don't ever do anything like that again, you goose!"

I knew he would forget my request and probably forget the entire incident by morning. He might wake with the unhappy sense that some problems had occurred the previous day, but he wouldn't remember the details. For a change, I envied him. I wished I could forget so easily. But that night, and more than once on following nights, I lay awake and again stumbled up that steep, dark embankment, feeling clumsy and powerless as I tried my hardest to get to a husband I knew would not be waiting for me at the top—as if in a bad, bad dream.

Eventually, the sound of John's blessed breathing calmed me down. He was still there. I was still there. Blake was safe in her room. What else mattered? With that decided, I turned against my husband's confused but sturdy back and fell asleep.

CHAPTER EIGHT

CHOOSING TO LIVE

The hardest decision John and I had to make in the first six months after the *status* seizure was whether to go ahead with the telemetry procedure that Dr. Kim had suggested. The purpose of telemetry was to locate the part of John's brain that was the source of his seizures—the focal point—so it could be surgically removed. A successful operation would mean an end to John's epilepsy. Without surgery, he would probably continue having major seizures, any of which might cause further brain damage. Of course, the focal point might be found in an area where an operation could not be performed without causing further harm. But there was no way to know whether surgery was a real option without telemetry.

If that was all there was to it, the decision for John to undergo the procedure would have been easy. But there was a crucial complication, which was the fact that telemetry itself was dangerous. To determine the source of the epilepsy, John's brain activity had to be recorded while he was having focal seizures. This required taking him off his medications, allowing the seizures to occur, and recording the results when they did. The problem was that without his medicines, he might also have one or more major seizures during telemetry, with unknown results.

It was a catch-22 situation. The condition for John to have a chance at getting better was for him to get temporarily worse. The question was, could the getting worse part be restricted to his having small seizures, and would it be truly temporary? Or would telemetry result in a major seizure—maybe even another *status epilepticus* event—that left him with even greater brain damage?

Doctor Kim admitted that there was some danger in telemetry. But he emphasized that he would be overseeing the process and that John would be under tightly controlled conditions. The procedure would take place at UCI, where John would be hooked up to brain electrodes and monitored for seven days around the clock. Though Dr. Kim would be home after hours, he would be connected to the hospital by computer and able to view John's brain data at all times. If a major seizure were to occur at night, the hospital could notify Dr. Kim immediately. He would then be able to monitor the event and direct the nurses in how to handle it.

John and I talked about whether to go ahead with telemetry several times, with the conversation always taking the same basic route.

"It scares me," I said. "I can't get over the idea that they want you to have seizures. It's asking for trouble."

"You just told me a minute ago that they only want me to have focal seizures."

"But what if one of those turns into a grand mal? And then goes on and on? It could injure your brain even more."

"You also just told me that the doctor said they could control any big seizure," John replied.

"That's what he says. But they weren't able to stop your *status* seizure at the hospital for over five hours. Has Medicine progressed so far in six months that now they've got it all figured out? I don't think so."

"Well, even if it turns into a grand mal, it's better to have one in the hospital than out on the street somewhere. And that's what will be happening unless I get the surgery. I think it's a risk worth taking."

"You're the risk taker," I said. "I'm not good at taking risks."

"It's my risk to take."

"It's mine too! You don't have to stand there looking at yourself while you're having convulsions, wondering whether you're ever going to come out of them."

"Melinda, I know it must be hard for you, too. But when you weigh both sides, the biggest risk is to do nothing. I don't want to die in the hospital, or to wake up and not be able to think any more. Which is as good as dying. But the chance of that is even greater unless they find a way to cure the epilepsy. I want to live. To have telemetry gives me the best chance to live."

After we had gone through the same argument several times, I capitulated. In the end, I had to agree with John. The greatest peril was to do nothing. To choose life—or the best chance for life—meant to choose telemetry. We gave Dr. Kim the go-ahead.

The procedure was set for October, only a few weeks following the meeting at which John's partners had suggested he move to insurance sales. After considering my offer of coming in to work with him, they agreed to try it. John also agreed. But the experiment would have to wait until after telemetry, and maybe until after subsequent surgery and recuperation. We left open the exact date for him to return to work.

Not long before John was to go into the hospital, we informed the naturopath Dr. Steenblock that we had decided to go ahead with telemetry. He strongly advised us to reverse the decision, saying that the procedure might be disastrous. We also briefly saw two other naturopaths at about that time, and they agreed that telemetry was not a good idea. One of them said that it might kill John.

This unanimity among three doctors scared me so much that I was tempted to withdraw my support for the procedure. But the arrangements were already finalized. The insurance company had given its okay, the hospital facilities had been reserved, and Dr. Kim had set aside the week in his schedule. More important, John was still insistent about moving ahead with it. Despite their misgivings, the naturopaths didn't seem to be offering anything as promising as the possibility of surgery. John, who didn't have a lot of trust in naturopathic medicine anyway, convinced me again that telemetry was our best option.

I tried my best to lay my worries on God's shoulders but found it hard to shake the specter of something bad happening during telemetry. When we arrived at UCI on the big day, I was full of trepidation. John was given a small room with two chairs, a table, and a television, with the remaining space packed with monitoring equipment. A technician came in to attach thirty or more electrodes to his head, placing bandages over the electrodes to help keep them in place. The wires were connected to a machine with a monitor showing John's brain activity. Dr. Kim would be able to see the same activity on his computer while at home.

There was also a video camera trained on John so that his behavior could be continually recorded. The signals from the electrodes and the camera were correlated so that Dr. Kim could later match what had been happening in John's brain at any moment with the video recording.

After the technician had finished attaching the electrodes, John looked like some weird hybrid creature from the ancient past. The chaos of wires sticking out of his head made him into a model for Medusa, while the wrappings that kept the electrodes in place reminded me of a mummy. The contraption was heavy and cumbersome. He immediately started complaining about how his head itched beneath, and I worried about how he would be able to sleep wearing such a get-up. I could already see that he was in for a long week.

Rock and Judy had come out to help support John during the procedure, and we agreed on a schedule for staying with him. I would be there after I got off my insurance work from about four in the afternoon until ten. Either Rock or Judy would then stay overnight, while the other would be with him during the day until I came in again.

On the first evening, the hospital staff kept John on his three anti-convulsive medications. This was a kind of control procedure to make sure that he wasn't having any seizures while taking his medicines. The next morning, when they found that he had had no seizures, they began withdrawing him from his medications by giving him smaller doses of each.

The idea, as Dr. Kim had explained it, was to get John to the point where he would have several focal seizures over the next week. Once the data from these were analyzed, the source of the epilepsy should become evident. What was not wanted was a full-generalized convulsive seizure. Not only would a grand mal be dangerous, the data gathered from it might be "off the charts" and not of much use.

While I was at work during the second day, I received a call from Rock saying that John had had a focal seizure. This was good news because it indicated that the telemetry was working as planned. If he could just have one more small seizure a day over the next five days, that should provide enough data for Dr. Kim to pinpoint their source. Then we could go home and arrange for John's surgery. Once that was completed, we could start walking down a safer, more hopeful path. It was beginning to look like my qualms had been groundless.

But the expected wave of focal seizures didn't develop. That night John was seizure-free, and I received no calls the next day. Now I started worrying that he would have no more seizures at all and that telemetry wouldn't provide enough data to determine the focal point of his epilepsy.

When I arrived at the hospital on the third evening, John was in good spirits, other than having to put up with the discomfort caused by his headdress. After he finished his dinner, we decided to watch television for a while. The bed rails were down, and I decided to get into bed with him on top of the covers. There were two buttons near the bed that I had been instructed to push if he began having a seizure of any kind. One was to set a mark on the recording that was being made of his telemetry. This would indicate the start of the seizure. The other button was to call the nurse.

"How many more days am I supposed to be here?" John asked as I cuddled up to him.

"Only four more. This is already your third."

"This thing on my head is driving me batty. I feel like I'm wearing a bunch of TV antennas. Maybe if you plugged me into the television, we could get more channels."

I laughed. "Somehow that doesn't sound like a real good idea."

We had been lying there for only a few minutes when John suddenly shifted his body, then put his head back and groaned. A second or two later he began making the telltale smacking noise that I had heard many times before. I fumbled for the two buttons, pushed them, and leaped out of bed.

Almost before my feet hit the floor, it was clear that this was not going to be a simple focal episode. John's body was starting to jerk violently, already in the throes of a full seizure. I pulled the rails up to keep him from falling out of the bed and ran to the door to call for help. "Nurse! Come down here! He's going into a full seizure!"

"Okay, I'll be right there," came a voice from down the hall, but its tone seemed to lack a sense of urgency.

John was shaking wildly, his head tossing back and forth, with the electrode apparatus threatening to start knocking against the head rail. I went to him, leaned over, and tried to push his body toward the foot of the bed, but as usual found it difficult to move him. I kept expecting hospital staff to come rushing through the door, but no one had yet arrived.

I turned and this time screamed for the nurse: "Someone please help me! He needs his medications to stop this! He's going to hurt himself!"

This was the first full-scale seizure I had witnessed since the *status* seizure, and I felt myself reacting in a way that I had never before responded to any of John's attacks—utter panic. The main reason was that since the *status* event, I had come to view his major seizures in a new way. Before, I had seen them as always taking a fairly predictable course. Despite their harrowing nature, they were short-lived phenomena whose worst parts tended to last no more than ten minutes or so. Immediately afterward came the post-ictal stage and then sleep.

But since April, all previous bets were off. I now knew how terrible a seizure could become, how long it could last, and what devastation it could cause. To see John again totally out of control and to understand that this could turn into another horrifying event that lasted for hours made me desperately want it to end as quickly as possible. It also created a panic in me that went beyond anything I had felt with any of his other seizures. What made the situation worse was knowing that it was through our own decision that this appalling thing was happening.

It had been over a minute since the seizure had started and still no one had arrived to help. John's arms were shaking with the rest of his body, but he seemed at times to be trying to raise them to grab at the electrodes, as if unconsciously he wanted to rip them off his head.

"John, don't do that!" I said. "You need to keep those on." As if he could hear me.

I again ran to the door and stuck my head out into the hallway. "Nurse! He's seizing! I think he's trying to tear his electrodes out! You need to come down here right now!"

I went back to the bed and did my best to try to get him to lower his arms, but he was too strong. "John, please Hon, don't," I begged him. I stood there helpless as he continued to flail, hoping that he didn't actually get hold of any of the electrodes and worrying that if he did, he would rip part of the skin from his scalp.

Again I screamed, begging and demanding that someone come take care of my husband.

"I'm coming, I'm coming," I heard the nurse call.

Finally, two minutes or more since the seizure had begun, the nurse entered the room. "Please calm down, Mrs. Wilferth," she said as she went to John's bed and started trying to talk to him.

"He can't hear you!" I said. "Call Dr. Kim!"

"Dr. Kim can see all of this at home on his computer," the nurse said, trying to placate me. "Please compose yourself. Why are you so upset?"

"Because I'm afraid you won't be able to stop this! You need to give him his medicine now!"

"I can't do that without Dr. Kim's authorization," the nurse replied.

"Then call him now and get his authorization!"

I don't know if the nurse had summoned them before she came in or had somehow contacted them from where we were, but a moment later, three security guards came through the door, crowding into the tiny room.

"Please calm down, ma'am," one of them said, echoing the nurse.

"How am I supposed to do that? My husband is having a grand mal seizure, and no one's doing anything about it. Look at him!"

"Ma'am, I'm sure they're doing everything possible," the guard said, repeating a standard line that seemed to have nothing to do with the reality that was taking place right in front of our eyes.

John was still in full seizure, the power of his paroxysms causing his bed to jitter on the floor. He still appeared to be spasmodically grabbing at the electrodes, though so far he hadn't succeeded in pulling any out.

The nurse was on the wall phone near the door, talking to someone. I assumed it was Dr. Kim. I expected her to put down the receiver quickly so she could get John's medications and inject him, but she just stayed on the phone. *What are they talking about? Why is everything taking so intolerably long!*

Finally, I asked the nurse to give me the phone as I practically took it from her hands. "Doctor Kim?" I said. "You told me you could control this! He went into a grand mal seizure over five minutes ago. You told us this would be all right!"

He asked me to take a breath and collect myself. He said that he was monitoring the seizure at that moment and that they, meaning he and the hospital staff, were in control of the situation.

"What do you mean you're in control? In control of what? He's in a full-generalized convulsive seizure. He's trying to tear his electrodes off. That's a far cry from a few little focal seizures. How do you know this won't do more damage? How do you know that?"

The doctor continued trying to convince me that they were in charge of what was happening, while telling me that my panicked reactions weren't helping. I knew that the latter part was true: the only thing that my spinning around like a whirling dervish had accomplished was to bring out the security guards. But even so, I couldn't understand in what sense either he or the staff had been or were in control of the situation. It was John's brain that was in control, and his brain wasn't taking orders from anyone.

After I gave the phone back to the nurse, I stood in the doorway and tried to stay out of the way. By that time, there were two nurses and three security guards in the room. One of the nurses gave John an injection, apparently on

Dr. Kim's order, but he continued shaking, his face strained and red from the terrible stress the seizure was placing on his body. *This man isn't going to wake up,* I thought as I stood there. *That other doctor was right. I've killed my husband.* In between my dire thoughts, I prayed over and over to God to make the seizure stop, to not let it go on any further.

A few minutes later, the shaking finally began subsiding. The seizure had lasted almost a quarter of an hour—the longest one I had witnessed other than the *status* event. Almost immediately, the post-ictal stage began, with John belligerent as always. He started raising himself, trying to get out of bed, while the security guards grabbed his arms and legs.

"Leave him alone!" I yelled.

"Ma'am," one of the guards said, panting from the exertion of trying to hold John, "we have to control him."

"Just let him rest! He needs to rest now!"

Realizing that I was still behaving frantically and wasn't helping anything, I turned and went out into the hallway, leaned against the wall, and felt myself sliding down until I was sitting on the floor. I then started bawling like a lost four-year-old, my cries echoing up and down the hallway as I listened to the struggles in the room behind me. After about ten minutes, I managed to pull myself together enough to get up and go back inside, where John had calmed down considerably. I saw that he had finally managed to pull off his entire headdress. It lay there on one side of the bed, a tattered skullcap with a few clumps of hair attached to its underside. If the electrodes were recording anything now, it could be nothing more than whatever charges might be in the room air.

I felt a little more in control of my emotions, probably partly due to my crying jag, but mostly just because the seizure was over. I began apologizing profusely to the nurses and the security guards for my behavior. Before, I had always prided myself on what I thought was fairly levelheaded thinking during John's seizures. This time I had turned into a basket case. At the same time, I didn't entirely see myself as the hysterical woman getting in the way of the wise medical staff. I still failed to understand why it had taken so long for someone to get to John's room, and I continued to question how much control over the telemetry process anyone had.

After John was fully pacified, I called his parents and told them what had happened. Just a few days before, they had mentioned that if he had a major seizure during telemetry, they hoped that one of them would be there. The reason was that in all of the years John had suffered from epilepsy, neither had ever witnessed him having a full-generalized convulsive seizure. Now I had to inform them that they had missed this one, too—though to me, that seemed to be a blessing for them. I prayed that none of us would have to witness it happening again during the remaining four days of telemetry.

A technician came in to reattach the electrodes and John, though very tired, had to remain awake while that was done. I helped him smooth down his hair, which looked like a mad barber had been at work, and I was able to talk to him a little while the technician worked. But he was groggy and confused. I hoped it was only a sign that he was exhausted and not a sign of something more ominous.

By midnight, the electrodes were all reattached, and John was finally able to sleep. Judy had come in to stay with him through the night, and I went home. The next morning, I came in to the hospital early. Rock, who was there, stepped outside for a few minutes while I visited with John. I found him very confused. He no longer seemed to understand what he was doing in the hospital.

"What's going on here?" he asked. "Are they going to put needles into my head?"

"No, Hon," I replied. "These are wires for your telemetry. The doctors are trying to find out the focal point of your seizures."

"But why are all these needles in my head?"

"They're not needles. They're wires. They're attached to your scalp to detect your brain waves."

I had to keep repeating to him the purpose of the electrodes and why he was in the hospital.

"Are my folks here?" he asked me at one point.

"Yes. Both of them have been sitting with you over the last few days."

"Are my brothers here?"

"No. Just your mom and dad, and me."

He was still confused when I left. In talking with him, it seemed to me that his short-term memory was much more tenuous than it had been before the previous night's seizure. In fact, he seemed to be no better now than the day he had arrived at UCI back in late April. I was angry. *We've lost five months of recovery,* I thought. *This is turning out to be a disaster.*

That afternoon, I shared my misgivings with Rock and Judy as we talked outside John's room. "Despite the assurances," I said, "I don't think Dr. Kim and the staff have much control over what kind of seizure he has. If they did, why did he have a grand mal? Without his medications, he's helpless against his epilepsy. It can do whatever it wants with him. I think he should go home today. The sooner the better."

They argued against that idea, saying that the medical staff would probably be able to adjust John's medicine to ensure that he had only focal seizures during the next four days. They agreed that telemetry was difficult to go through, but they still thought it would be worth it once the source of the epilepsy could be determined.

It seemed to me that if Judy and Rock had actually witnessed this last seizure, or any of John's other major seizures, they might not feel so confident that moving ahead was the right thing to do. At the same time, I realized that my doubts were colored by the fact that I had been there when it happened. Maybe it was me who had the skewed perspective.

The final decision was John's. I was worried that he wouldn't be able to address the question rationally, but when we went in to talk with him, he seemed considerably less confused than he had been that morning. I realized that maybe the seizure had done no permanent damage after all. I told him of my doubts, but he insisted on moving ahead, so I again relented. *All we have to do is make it through three more days,* I thought. *Please God, keep him safe until I can get him home.*

He had two more focal seizures over the next three days, both while I was there. That made a total of three focal and one grand mal seizure that he had experienced through six days of telemetry. Whether that would provide enough data to enable Dr. Kim to identify the source of the epilepsy we didn't know, but we were hopeful when we met with him in John's room on the sixth night.

The verdict was not what any of us had wanted to hear. The doctor told us that from the data he had gathered, it appeared that John's seizures were originating from a part of his brain that had so far remained undamaged. To remove that part could further incapacitate John, possibly turning him into a "vegetable."

The word shocked all of us.

"What do you mean 'a vegetable'?" John said loudly. "I'm not having surgery if it's going to leave me brain dead!"

I was as troubled by what the doctor was saying as John was. "Do you mean there's no way surgery can be performed? Are you saying that nothing can be done?"

Rock and Judy urged me to calm down as I found myself starting to become upset again.

The doctor repeated that the focal point of the epilepsy appeared to be in a part of John's brain that was indispensable to his ordinary functioning. If so, to operate it would be very dangerous. But he added that his conclusion was only tentative because his database was weaker than he would like due to John's having experienced so few focal seizures. More data might or might not corroborate his conclusion.

"How do you get more data?" I asked.

"We would need to keep John in for another week of telemetry. That's the only way to be sure."

"Another week?" I asked, immediately balking at the idea. "You just said you thought that John probably could not be operated on without him turning into a vegetable. Now you say you want another week to confirm that?"

He replied that new data might either confirm or disconfirm his initial conclusion.

"Well, what's the probability you'll find something to make you change your mind?" I asked. "Isn't it likely that the new data will only agree with the old?"

He said that it was impossible to say at that point.

I kept asking him to give me reasons why John should go through seven more days of possibly having another major seizure, but I wasn't hearing what seemed to be adequate reasons. Based on what he knew, the doctor had concluded that John's focal point was probably at a certain location, and there seemed to be no good reason to think new data would tell him something different. If he had said that further telemetry gave a pretty good chance of finding out he was mistaken in his initial conclusion, I might have felt differently. But that's not what he was saying.

"It's too big a risk to take," I said, "just for a slim possibility that you might find out you were wrong the first time. I say no."

"Wait just a minute," John said. "It's my brain we're talking about here. I have some choice in this."

I turned to John and saw tears in his eyes. In grilling Dr. Kim about reasons why telemetry should continue, I had neglected to pay attention to how John was taking the doctor's evaluation. I could see now in his face how hard the news was hitting him. And he was right. I felt so adamantly that the telemetry shouldn't continue that I was trying to make the decision without consulting him or anyone else.

"I'm sorry, John. What do you think? What do you want to do? Please tell me."

"I don't know what to do. I just want to make sure that we do the right thing here."

"I do too," I said, and tears were now forming in my own eyes. "I just feel that with what we know now, the chance of something good coming out of further telemetry is small. And the chance that something bad will come out of it is too big. I don't think it's worth the risk any longer."

Rock and Judy had not been saying much, but now they stressed the importance of not rushing into a decision. I wiped my eyes, and after I had regained my composure, I asked Dr. Kim about other possible avenues for ameliorating John's epilepsy. I had learned about a kind of electrical implant for the brain similar to a pacemaker that could detect and short-circuit a seizure when it begins occurring. Might John be a candidate for such a device? The doctor did not recommend it. Nor did he offer any other alternative.

Rock and Judy asked him if there was any way he could guarantee that John wouldn't have another full seizure if he underwent further telemetry. He replied that there was no way to be sure that it wouldn't happen again.

"Well, suppose he did have another major seizure," I said. "How can you know it wouldn't harm his brain? For that matter, how do you know the last one didn't do damage?"

He admitted that at that point, he couldn't say for sure whether John's latest grand mal seizure had left him with further injury.

That admission pretty much sealed it for me. The discussion continued for a few minutes more, but it became increasingly clear that Dr. Kim was not going to offer any assurances. It was also evident that John was unprepared to make a decision one way or the other.

"I just can't see the value of putting John in further jeopardy," I said. "I think it's time we go home." I stated it with some finality, then looked at John. He made an uncharacteristic sign of acquiescence, indicating that he was leaving it up to me. Rock and Judy also seemed to accept the decision.

With that, telemetry was over.

We would have to wait until the next morning, though, before John could check out of the hospital. The staff would first have to bring him back up to his regular medication levels while observing him for any unexpected reactions, and the technician would have to remove the electrodes. As I sat with him that evening and felt his dark mood, I had second thoughts about the decision. Though the others had accepted it, I had been the main instigator. It rested mainly on me.

Ironically, what had led John to insist on telemetry in the first place was the same consideration that led me to conclude that it was time for the procedure to end. In each case, it had been a matter of choosing to live. Initially, that had meant choosing telemetry, a procedure that might pave the way for surgery. But after initial results indicated that surgery was out of the question, choosing to live meant choosing against further telemetry and the possibility that it would worsen John's condition.

There was no satisfaction in the decision, though, and I wasn't even sure it had been the right one. It was like so many other decisions in life, often very important ones—you make them on the run, without enough information, trying to listen to your heart and your brain at the same time, hoping you've got it right and that it agrees with what God wants.

After Rock and Judy had left, John received a phone call on his room phone. It was from his son Briggs, who knew that his father had been scheduled to receive the telemetry results that evening.

"Hi Son, it's good to hear your voice," John said. What followed was a brief but heart-wrenching conversation.

"Yes, we got the results. I'm sorry, Son. I'm so sorry. They're not going to be able to do the surgery. I'm not going to get well."

As I watched John's eyes fill with tears again, I realized just how devastating Dr. Kim's evaluation must have been for him. To say that he saw it as a kind of death sentence may be going too far. On the other hand, he now knew that he would have to continue living every day with the possibility of a major seizure occurring. And he realized that any one of those might lead to further brain damage, which, for him, might be synonymous with death.

"Thanks Briggs," John said as he responded to what seemed to be an effort by his son to encourage him. "I'll stay strong. Don't worry. I will be okay."

Not long after the conversation was over, I got a call from Charlotte on my cell phone. She told me that Briggs had indeed tried his hardest to console his father during their talk, but that after he had hung up, he himself had been inconsolable.

The technician came in to remove John's electrodes and get us one step closer to home. Afterward, as I lay beside John, I kept silently running through the arguments for canceling telemetry, still unsure of whether it had been the right decision.

I realized that in the end, for me, it had boiled down to wanting to take what was left of my husband and get out of there as soon as possible. Before I lost any more of him.

CHAPTER NINE

IN THE MOMENT

How to go on. That was our immediate problem after telemetry. How to move ahead knowing there would be no surgery to cure John's epilepsy.

Nothing we had so far faced had been so demoralizing. Despite everything that had occurred over the past six months—the *status* seizure itself, the resulting brain damage, the neuropsych testing that had indicated little chance of John's memory function returning—through all of that, we had remained hopeful that significant healing could occur on one front or the other.

Telemetry had been at the center of our latest hopes. Despite my initial misgivings, I had begun seeing it as a huge step on the road to finally ridding John of epilepsy. How wonderful that would be after all we had gone through! No more fear that a seizure might strike him at any time. No more freeze frames where he reported feeling odd and everything else in the world stopped while I waited to see what would happen next, a dozen questions racing through my mind: *Is this a focal seizure or something worse? Did he take his medicine? Are there appliances or basins or pieces of furniture nearby that he might strike if he falls? Please, please, please God, let this be only a focal seizure.*

But telemetry had proven to be a step on a road to nowhere. There would be no surgery, no alleviation of John's epilepsy. And if a really bad seizure were to erupt and cause further brain damage, the future might become very, very grim.

Finding a way to accept the results and move forward was actually more my problem than John's. He remembered for a while that something bad had occurred. It showed in his mood for days after we were home. But he quickly forgot the details of what the bad thing was.

"Are you feeling all right?" I asked him the morning after we got back from the hospital. He had seemed distracted and unhappy since waking.

"For some reason I feel like I've been drug through a swamp and left for dead," he replied. "Was there some kind of problem yesterday? I seem to remember something happening that caused a big problem for us. But I can't get back what it was."

I didn't want to remind him of the telemetry or its results, but I also didn't want to treat him like a child by lying to him. "A couple of days ago something did happen," I said. "We got some results about your epilepsy. Maybe that's what you're remembering."

"What results?"

"That you can't have surgery for it."

Somehow that triggered his memory. "That's right," he said. "That's what it was. No surgery. No cure." He shook his head angrily. "I can forget any stupid dreams I might have had about getting better. I can forget all my dreams. They're destroyed now."

"We'll create new dreams," I quickly said. "And we'll make them come true."

Thankfully, after a few days he stopped asking questions like that, and I didn't have to remind him of what had happened.

As for me, I went into a blue funk for the first week or so, a dark mood in which I found it hard to believe my words about new dreams. I continued to work at insurance sales when someone else could stay with John, but the initial enthusiasm I had felt for the job waned. No longer was it one element of a big, bright picture in which our family got healthier financially while John got healthier physically. With the second part of the picture crossed out, the entire image was compromised. The future, whose outlines had seemed reasonably bright and distinct, now became a dark blur, tailing off into a blank. Even when I had the time and freedom to make sales calls, I often found excuses to go home early, too mentally tired to face one more prospect. At home, I escaped with John into television and sleep. In the morning, I woke feeling hollow.

I knew that couldn't go on. I had to find a way to regain my strength, and I began understanding that the only way to do so was to reorient myself in time. For six months I had been living for the future, hoping and praying incessantly for John's healing. But after telemetry, it was no longer possible to live mainly for tomorrow. It was too dark there, too unknown. It was finally clear how little control John and I had over what the future would bring. To keep focusing on it was a recipe for anxiety, feelings of powerlessness, and even depression.

But there was only one thing other than the future to attend to, and that was the present. I started realizing that I had to pay more attention to what was on our plates right now. Tomorrow would have to take care of itself. Or, better, God would have to take care of it.

With that realization, which was practically forced on me by the situation, I started coming out of my funk. I was also able to take one more step toward understanding how to hand the burden of our family's future over to God.

Lord, thank You for keeping John safe yesterday. Please keep him safe again today. I don't know what You have in store for us. I don't know what's going to happen. I'm going to leave the big questions to You. I'm going to live for this day and try my best to get everything sorted out for the moment. Please reveal to me what I can do today to further this family. As for what comes after, I'm just going to keep watching for what You want.

Prayers like that, in which I gave the problem of our future fully to God, took a great burden off my spirit and gave me some serenity. If it was in God's plan that we would someday find a way to alleviate John's epilepsy or his memory problems, then that's what would happen. If it was not in His plan, then so be it. Of course I hoped for the latter, but now I knew better than ever that the future was in God's hands.

My decision to live more fully for today not only enabled me to accept our situation and move forward, it also had another big benefit. It helped me to grow closer to my husband, whose natural habitat was the present moment.

John had been learning to live in the present for half a year, and it hadn't been easy for him. Previously, he had been a man on a mission, striving hard, like so many others, for success. He still longed to regain what he had lost. But he lacked a skill that most of us take for granted—the ability to spend hours, days, and weeks developing, refining, and acting on plans to achieve his desires.

It wasn't that he hadn't tried, countless times, to redevelop that skill. Sitting in a chair, seemingly half asleep, he would actually be trying to pry open his mind and force it to do his bidding. But trying to find a way to organize his mind and retain memories long enough to make firm plans for the future led only to frustration. Gradually, he had learned that only when he let the future go and lived in the present could he have some peace.

Now I, too, was being forced to stop focusing on and trying to control the future. Instead, I joined my husband in the present moment, a change that was good not only for me, but for us as a couple. By being so focused on the future, wishing and praying for John to get better, I had forgotten something essential—that life is made up of present moments, and when we miss the experiences and possibilities that are here right now, we miss life.

It wasn't that either of us started living totally in the present. John was still oriented toward the future through his desires to restore his memory and to find a way to do well at work. And sometimes I still put myself into a state through worrying too much about what would happen to us. But the proportions changed. I spent much less time fretting about and trying to predict the future and more precious hours appreciating what John and I had at the moment.

And that was a lot. God had given us a lot. Aside from John's epilepsy, our family had its health. My dear daughter Blake was a constantly bright and beautiful gift, like the sun rising in my life every day. And John, by living more in the present, was calmer and easier to get along with. He was more like the gentle man I had married than the high-powered, stressed-out financial advisor I had been constantly arguing with a year previously. He still sometimes became frustrated, and his temper occasionally got the better of him, but these outbursts were fewer than during the first months after the *status* seizure.

One way in which John and I drew closer in the moment was through trying to make sure that we extended our special times together. Such times could be anything from watching a basketball player make a spectacular play in a televised game, to going out to dinner and enjoying a nice meal. Once the event was over, we would often replay it repeatedly in our conversation so that we could share it for as long as possible before it disappeared from John's memory.

"I really loved that meal," I might say on our way home from a restaurant. "Were your enchiladas good?"

"They were great," John would reply. "I liked the atmosphere of the place. We should go back there again."

"I think so too. The food was excellent. Food, service, everything."

After a minute or two of silence, we might start again. "What did you like best about the restaurant?" I would ask.

"The food was the best. At least my enchiladas were great. How about you?"

"I loved my chicken chimichangas. Absolutely filled with meat and the sauce was wonderful."

"I'll try them next time if I can tear myself away from the enchiladas."

"The service was very good, too."

"Did we leave them a nice tip?"

"Yes, twenty percent."

And so it might go. Of course, millions of couples have such conversations in which they share life together. The difference for John and me was that we might say the same basic things four or five times before we arrived home. I visualize those kinds of conversations as being like John and I sitting together looking at a photograph of the two of us experiencing something together. By talking about the experience, we keep the photograph vivid for both of us. And that's very important, because it will only be a little while before the image on the photograph fades into nothing for John. And at that point, I will be looking at the picture alone.

Even after we got into bed half an hour later, I might bring our dinner date up again, hoping that John hadn't forgotten.

"Did you enjoy your meal at the restaurant tonight?" I might say after we turned off the light.

"What did I have?"

"Enchiladas."

"That's right. Yes, they were good."

"I'm glad," I would say as I snuggled close to him. Somewhere inside I would be sad in the knowledge that by tomorrow morning he would probably have forgotten all about our night out. But for the moment at least, we still shared the memory.

It remained to be seen whether the relatively peaceful life that John and I were starting to enjoy would continue once he went back to work and I began tagging along to serve as his assistant. Soon after telemetry, everyone involved agreed that John would return to CMS in late October. A few weeks later, I would join him. We would start working together five days a week, for anywhere from six to eight hours a day, depending on doctors' appointments.

With that schedule, I would have little time for insurance sales. And if the experiment proved successful, the schedule might continue for months.

My supervisors at the insurance agency were understanding and seemed desirous of keeping me there. We agreed that once I started working with John, I would continue servicing my current accounts but would spend little time on new sales.

At that point, the improvement in our finances that had started flowing from my efforts in insurance would slow to a trickle. But hopefully, the loss in my income would be compensated for by an increase in John's. Of course, money wasn't the main consideration. The most important aspect of my helping John was that it would give him the best possible chance to continue in his job. The alternative, for him to be laid off or demoted, was too heart-rending to entertain. Not because of what it would do to our finances, but because of what it would do to John.

But would I really be able to help him? I realized that working with him would be the ultimate test for how successfully we could live together in the moment. At work, being in the moment with him would mean being aware of both his long—and short-term goals at all times and helping him stay focused on his immediate objectives. Most of all, it would require me to understand and help him to take the steps needed to achieve those objectives.

One morning in late November, the experiment began with John and me getting into the car and heading for Newport. When I reminded him on the way that today I was going to be doing more than just driving him into work and picking him up, he immediately objected.

"You're going to stay and help me out? What are you talking about? Are you trying to do my job for me now?"

"I don't want to take over your job," I replied. "I'll just be there to help out. I'll be your memory."

"You don't know anything about my work."

"That's not entirely true. But what I don't know, I'll do my best to learn. You'll teach me."

"What will the guys at work think about you coming in to help me?"

"They know all about it. They approved the idea."

"They did?"

"So did you."

"I did? I must have been crazy!"

Once we arrived, it was as if John was embarrassed at my being there. Like a student whose parent has decided to attend school with him to learn about his classes, he seemed to want to hide me from his peers. We went quickly to his office, and I watched him begin setting up his computer and desk for the day's work. He continued trying to ignore me, but he found it difficult because I kept asking questions about his computer files.

Over the next few days, I spent most of my time trying to understand the flow of information among John's files and programs and how he made decisions about whom to call and what to say on the phone. That was his main job—to call prospects, interest them in the financial services of the company, and set appointments so his partners could explain more about what the company offered. He had been very good at that job prior to the *status* seizure, but he had found it hard to perform ever since. The measure of success for John—and for me as his assistant—was whether he would become more productive in setting good appointments for his partners.

One thing I discovered during those first few days was how much time he spent each morning trying to understand the various files and programs on his computer. I had taken it for granted that because these had been key features of his job before the *status* seizure, and because he had continued dealing with them since his return to work in June, they would be part of his long-term memory. But I was wrong. Each day he had to start almost from scratch, spending an inordinate amount of time reasoning out how various elements on the screen related to his efforts. I now understood one main reason he had been so unproductive. It was because half his day was spent trying to understand his computer setup well enough to determine whom he should be calling.

That was an area in which I felt I could definitely be of use. Since the *status* seizure, there had been many days when John had managed to call only a few prospective clients. This was in stark contrast to his pre-*status* efforts, when he had been able to make a hundred or more calls a day. If I could help him achieve half of what he had once been able to do, or even a quarter, it would be an enormous improvement. And it would show his partners that he was regaining something of his old form, with even more improvement to come in the future.

But when I first started trying to help him understand which files he should be focusing on and how he might make more efficient use of the information in them, he didn't want to hear it:

"Who do you want to concentrate on today?" I asked him one morning while I sat on the opposite side of his desk with my laptop, looking at the same database that he was observing on his desk monitor.

"People I haven't called before."

"Do you have your database set up so you can mark the ones you've called?

"I'm not sure."

"I don't see a column for that," I said.

No reply.

"Maybe it would be a good idea to set up a column or field so you could flag it after you've called the person."

No reply.

"Would you like to do that?"

"Melinda, just let me figure it out for myself, will you?"

So that's what I did. Often I sat there, biting my lip and biding my time, waiting for him to come to a conclusion about how he wanted to proceed in the day's work. If I waited long enough, he usually would finally ask for my opinion about something.

I understood his resistance. At home each day, I had to remind him of a dozen ordinary household matters—when to take his medications, where he could find the household tool box, where he had left his cell phone. Though both of us took this as a matter of course by now, and though he often sought my help at home, I knew it was difficult for him to have to rely on me so heavily. At work, it had been different. There, he had been free of Melinda the Reminder. Of course, work had its own serious problems, but at least he didn't have to put up with someone telling him what he needed to do and making suggestions about how to do it.

I understood all of this, yet we had no choice. His partners had spoken: without my help, John would have to go to the insurance sales side of the firm, something that was unacceptable to him. With my help, he might be able to get organized enough to make more calls per day. If a few of those turned out successful, that would breed confidence. And greater confidence would breed greater success.

As I gradually became familiar with John's system and we learned to work together, he was able to spend more of his day on the phone. That was crucial, because each phone call was a time-consuming project, taking as much as half an hour to accomplish. Once he had decided whom to call, I would help him arrange his notes and files so that any information he needed during the conversation would be right in front of him. Then came the call itself. In almost every case, that was the shortest part of the procedure, lasting for only a few minutes. As I listened to John's side of the conversation, I took furious notes on my laptop. Then came the debriefing period, where I added any other pertinent information he had gotten from the contact. Was the individual interested in the services being offered? If so, in what? Was there a callback time or any other information that would help when contacting the person in the future? After everything was duly recorded, we could finally go on to the next prospect.

In listening to John's end of the conversations, I quickly realized that though his initial presentation was generally good, he sometimes lost his bearings. This tended to occur if the prospect started asking him questions about the product. To try to counteract this, we rehearsed calls beforehand and went over the kinds of questions the individual might ask and how to reply. These efforts buttressed John's natural ability to engage people in conversation. He still sometimes stumbled, but in many cases he was able to talk smoothly and informatively to the potential client.

This was crucial for his confidence. Previously, he had often found it hard to make calls because he was afraid he would not be able to reply to the other person's questions rapidly and clearly enough. He worried that the contact would discern his memory problem. But as he got smoother on the phone, he started sounding more like his old self as he talked about the advantages of learning about the financial strategy packages his company offered.

There was always a letdown for both of us, of course, if the individual on the other end didn't show enough interest to want further information. And that was almost all of the time. But we kept at it. Or I should say that John did. I was proud of him each time he picked up the phone again, dialed a number, and suddenly stepped fully into the role of John Wilferth, expert financial advisor who radiated friendliness, confidence, and good will. And that was the thing—he *was* an expert at his field. His knowledge about business and financial planning was something that the *status* seizure had failed to take from him. Yes, it was sometimes difficult for him to deploy that knowledge at a moment's notice. But if given a little time and space, he was still capable of bringing his expertise to bear for the sake of clients.

During the second week, we got to the point where he was completing about a dozen calls a day. This was still far fewer than he needed to be making, but it was more than when he was working alone. If we could only reduce the time required for each call, the daily number would go up. To my mind, it seemed likely that within a few weeks, we could reduce the time to fifteen minutes per call and get the number up to twenty or thirty a day. Then further reductions would lead to even more calls.

What was of more immediate concern was the fact that after more than a week, he had not been able to set even one appointment. And we knew his partners would not be impressed with any progress we might be making unless it included appointments.

Then one afternoon it happened. John was on the phone and the conversation seemed to be going well, but I expected the same result as with all of the other calls. Then I heard him say something like, "How about Thursday afternoon? My partners would be happy to visit with you, learn more about your needs and expectations, and talk with you about possible financial planning strategies."

I perked way up. And I got even more excited when John said, "Four o'clock sounds fine. I'll have one of our senior partners call you tomorrow to confirm that."

When he set the phone down, I jumped out of my chair like a cheerleader whose team's star quarterback has just made a touchdown. Or maybe I should say whose team's star swimmer has successfully completed an important leg of a race.

"Is it an appointment?" I asked. "Confirmed?"

"He wants to learn more," John replied. He was smiling, but he wasn't ready to celebrate quite yet. "Hurry! Let's get down all the information right away before I forget anything."

I parked myself back in front of my laptop and recorded all of the pertinent details of the call. I hadn't had so much fun in a long time.

Then—wouldn't you know it?—a little while later that same afternoon, he made another appointment.

The whole day was turning out to be a special event, and we made it last all evening by reliving it in our conversation over and over. There was no way I was going to let him forget those successes in a hurry! And every time I reminded him of his accomplishment, we celebrated again.

It was a good thing we made the most of our opportunity to congratulate each other when we could, because the next day and the next and the next after that there were no more bites as John continued throwing his voice out into the telephone lines like a fisherman tossing a fly into a river. He now seemed stuck at completing no more than a dozen calls a day. At that rate, if he got a positive response every hundred calls or so, it would take nearly two weeks to generate another appointment. That wasn't good enough. It became increasingly clear that we had to find a way for John to make more calls.

It seemed to me that one way to do that would be to make John's system as automatic as possible. The idea also made sense from the perspective of his eventually being able to work on his own. Determining whom to call, for example, could be made more automatic by marking a potential client's record so that an alarm sounded from the computer on the day John was to make a follow-up call. That way, he wouldn't have to spend time reviewing files to determine which contacts he needed to call back later.

With this in mind, we created a phone reminder file on John's computer. After a call had been made, if we decided that a follow-up call would be appropriate, say a week later at ten in the morning, we would input the individual's name and callback time in the file. Then, at the appointed time, a computer alarm would sound and the prospect's name, phone number, and other information would be right there.

It seemed like a simple, elegant solution. The problem was, it failed to take into account the realities of John's disability. For one thing, he would forget to input contact names and callback times into the reminder file. For another, when the alarm sounded, he sometimes forgot what it was for and how to access the information that it was signaling. He had understood the system when we first set it up, but later I had to keep explaining it to him. The net result was that instead of saving time, it interrupted the continuity of the work flow.

Grueling. That's what I remember most about our experiment as the second week merged into the third, then that into the fourth. Day after day, John had to remake the same discoveries about how to use this program or how to access information in that file. Often, he still insisted on finding an answer himself, with no help from me. And when I was offering input, it was often to explain something I had explained a dozen times before. Sometimes he became very frustrated—with me, himself, the entire situation. When that happened, I did my best to encourage him: "I know it's hard," I would say. "But I also know we can figure out how to do this more efficiently. We just need to keep at it." As time went by, though, I found it increasingly difficult to speak those words with conviction.

It was during those grueling days that I came to better appreciate how profoundly John's short-term memory dysfunction affected his ability to reason through a process or problem. I don't mean to suggest that his native reasoning capacity had been affected. For the most part, he was no more illogical than most of us in his thinking, and he was more logical than many. But to apply reasoning power effectively, a person needs information to work on—and John kept losing the information he needed. Someone can be good at arithmetic, so that adding a series of numbers together is a piece of cake. But if he or she keeps forgetting which numbers are to be summed, then the power can't be put to work. John remained a very smart man, but one with a very limited memory. As a result, he was like an athlete trying to swim fast while burdened with intolerably heavy weights.

As the days went by, efforts to automate the system fizzled, and we made no appreciable advance in shaving more time off the average phone call. Somewhere during what was probably the third week, John set another appointment, but this time there was no strong sense of celebration. Three appointments, that's what our joint efforts had produced so far. For a man who often used to set several appointments a day, it was a drastic reduction. Worse, his partners had been unable to convert any of the three appointments to new business for the company. Though they remained supportive of both of us, it was clear that they weren't impressed with our productivity or the quality of our appointments.

At home, we were so weary from our day at work that we had little energy left. Thankfully, we were able to leave behind whatever disagreements or problems we may have had on the job and enjoy each other's company. But much of the time, being together just amounted to vegging out in front of the television and going to bed early to get ready for the next round.

As we got into the fourth week, our spirits at work were sinking lower and lower. On one especially frustrating day, John said, "Melinda, I don't know if I can do this."

It was shocking to hear those words from him. John never admitted defeat. Yet a day or two later, he repeated virtually the same thing.

"Do you mean your job?" I asked. "Or working with me?"

"I mean we're not getting anywhere. I don't know how to do it right anymore."

I had begun to doubt the experiment, too. "I don't know how to do it either," I confessed. "The idea of me being your memory seemed so simple. But in reality, it's not. And I don't know what else we can do to make it work."

Adding to my doubts, John had a frightening focal seizure one evening about that time. He was suddenly very dizzy, then became belligerent until he took his medicine from me. Soon, he went to sleep. I discovered that he had missed his medications, and I attributed the seizure to that fact, but I still wondered if the stress at work might have contributed to it.

The holiday season was well upon us. It was prime time for jewelry, toy, and sweater salespeople, but not so much for those who market financial planning strategies. Few potential clients wanted to talk about putting together a financial package when there were packages to buy for their spouse, kids, and business associates. The chances that John would make any more appointments before the beginning of the new year seemed slim. So when I suggested at work one day that maybe we should think about staying home for a while to just focus on Christmas, he was immediately with me on it. And when we passed that idea by his partners, they agreed—maybe a little too quickly, I thought.

It meant that at least for the time being, our experiment was over. I told myself that it was time for a break anyway. Maybe a couple of weeks at home would give us some perspective. Maybe we would be able to develop a strategy to simplify John's work system. Maybe after the first of the year, we would go back in, implement the new plan, and see John's phone calls climb steadily each day.

Maybe. But I couldn't really see what we could do later that we hadn't already tried. And I couldn't quite believe that a few weeks at home were going to give us the answer. Somewhere in the back of my mind, I think I knew it already. And I think John may have known it, too—that our experiment was over not just temporarily, but for good.

If so, then we would soon have to face a horrendous new challenge, one that I had deeply dreaded—the end of John's career as a financial planner. But for now, we would not think about it. We would go home, be together as a family, and get ready for Christmas. We would live in the moment, trying to squeeze every drop of goodness we could out of the Holidays, to help strengthen us for what came after.

CHAPTER TEN

SABOTAGE

We can do this. We can find our way out of this dark place. With God's help.

I think that for most of us, there are times when we need to cling hard to such words, periods when we feel lost and need to embrace, with our entire being, the tenacious hope they express. For John and me, the first few weeks after Christmas 2003 were such a time. In fact, in some ways it was the most difficult period we had endured since the *status* seizure.

I don't like to admit it, but there were a few days back then when despair overtook me and I nearly gave up the idea that we would ever gain clarity about the main issues we were confronting. But I could never really believe that God would abandon us, that He would not lead us to the light. And sure enough, by the time that arduous period was over, our dear Lord was beginning to show us, in the most unmistakable terms, the direction we should take.

First, though, we had to get through some very dark days.

After Christmas, it was time for John to decide whether to go back to work at CMS. When we talked about it, I reminded him that we would have to work together again, and unless we could quickly find a way to do much better than we had done so far, he would have to transfer to the insurance sales side of the business. I also reminded him of what it had been like working together, and told him that I honestly thought our chances of doing much better were slim. He trusted my evaluation, but it was clear that he still wasn't willing to transfer to the other side.

"Let's stay home," he said. And just like that, with no fanfare, the momentous decision was made.

It was something I had feared for months—that he wouldn't be able to continue in his career. But given the results of our experiment, I didn't see what else he could he do. For months, he had tried his hardest to function effectively in a position and a place he loved, with people he loved to work with, and to retain his role as a major breadwinner for our family. Day after day he had faced his fears and the cacophony that must have been going off in his head, and had made heroic efforts to marshal his cognitive faculties and stay a productive member of his team.

But his memory had continued to fail him no matter how much he tried to capture and hold the fading substance of his thoughts. And my entrance into the scene had helped little. So, rather than taking what he considered to be a demotion and having to train for a new job that may have been even more demanding, he recognized that it was time to retire.

It was the right decision. The only problem with it was that when he stopped pursuing his profession, a major part of his identity disappeared.

As if he hadn't already lost so much.

After the first of the year, we went to his office one day to clean out his desk and files. I helped some, but he wanted to do most of the boxing up of his papers and books himself. When it was done, I asked him if he wanted to say goodbye to his partners.

"I don't want to say goodbye to anything here," he answered. "Least of all them."

He spent a few minutes with the men who had proven themselves to be true friends by allowing him to continue at his work until he was able to decide for himself that it was time to move on. Then we left for the final time.

I remember how proud of him I was that day—the brave manner in which he faced the closure with his partners, the way he held his head high as he carried the boxes down to the car. Maybe his brain had let him down, but his spirit had not.

Still, during the following days he was often sad, now that the prospect of returning to work was conclusively gone. He slept more than ever and was frequently lethargic when awake. It was obvious that his confidence in himself and the future had been profoundly shaken. He remembered the job and the fact that he had been a financial planner. And he knew that he could no longer define himself as that. He often commented about how he couldn't be himself any more, how he had lost himself.

I tried to encourage him, to lift him out of his melancholy as much as I could, but I wasn't doing so well emotionally myself. I often felt I was floundering in a sea of ambiguity, where nothing was clear, the way to shore and to safety blocked by heavy waves constantly rising all around me, cutting off my vision. In my journal I would ask God to help me, to guide me and take my fears away, to not let me give up. On one day like many others, I told the Lord what He surely already knew—that I was shaking as I was writing: *Please Lord, put Your arms around me and comfort me.*

Awash in ambiguity, drowning in sadness.

One thing that helped me keep my head above water was the fact that there was so much to do. A household to keep up. Doctors to see. Insurance accounts to service. A few small interior design assignments coming in. There was no time to wallow in despair. So I would shove my anxiety as far back into my mind as I could and just try to focus on what needed to be done.

Thankfully, there were also a few happy moments during that period. Joe and his wife Anna and their two boys had come out with another couple and their young son to visit Anna's relatives for the holidays, and just before the new year we all went to stay in the desert for a couple of days at the vacation home of Anna's grandparents.

The first night we were there, I made my "famous" seafood bisque, which everyone seemed to enjoy. That made me feel good, appreciated.

And it was great to see John with no worries for a change. There were incredible citrus trees just outside, with lemons like softballs and oranges as big as cantaloupes, and John was like a kid himself out there as he and the other men and boys played catch with lemons and chased each other around the yard with water guns.

John also took on the role of Carnival Ride Master as the boys lined up to have him swing them around. He would take the first boy in line, hoist him up in the air by the waist, flip him over, catch him by the feet, and swing him in a big circle a few times. Then he would pull the boy up, flip him over again, and set him gently down on the ground. "Next!" he would call after the thrill ride was over, with the now-dizzy but widely grinning boy taking his place at the end of the line to wait for his next turn. It was wonderful to see John with that big trademark smile back on his face, where it belonged.

Another high moment was when Briggs came to stay with us for two days in early January, an event that lifted John's spirits enormously. At one point, John mentioned to Briggs that he had been looking for a watch with as many functions as possible, including day of the week, date, and month. He felt that such a watch would enable him to better locate himself in time, that most elusive aspect of his reality.

After hearing that, Briggs was immediately off to the chronological races. He started looking everywhere for a watch like the one his John-Daddy had described. On the second day, we went to Downtown Disney, and at every store that looked as if it might carry watches, Briggs was running in ahead of us to ask if they had a watch like the one his father was seeking.

Though we all helped Briggs look, he unfortunately wasn't able to find the right watch during the visit. But not from lack of trying. And you could see the pride in John's eyes every time his son ran into another store to try to find a special timepiece for him.

Our two days in the desert and Briggs' visit gave us welcome respites. But even during those brief periods it was impossible to forget the pressing questions that were demanding our prompt attention. There were three of these—three crucial, interrelated questions that had to be answered very soon.

The first concerned our finances. Some residuals were still coming in from ongoing contracts that John had previously shepherded, but they weren't nearly enough to pay our living expenses—which meant that it was up to me to make up the difference. I was trying to maintain my insurance accounts, but I had little time for new sales because of having to stay home with John. I was also still doing occasional contract interior design work and selling my jewelry. That helped, but it was still not as much as we needed, and none of it amounted to a steady, dependable paycheck each month.

Nor did any of that work offer the kind of health insurance benefits we needed. This had become a matter of critical importance with John no longer working. The costs of John's doctors, pharmaceuticals, tests, and treatments were substantial, to say the least, and though his insurance through CMS would be in effect for a while, it would not last forever. When that point came, financial calamity and our possible inability to provide John with the best medical care would threaten unless we found some reasonable substitute.

So the question was, Where could I find a steady job that would bring us the income and health benefits we needed? To try to answer that question, I was constantly checking the newspapers and the Internet for job opportunities and sending out resumes right and left for any work that I thought I might qualify for. But the only positions for which I was even being offered an interview were ones with no adequate insurance benefit. Despite my efforts, nothing was opening up on the financial front, and every day I could feel that ogre named "Fiscal Disaster" creep one step closer.

The second important question was to decide what steps we should now take in John's treatment. With the idea of surgery for his epilepsy having been put to rest, two options still seemed to remain for possibly restoring his lost brain function. One was the hyperbaric oxygen treatment we had discussed with Dr. Steenblock in August. But the iron concentration in John's blood was still too high to consider that procedure now, and we also had serious doubts about its potential benefit.

The other possible avenue was stem cells. I had started reading about and talking to John about stem-cell treatment in the early fall, and he and I had discussed it with Dr. Steenblock in November. The doctor thought such treatment might hold promise for John, but he made clear that it was not an approved procedure in the United States. He did mention a physician in Mexico who used stem cells for treating brain trauma, though he stopped short of recommending him to us. It appeared that the cost for the treatment would be at least $20,000. Where such money might come from if we decided to pursue that option wasn't clear—but it certainly wouldn't be covered by insurance. Here, too, the financial problem was raising its insistent head.

The third important question we were facing was closely connected to the first two—Should we move? We loved Las Flores, but our living expenses were high there, and we wondered if perhaps it was time for us to retrench. We had done so once already when we sold our previous house and bought the smaller one before the *status* seizure. The world certainly hadn't come apart then—why should it now? We could sell our home and use the profit to make a substantial down payment on another, less expensive house in some other part of the country. Then we could start over with fewer financial pressures.

Two options for relocation seemed most reasonable. One was to return to southeastern Missouri, perhaps to Cape Girardeau. The second was to move to the Vail Valley in Colorado, where we could be near John's sister Jill in Eagle. Several times she had encouraged us to relocate to her area, and though living expenses there might be higher than in some other places, they seemed less than in South Orange County.

The biggest problem with both options was that the prospect of moving from where we had put down substantial roots just struck all of us—John, Blake, and me—as a bad idea, on several grounds. First, there was the issue of John's doctors. At that time he was seeing five main physicians, including two epileptologists, a naturopath, an internist, and a neuropsych examiner. We were happy with all of these doctors, so why do something that would require us to find new ones that might not be as good? In addition, UCI Medical Center was nearby, and not only was it a respected research institution, many of the center's staff already knew John from his stay there. For these reasons, the idea of moving seemed wrong from the purely medical standpoint.

Second, John had many anchors in the area. By the term "anchors," I mean friends, acquaintances, and places that he had known before his *status* seizure and that he still remembered and recognized. It's true for virtually all of us that proximity to familiar people and places tends to help us feel comfortable and to remain psychologically stable. For John, such familiar touchstones were even more important due to his memory deficit. Because he had difficulty remembering what happened a short while ago, his consciousness tended to be more free floating than most, and he had a harder time finding his bearings in his surroundings—which is again to say that he tended to feel lost in the here. So anything in his environment that he was able to remember helped him to locate himself within the world and contributed to his sense of self. To take him away from those anchors to his past could set him even more adrift in the present moment. Worse, it might negatively affect his potential for recovery.

Those were probably the two most important reasons against moving, but there were others. Our home, our friends, and the beautiful area in which we were fortunate enough to live had been some of our main blessings through times when other aspects of our lives were falling apart. There was also Blake's school, which she liked a lot and, of course, Saddleback Church. We really didn't want to leave any of those blessings behind.

How to address the three questions was a matter of constant concern for me, and the topic of numerous discussions with John. Each time we sat down to talk about what to do in this or that matter, I would need to refresh his understanding by carefully explaining where we were at the moment and what our options were. He would quickly grasp the details, and the resulting conversations were generally to the point, but we never came to firm conclusions on any of the issues. About the only thing we seemed to be settled on was that we really didn't want to have to move from Southern California.

I was tired to my bones of the uncertainties we were facing, and I often called on God to help us, to show us which doors we should go through. *Please Lord, let Your answer be clear,* I would ask Him. *If there are doors You don't want us to go through, please close them firmly and decisively so that we will know. Just slam them shut. Then, please open wide the doors that You do want us to go through.*

I would sometimes get impatient to have my prayers answered, then would get upset at myself for not having enough faith to just be calm and wait for God's reply. It seemed to me that I was doubting Him at times, and I felt terrible about that. So I would ask Him to give me composure and grace in my heart. *I am going to be quiet and still,* I told Him one day in my journal, *waiting for You to reveal what I need to know.*

That's not to say I waited passively for God to provide answers. Every day, I kept searching for work, sorting through our options, trying to understand what He wanted for us. But in doing so, I tried my best to stay patient and to place all my trust in Him.

Then one afternoon my friend Nancy called me with information that looked like it might be the beginning of the revelation I had been asking for. Nancy worked as a representative for a large paper products company, and several times I had discussed with her the possibility of my obtaining a similar position for some such enterprise. She knew that I had had some success in sales, and she had been keeping her ears open for any local opportunities in her industry that I might qualify for. Her call was to tell me that she had learned that a rep position was opening up for another large paper company with nearby offices, Boise Cascade.

"You would be representing envelopes to commercial clients," she said. "I don't know if that interests you, but it might bring the kind of income and benefits you've been looking for."

"You just said the magic words, my beautiful friend," I told her. "Of course I'm interested." *For that kind of opportunity,* I thought, *I could sell forty pallets of envelopes to a convention of stone carvers.*

This could be it, I realized—the door I'd been asking God to open for us.

After I learned more details from Nancy, I contacted the employment agent handling the position applications, and soon I had an interview with Boise-Cascade scheduled for January 14. I was very excited about this turn of events. I started searching the Web and trade journals for whatever information I could find about the company. I also spoke with Nancy several times about what she thought the position might entail, given what she knew of the industry.

By the time the big day arrived, I was confident I would do well. Not only had I done my research, I was sure my interview skills were well honed. Over the years, I had learned how to present myself effectively—to go into the interview prepared and with enthusiasm and to answer and ask questions in an organized, coherent, and positive way.

I also felt confident because it looked to me like God's signature was written all over this job opening. It had arrived while I was praying hardest for Him to show us the way, and it had come via my best friend, which struck me as significant. And surely, God recognized that remaining where we were was our best option, but that I needed a good job to enable us to stay. So it just seemed obvious that this opportunity was a matter of God answering my prayers by opening a door for me. And of course, because he wanted to see me step through that door, He would help me, or at least allow me, to do well in the interview.

So, having figured out so cleverly just what God was up to, I walked into the interview office on the afternoon of January 14, all confident and sure of myself, smiled, shook the gentleman's hand, sat down, and totally self-destructed.

To this day I'm not sure what happened to me during that hour. It was so odd. It's not that the interview was blatantly horrible. But I kept making this erratic series of small glitches, the like of which had never occurred in previous interviews. Off and on throughout the meeting, my replies, my facial expressions, even the tone of my voice seemed slightly off kilter. I stumbled at simple questions for no reason at all, mispronounced words that I had spoken a thousand times, felt my expressions stuck on my face as if they had been painted on with glue, and just generally felt as if I were a frame or two displaced from where I ought to be.

Near the end, I finally remembered to tell the interviewer that I definitely wanted the job—something that, amazingly, I had almost forgotten to say. A few minutes later we shook hands again. He told me there were several other candidates for the position and he would make a decision within a few days about whom to select for a second interview. I gave him another of my frozen smiles, thanked him, and left the office.

All the way down in the elevator, to the car, and out of the parking lot, I managed to hold it in. But a block away from the office, I pulled over to the side of the road and just sat there for five minutes, bawling.

Sabotage. That word kept going through my mind. And that's what it felt like—as if someone had silently entered the room at the moment I sat down and had fiddled with my brain enough to slightly undermine my responses throughout the interview. Just enough to sabotage me. And the saboteur, I couldn't help but think, was none other than our dear Lord.

I called Mom when I got home and told her that the interview had gone terribly. I even mentioned my feeling of being sabotaged. But she wouldn't have it: "Oh, Melinda, you're probably just being overly critical of yourself because you've invested so much hope in getting that position. I bet you did much better than you think. Knowing you, I wouldn't doubt that you nailed it. I'm sure you at least impressed him enough so he'll give you a second interview. And then you can really shine."

As always, my dear mom was a great cheerleader, and after a while she had me convinced that there was probably a brighter side that I wasn't seeing. By the time we hung up, I had decided that maybe she was correct, maybe I was being too pessimistic and would get a second chance.

One thing she was certainly right about was how strongly I was pinning my hopes on getting the job. The importance of doing so had been further underlined by an experience that had happened several days before.

John had asked me to take him to get his cell phone repaired, so I had dropped him off at the cell phone store and gone on to do another errand. When I returned, I learned that the phone had been fixed and that John had gone across the street to a fast-food restaurant. When I drove over there, I found him standing outside the building, and when he got into the car there were tears of anger and frustration in his eyes.

"What happened, Babe?" I asked him. Then he told me a horror story.

He had tried to order something to eat inside, but he had found he only had a dollar in his wallet, and the boy behind the counter had refused his credit cards.

"We can only take debit cards," the boy said, so John pulled out his bank card but couldn't remember his PIN number. He kept trying to punch in the right code, but nothing worked.

Embarrassed, John said, "It's not stolen, you know. I'm not a crook. I've got a law degree. I have an MBA."

"Maybe you could find some change in your car," the boy said.

"I don't have a car."

"How did you get here, then?"

"I don't remember," John replied. Then he turned and walked out of the restaurant.

After he had finished the story, there was anguish in his voice as he said, "I feel so retarded."

It was a horrible experience for him, and very disturbing to me. I was angry with myself for allowing him to get into such a situation. As for him forgetting the pin number, I don't know what I could have done about that. Even if he had been carrying a piece of paper in his wallet with the number written on it—which could be a problem if he were to lose the wallet—he probably wouldn't have remembered that he had the paper. But I should have checked with him to make sure he had some cash, and I shouldn't have left him for so long.

The incident shined another bleak light on the cage in which John found himself—a place where it was difficult to engage in activities that most of us take for granted. And it dramatized once again the importance of finding some effective treatment that could restore his memory function. Of course, my getting the rep job wouldn't do that in itself, but it would allow us to go on living where we were so that John could continue with his present doctors. And the position's good insurance benefits might eventually enable us to afford some treatment that could improve his short-term memory, or cure his epilepsy, or both.

Ultimately, that was the biggest reason why I hoped God would keep the door open for us—John's health. So, over the next several days, I called on Him to help the interviewer look favorably on our meeting. *Please Lord, make my numerous misfirings seem unimportant in the evaluator's eyes.*

On the morning of Monday, January 19, five days after the interview, I received a brief phone call from the employment agent. Its gist: "You were a strong candidate, but there were others even stronger. The company has decided not to invite you to the second step of the process."

I thanked the agent and set the receiver down. Suddenly sick to my stomach, legs trembling, I managed to make my way to my bedroom. I don't think there had been a time over the past nine months when I felt so defeated. The word *sabotage* drifted back to me. Obviously, I had gotten it all wrong. God hadn't wanted me in that job. He had made that perfectly clear. In fact, He had done exactly what I asked Him to do—He had slammed the door shut in my face so there would be no mistake that it was not the door we were to go through.

He had answered my prayers. The problem was, I hated the answer.

I flopped down on my bed and lay there in a haze, feeling like I weighed a ton and would never have the strength to get back up. And that's where I stayed for the next several hours, holding a little pity party for Melinda. The theme of the party at first was simply "Poor Me." But after a while, interspersed with feeling sorry for myself, I started trying to understand what it all meant.

Why would God close down that door? Was there a better job out there that He was setting me up for? Or was He telling us it was time to move on?

I couldn't figure it out. Not any of it. But I did know that the idea of getting up and going to my computer to start looking for another job struck me as about the hardest thing in the world to do at that moment. So I just lay there, realizing how foolish I had been to think I had God's plans all figured out. And on no basis, really, other than the fact that I had wanted all of our problems to be solved by the job and had convinced myself that God wanted the same thing.

But then He had shown me that He had different ideas. At the same time, maybe He was reminding me of a few general principles that I had managed to conveniently forget: That it's often not simple to know God's plans for us. And that it's easy to substitute our own personal desires for His will. At least it was for me.

After a long while of brooding over what had happened, I finally mustered enough energy to reach over and pick up the bedside phone to call Mom—so often not just my cheerleader but my conduit to our dear Lord. I told her what had happened, and she let me cry on her shoulder for a few minutes. Then I said, "Can you read me something, Mom? Some inspirational words to help get me out of this funk?"

She quickly found a text that she had read to me a couple of weeks before when I had been feeling down, a passage from the writer Max Lucado. It was about never giving up. "The God of surprises strikes again," she read to me. "Is the road long? Don't stop. Is the night black? Don't quit . . . . For if you do, you miss the answers to your prayers."

There was more to the passage, but those few words revealed its central message. And Mom reinforced them by saying, "You can't quit now, Melinda. You have to keep going. You have to have faith."

I thanked Mom and told her I would do my best and would call her the next day. Then I lay there with her words running through my mind. *She's right,* I thought. *I can't quit. How horrible for God to have an answer to our problems that we never find because I gave up. I have to have faith.*

But even with that, I still couldn't drag myself out of bed and back to a chase that so far had proved fruitless. I prayed for strength: *I'm so tired Lord. Paralyzed. Please help me move my legs. Please just pick me up, lift me out of this bed in Your strong arms, and take me in to my computer.*

I kept praying that same thing, over and over, I don't know how many times, until at some point I was slowly pulling myself up, rising from the bed, then making my way to my office. It felt like my body was on automatic, as if I wasn't doing it myself, as if God really was carrying me.

At any rate, I was finally up. And my little pity party over.

I sat down at my computer and connected to the Web. But instead of looking at employment opportunities in the local area, I logged onto the Vail, Colorado, *Daily.* *Who knows?* I thought. *Maybe there'll be something there for us.*

I'm not sure I really believed that, or even wanted to believe it, because the idea of leaving California was still unwelcome. So I was surprised when I found a couple of openings where I might be able to use my interior design experience. *Well, this is interesting,* I thought. As I continued searching, I got the impression that the Vail employment market was thriving in my area of expertise. More so, it seemed, than the local market.

I decided to give Jill a call. We had talked a couple of weeks previously about the possibility of our moving out to be near her and her family, but at that point the Boise Cascade interview was still in the future, and our relocating to Colorado had seemed no more than a theoretical option. Still, both she and her husband August had been positive about our coming out there, and she had generously volunteered to stay with John for much of the time if I were to find work.

When she answered, I told her about the job rejection, then mentioned what I had discovered about the employment market in the Vail area. I asked her if she still felt positive about the idea of our moving there.

"Absolutely," she said. "I would love it if you guys would come out and live close to us."

"Do you really think I could find a job out there?"

"Melinda," she said. "Come out here. I will find a job for you in a heartbeat. I'll get everybody I know on it. Just sell your house and get here."

Jill's enthusiasm caught me off guard. I had been wallowing around all day in ultra-negative energy, then suddenly here was this earth angel somewhere out in the Rocky Mountains, singing this beautiful *can do* song in my ear. For the first time that day, I actually smiled.

"But what about John's doctors?" I asked. "We would have to leave them."

"I'm sure you can find very competent doctors in this area," she replied. "Augie's a pharmacist. He can help you locate good doctors. And just think! I'll be able to help you look after John while he's getting better. I know how difficult it's been for all of you. I would love to help you guys."

By the time I set down the phone, Jill's enthusiasm had started rubbing off on me. More than that, I was beginning to see light from a door that seemed to be cracking open for us.

Is this what You want, Lord? I asked. *Is this the door You want us to go through? For us to sell our home here and go to Colorado?*

I reminded myself that if we decided to go in that direction, it would take time to make it happen. Selling a house isn't something that can be done overnight. We would also need to find a new house in Colorado, and I would have to do my best to find a position before we actually relocated. And there were many other important logistics of a move to consider. With all of that, I figured it would probably take six or eight months, maybe as much as a year to make the move, even if we started working on it tomorrow.

Still, everything takes time, and if this was the door our Lord wanted us to go through, we should start going in that direction as soon as possible. But was it the door in reality? And how would we know? Before, I had interpreted a few meager signs as God wanting me to work for a paper company. Was I now doing the same thing with the idea of moving to Colorado?

I had to admit that maybe it was true—that I was getting worked up over what would turn out to be another mirage. But still, I had asked God to close tightly all false doors, and that's just what had happened. Then suddenly there had been that uplifting conversation with Jill. It seemed to me that if the Lord wanted to make clear that we should move to the Vail Valley, a great way to do so would be through such enthusiastic and loving words.

I decided that the bottom line was that it was impossible to know for sure whether God wanted us to go to Colorado. But He doesn't want us to be quiescent or afraid to take a risk. At least I don't think He does. I believe that He wants us to use our best understanding and patience to discover what doors He is opening for us, and then to apply our energy to go there. If I was wrong about moving, we would somehow find out soon enough. If I was right, God would open the door even wider. But we wouldn't find out, one way or the other, by doing nothing. The only way to discover whether it was the right door for us was to start moving toward it—at least in our minds.

That meant the three of us had to talk it over. After all, it wasn't my decision to make alone. If we were going to do this, we would have to do it together. I had to explain to John and Blake what I was thinking and to find out how they felt about it. And to do that, we needed to schedule a family conference for that evening.

I was nervous as I got ready for the meeting, expecting a lot of resistance from both John and Blake to any suggestion of moving. I spent ten minutes alone in my room beforehand, praying that we would have a good talk. *Lord, if this is the door that You are opening for us, please bless our discussion and make it productive. Soften John's and Blake's hearts to the idea of moving to Vail. Please soften mine, too, as You know I still have some misgivings about the thought of leaving our home here. Thank you, Lord.*

At 7:30, we gathered in the living room.

"What's this about, Mom?" Blake asked as she settled on the couch, wearing a dubious expression.

John just looked at me quizzically, waiting to see what I had to say.

"I want to talk about something that's a little difficult," I said. "And I don't want you to say anything before I'm finished explaining."

I began listing the problems we were facing—my having lost the Boise Cascade opportunity, the difficulty of finding a good job in the area that utilized my skills, the cost of living, our eroding finances, and the fact that we had to make some tough decisions quickly. Then I told them I thought we should seriously consider the possibility of moving.

I immediately saw some resistance in John, and a lot in Blake. She pursed her lips in a way that showed me she really didn't like the way this conference was going.

"Please be patient, guys," I said. "Let me tell you a little more. There are several options open to us. One would be to go back to Missouri—either to Cape Girardeau or Sikeston. That would mean being near family, which is a big advantage. But the job situation there is probably not so great in the interior design area—a definite disadvantage."

My husband and my daughter were still regarding me skeptically.

I continued: "Another option would be to go to the Vail Valley, where we would be near Jill. Again, being near family is a plus. In addition, the job situation in my field looks strong there." I told them about what I had discovered on the Vail *Daily* Web site. "So, that makes two big advantages."

I then took a deep breath: "Everything considered, I think we should consider moving to Colorado."

I stopped to wait for my audience's reaction. John, I saw, seemed to be considering the idea. After a few seconds, he surprised me by saying, "You may be right, Melinda. We have to do something. And if there are good job prospects in that area, we should consider going there—especially with Jill nearby."

But Blake, my beautiful, darling daughter who had been so strong throughout all of this—who had understood that her John-Daddy was ailing and had done her best to care for him in her own ways—started tearing up.

"Oh dear," I said. "Don't cry, Sweetheart." I grabbed a tissue and gave it to her.

"I don't know, Mom," she said. "It's a big thing. A little scary."

"I know, Love," I said. "But there are some very good points to it that I hope you'll think about." I talked to her about the importance of my getting a job that could help make us more financially secure and of having the support of family nearby.

"And Colorado's a great place, Blake," John added, recalling the year he had lived there before we were married. "Beautiful mountains and meadows everywhere," he said. "And you can learn to ski. And that, believe me, is something you'll just love."

I had to smile. I had expected resistance from John, but here he was helping me convince Blake that we should consider moving to Colorado. In fact, he seemed already sold on the idea.

After some more discussion and explanation, I could see that Blake was starting to accept the idea, though she was still hesitant. "Mom and John-Daddy," she said, "I understand what you're saying. It's just a little hard to think about leaving here."

"I know it is, Darling," I said. "It will be difficult for all of us."

"But the main thing is that we're together," she said. "I know we'll be fine if we're all together."

"Oh, that's so wise of you, Blake," I said.

Then she really surprised me: "So if we're going to go, we should leave right away. How quickly can we move?"

John was looking at Blake with a rosy smile on his face.

I couldn't help but laugh. I had been worrying about how my husband and my daughter would receive my thoughts, and here they were one step ahead of me. The Lord, my wonderful Saboteur and door closer, seemed to be proving Himself also to be the greatest of all door openers by freeing my family's hearts to the possibility of Colorado.

"Slow down, you guys," I said. "If we do this, it can't happen overnight. It will take time."

But John was ignoring me and talking to Blake: "You know you are an amazing girl. Truly amazing."

And he was right. In the space of less than half an hour, she had turned on two dimes. First, she had moved from resistance to begrudging acceptance. And now she was actually spurring the process on. Wanting the best for the family, she had gathered her courage and quickly gone from denial, to acceptance, to empowerment.

I had thought I was going to be working a tough crowd that night, and that the best I could hope for was to get the idea of moving to Colorado fully out on the table. But the reception that John and Blake were giving the idea, combined with my own thoughts, made it clear to me that going to the Vail Valley wasn't just something we were talking about. It was probably going to happen.

And maybe sooner than I had thought, if what was said next was any indication.

"Mom," Blake asked, "are you sure that moving to Colorado is the best thing for us?"

"No, Sweetheart," I said, "I'm not sure. But I think it is. I really do."

She looked at me with those beautiful hazel-brown eyes and set her jaw: "Then let's go."

At that, John reached up and pulled a big Yes! down from the air: "We are so outta here!"

CHAPTER ELEVEN

DOORS WIDE OPEN

Many times since John's *status* seizure, I had asked God to show us what He wanted for our family. Often, I phrased my prayer by asking Him to close doors leading to pathways He did not want us to travel down, and to open doors that would take us to where He wanted us to go. For months, we seemed to be receiving answers only to the first part of the prayer, with one after another promising door suddenly shutting on our noses. Now, finally, it seemed that the Lord was answering the second part of my prayer by opening the door that would lead us to Colorado.

But even after our family conference that night, I wondered if I was misreading what God wanted for us. To take John away from the area, the friends, and the doctors that were familiar to him would be such a huge step. And once made, it couldn't easily be reversed. We didn't have the money to be able to move from one place to another at will. If we cut our ties to the area that had been our home, it would probably be for good. Would that be a horrible mistake? With questions still lingering, I found myself wavering about a move to Colorado.

But God, in His wisdom, wouldn't allow me waver for long. Soon, matters began playing themselves out in such an incredible series of unlikely, providential events, that I could no longer doubt that our Lord was thrusting wide open the doors that He wanted us to go through. The result was that by early March, a mere six weeks after my "pity party," we were well on our way to Colorado and a new job for me. Also, an exciting new opportunity for possibly healing both John's epilepsy and his memory dysfunction had opened up for us.

The amazing series of door openings began with a call from Jill a day or two after we held our family conference. She told me that she had a friend who knew the head of a large design firm headquartered in the Vail area. She thought that this company, Slifer Designs, might be perfect for me, given my training and interests, and she urged me to send them my qualifications. I shot off a letter and my resume to the company right away.

My thought was that if I could find a job or the promise of a job in Colorado, then we could put our house up for sale. I wondered, though, if anyone would be willing to take a chance on me, given that it would probably take months to sell our house and relocate to Colorado. But the only way to find out was to get my name out there.

While waiting for a reply from the company, I located a few other potential employers in the Vail area and forwarded my qualifications to them, too. It took only about a week before I received a reply from Slifer. They seemed to like my resume and were interested in talking to me further, but they had nothing to offer me at the moment. Still, all in all, it was a positive reply.

The letter became even more encouraging when, in checking the *Vail Daily* online the next day, I discovered a new advertisement for a position in Slifer's design department. The timing was wonderful, and I felt that God was using the ad to ease open the new door a little further. If I could just find a way to get to Colorado and speak to the people at Slifer in person, maybe I could get that job!

But again, there was the question of selling the house, where we faced what seemed to be a paradox. The condition for having a good chance at getting a job somewhere in the Vail area might be to first sell the house so that we could all go there. But how could we do that before I had a job? Despite the fact that the door to Colorado seemed to be opening more and more widely, and my resulting excitement, we still seemed to be stuck right where we were for the time being.

Then, on a Sunday night in late January, John had a focal seizure. It was no worse or better than many others he had had, but somehow it changed my thinking. It brought me back to the urgency of our situation: John was still prone to small seizures and could have a major one at any time, and his memory dysfunction remained. He was out of work, and I was having to cut back on my insurance sales to care for him. All the doors in the area had been closed, and we were going nowhere. At the same time, God seemed to be showing us a new way. Yet here I was still only dreaming about a better life in Colorado, not yet willing to commit myself to it. I realized that it was time to put aside my indecision, take the handle to the door firmly in my hand, pull it further open, and start moving.

The next morning, John and I talked, and I told him I thought we should put the house on the market now. He surprised me by agreeing immediately. He was ready to move forward, too.

The question was, how could we sell the house quickly and for the right price? It was important for us to make a reasonable profit from the sale because after paying off our loan, the money left would have to pay our moving expenses and cover the down payment on a house in Eagle. For that reason, we felt we couldn't afford to sell our home through a real estate agent and pay the customary commissions. We would have to do it ourselves. Though that would probably make the process more difficult, we felt we had no choice.

After checking on several recent home sales in our area, we decided that $500,000 was about the right asking price given the neighborhood and the size of our house. After the loan was paid off, that would leave us $100,000 for taxes, the move, and a down payment. It was a pretty slim margin, especially since it might also have to cover most of our living expenses for a few months after we got to Eagle. But I couldn't imagine anyone paying much more than $500,000, and we didn't want the house to sit unsold for months and months.

Once we had settled on the price, we went to a hardware store to buy a couple of "For Sale" signs. That was the easy part. Next, we had to actually go out and hammer the signs into our front lawn. It was scary. It felt like we were at the point of no return.

And we were. It was eleven in the morning, and I had no idea, as I helped John pound the signs into the ground, how quickly events would transpire. That simple act put in motion a series of occurrences that still boggles my mind when I recall them.

First, just a little while later, as I was inside creating and printing out price posters to put on the signs, two women knocked on the door. After introducing themselves, one said, "We were just driving by and wondered how much you were asking for your house."

"Well, we are just putting it on the market," I said. "And I think we're going to be asking about $525,000." I don't know why I said that, given our earlier decision, but I was very encouraged when the women seemed excited about that price. With John's okay, I went back to the posters and changed the price to $525,000.

But before I could put them out, one of my neighbors who had noticed the sign came over and asked if we were moving and what we were going to sell our house for. When I told her that we were hoping to get at least $500,000, she said that she thought that was far too low.

"You should be asking at least $575,000, Melinda," she said.

"Really?" I was a little shocked by her estimate.

"Definitely. This area is very popular. And you have a nice house. I think that's the minimum you should ask."

I was soon back in the computer room changing the price again, to $575,000 this time, and re-printing the posters.

Thank you, God, for not letting us make a huge mistake, I thought as I went out to attach the posters to the signs. I wondered what else was going to happen. How else would God help make our sale a success?

I didn't have to wait long to find out. Another neighbor on the street, Lori, called to ask what we were up to. After I told her, she said she had a friend who might be interested in helping us, a realtor who would possibly charge us a lower fee. I said that I would be happy to talk with the person, and when she told me the realtor's name, I realized it was Cindy, a friend I had known from our old neighborhood.

A little later, Cindy called and asked if we needed a listing agent. I told her of our qualms about paying a full six percent for others to take care of selling the house, and she replied that she had heard about John's illness and would like to help us out at a much-reduced rate. By that time, I had realized that we should probably let professionals handle the sale in order to get the best price. Also, Cindy was very kind on the phone and genuinely concerned about our situation. It seemed clear that reversing our earlier decision and allowing her to list the house was the way we should go.

Cindy came over that evening, and we spent some time convincing John about the wisdom of listing the house with her. As was typical for John, he saw the sale of the house as a challenge that he would prefer to handle himself. But we eventually convinced him that we were being offered a very fair deal and that the new plan would simplify the sale greatly. Eventually, he agreed. No doubt, one main reason was that Cindy thought that given where the market was at the moment, our actual asking price should be about $620,000.

At ten that evening, the house went onto the multiple listing service for that price. The results were almost immediate. The next day, we received an offer for $3,000 over the asking price, and with that, a bidding war began, with several offers trying to top one another. Within forty-eight hours of putting up the sign, we made a counter-offer to one of the potential buyers, and the house was in escrow by Thursday. The final selling price of the house was almost $630,000, over twenty-five percent more than we had originally thought we could sell it for. Just as wonderful, instead of it taking months to sell our house, it had been accomplished in less than four days. Another happy result was that the house was bought not by strangers, but by a nice couple who owned a nearby restaurant that John and I had always loved. It felt especially good to be selling our house to people we knew and liked.

At that point, I was in a state of blissful astonishment. God was not only opening the door to Colorado wider all the time, He seemed to be paving the road for us to make the journey as smooth as possible.

The next step was to locate a house in Eagle, as close to Jill as possible. I called her and said that we would all like to come out the next week. Could we stay with her and her family until Friday while we tried to find a house? Maybe I would even have the opportunity to look for a job. She was overjoyed at my news and said they would have beds and a warm meal ready for us whenever we wanted to make the trip.

Then came another occurrence in what was becoming an increasingly incredible series—a phone call from Slifer Designs. The person on the other end told me that the owner of the company was interested in my resume and would like to meet with me if possible in the near future. I replied that I was planning to be in Eagle the next week until Friday. Would sometime then be convenient? They called back a little later and said that Friday would work. So now the employment door seemed to be opening wider, too!

But there was a problem. Regular airline tickets for all three of us to Denver would cost over $3,000, and we didn't have that money available. The only way we could go would be to use the free miles we had accumulated with a certain airline to purchase tickets at a reduced price. But there was only one seat available to Denver before the interview for which I could use the miles credit. I briefly wondered if the door was closing a bit, but I couldn't believe it. Too many good things had happened in the last few days. Maybe God wanted me to go out to Colorado alone.

With that thought in mind, I booked the flight, which would leave in just a few days, on Monday, for myself only. That meant leaving John and Blake by themselves, and I didn't really see at the moment how I could possibly do that. But by this time I believed so strongly that God was leading us, that I felt He would somehow make it right.

I didn't have to wait long to find out how He would do so. That night, Melanie called from St. Louis. I told her what had been happening, about my upcoming trip to Colorado, and about not knowing how I could leave John and Blake by themselves for five days.

"Maybe I could come out there and stay with them," she said.

"Really? You could take the time off work?"

"I don't know. I'd have to ask my boss. But it's worth a try. What's a twin sister for if not to help at a time like this? I might have a little problem affording it, though. I don't know how much a ticket would cost at this short notice."

"A lot," I said. "But I'll tell you what. If you can get out here, I'll find a way to pay for the trip."

"Deal," she said.

When I got off the phone, I immediately went online to see what kind of ticket I could find for Melanie. I knew she still had half of a round-trip ticket left from a previous visit to me. All I needed to do was get her a flight back to St. Louis. It turned out to be another dollop of ice cream on our plate. I quickly found her the ticket she needed for only about four hundred dollars, a very low price given the short notice.

It got even better when I called Rock and Judy to tell them that Melanie might be able to come out to stay with John and Blake while I was in Colorado. They were so happy about the news that they offered to pay for Melanie's ticket.

The next day, Melanie talked to her boss and got approval to take a week off work. She arrived two days later, on Saturday. My dear twin came through in the pinch as she often has. And my decision to buy a ticket to Colorado only for myself looked like the work of genius.

And it was, of course. It was God's genius. All I did was to continue putting my trust in Him.

When I landed in Denver on Monday afternoon, Jill was there to pick me up and to make me feel immediately at home. When we arrived in Eagle, I found a small town sitting amid beautiful hills and mountains. Both John and I had grown up in small towns, but we had lived in and near big cities for most of our adult lives. How well would we fit now into such a quiet, out-of-the way community? *Maybe small town life is just what we need at this time of our lives,* I thought. At any rate, it looked like we were going to find out soon.

The next couple of days went by like a controlled whirlwind. Working through the same mortgage company that we had in California—which made the entire process much easier—I committed part of the proceeds from the sale of our old house to a down payment for a new house to be completed in the summer. The house would be located just across the street from Jill and Augie's new house, which was also to be completed in a few months. At the same time, I arranged to rent a small house that was very close to where Jill and Augie now lived. We would stay there while our new home was being completed. Of course, it just so happened that the house I rented was the only one in the area that was up for rent at the time.

By the time Friday came, everything had been arranged for our move except for one vital ingredient—a job. My appointment was for Friday morning, and after the interview was over, I felt that I had done much better than I had at the one only three weeks previously. As important, my interests and skills seemed perfectly matched to Slifer, and it struck me as just the kind of company I wanted to work for. It would be a week or two before I would find out for sure if I had a job with them, but with everything that had been happening, I felt strongly that God would open this door for us too.

Though it was a great trip, I was happy to get back to California and my family. All that was left to do now, I decided, was to wait for a letter offering me a job, and then wait for all the necessary paperwork to go through on the sale of our old house and the purchase of the new one. In the meantime, we could start packing up. Soon, we would be on our way to our new life.

But I quickly discovered that it wouldn't be quite that simple. I didn't know it at the time, but another door was about to open up for us. It was something totally unexpected, an opportunity at once exciting, frightening, and full of hope.

It began with another call from Jill soon after I got back.

"Melinda," she said. "A friend of mine has been telling me about a German doctor who has been visiting in the Vail area. His name is Dr. Scheller, and my friend is acquainted with a woman who knows him well. Apparently, he's involved in stem-cell treatment in Germany. You told me that at one point, you guys had looked into the possibility of using stem cells."

"We did," I replied. "But nothing much came of it. It isn't officially approved in this country, and the cost is very high."

"Well, would you like me to find out more about him? Or should I just drop it?"

"Definitely, find out more. Any information you can get might be important."

"I'll put my bloodhounds out," she replied.

A few days later, she called again: "You'll never guess what! I got in contact with Dr. Scheller through my friend, and found out he was giving a dinner. The dinner was last night. It was for only eleven people. And guess who was there?"

"Who?"

"Me! I finagled an invitation."

"Really? You actually spoke to him?"

"I did. I told him a little about John's case, and he was very, very interested."

"Oh, Jill, I can't believe it! Does he think he might be able to do something to help John?"

"All he would say was that stem-cell therapy is a very promising field, and he thinks it's possible that John would be a good candidate for it. But he has to know a lot more."

"What does he need to know?"

"I'm not sure. But we made an appointment to meet for lunch tomorrow to talk more. He also said he would like to talk to you. I took the liberty of giving him your phone number. He said he would try to call you tomorrow after lunch, if that's all right."

"That's so exciting, Jill. Of course I want to talk to him. And I hope you'll find out everything you can, too."

The next day, Dr. Scheller called me, and we talked for almost an hour. I filled him in on what had been happening with John over the past nine months, and he had many questions. Afterward, he said that it sounded as if John might be a perfect candidate for stem-cell therapy. He explained a few of the basics of the process and said that to undergo it, John would have to travel to Germany and stay for several weeks. The total cost for the treatment could be thirty to forty thousand dollars.

My feelings were all over the place when I hung up the phone. Was this a real possibility? Doctor Scheller seemed to have good credentials. He had a Ph.D. in chemistry, was a registered pharmacist, had studied medicine at a Budapest university, and had done an internship in oncology. He had also received a prestigious German medical prize for work in a cancer-related area. Currently, he was the Chief Medical Administrator of a hospital in Germany.

In our conversation, he had talked very positively about the use of stem-cell therapy for brain trauma. The treatment would involve replacing damaged brain cells with stem cells that would grow into new, healthy neurons. He had also mentioned that the therapy might have a positive effect not only on John's memory dysfunction but on his epilepsy, too. It was all very exciting. But at the same time, he had pointed out that there were risks involved. It was possible that John's body would reject the stem cells or that he would have some other kind of negative reaction. To me, the thought of him being injected with hundreds of thousands or millions of the stem cells was in itself very daunting.

The idea of paying up to forty thousand dollars for the treatment was also unnerving. Still, the financial aspect was less of a roadblock than it would have been a few weeks previously, before we had sold our house for more than we expected. Did God want us to use some of that extra money to enable John to get this new treatment? The facts that a renowned doctor involved with stem-cell therapy just happened to be in Vail at this time, and that Jill just happened to make his acquaintance, struck me as almost too auspicious to be a coincidence—especially considering all the other favorable events that had been occurring.

But I still had many questions. For one thing, how could John go to Germany alone? Surely, I would have to travel with him and stay by his side as long as he was there. And maybe Blake would have to go, too. All of that would make the undertaking considerably more expensive and difficult to arrange.

I was also aware that stem-cell treatment is a controversial issue, especially if it involves stem cells obtained from an embryo. I didn't know whether the ones that the doctor had talked about were embryonic stem cells. If they were, would God be opening up that door for us anyway?

I told John about my conversation with Dr. Scheller, and though he was cautious, I could tell he was excited. But like me, he had many questions.

Fortunately, we would soon have the opportunity to talk it over with John's parents and my own mom and dad, because we had decided to go back to Missouri to visit them all. This was something that we had not been able to do since the *status* seizure. But Blake's father was coming out with his wife to visit Blake in mid-February, and that provided John and me an opportunity to go home for a few days. There, we would be able to get our respective folks' opinions about this new door that seemed to be opening.

———

It was a great visit, with both sets of parents keenly interested in our news about the possibility of John undergoing stem-cell therapy. Rock and Judy grew increasingly enthusiastic as they came to understand the basics of the procedure, learned of Dr. Scheller's qualifications, and finally spoke with him on the phone. They then surprised John and me by offering not only to pay for the procedure but also to fly over with him and stay with him throughout the treatment if we decided to go ahead with it.

Later, when John and I were alone, I asked, "What do you really think about undergoing stem-cell therapy, Hon?"

"Will it help me get better?"

"I don't know. That's the idea. But there's no guarantee. And it could be dangerous."

"How dangerous?" he asked.

"I'm not sure. The doctor says they would first get you very healthy and that the treatment should then be quite safe. But they would be sticking needles in you and injecting a lot of stem cells into your brain. There's bound to be some risk."

"New cells for old," he commented.

"That's the idea."

"The old ones aren't doing much. Maybe it's time to kick them out."

"You would have to spend a few weeks in Germany."

"Beer! Wiener schnitzel!"

"Is that all you care about?"

"Frauleins! Will the stem cells make me young again?"

"Not that young."

"Well, if it's got a chance to work, I'm for it."

We talked more about the treatment, but it didn't take long for the potentially life-changing decision to be made. Not for the first time, it felt as if we were on a roller coaster, with my breath being taken away yet again. *Germany. Stem cells. Possible brain rejuvenation . . . .*

What next?

I found out what was next a day or two later when another amazing "coincidence" occurred. We were at my parents' house and John had gone into town with my dad, who had to get something at the local hardware store. I wasn't with them, but they later told me—as my jaw dropped open—what had happened on their brief trip.

When they entered the store, John immediately recognized one of the men working there. "Eugene!" he said. "I can't believe it, it's Eugene!" He rushed over to the man and grabbed his hand. "Eugene, do you remember me? I'm John Wilferth!"

John then turned to my dad, who was standing there puzzled by his son-in-law's reaction. "Eugene's the guy who gave me this!" John said as he pointed to the scar that angled from the crown of his head down the right side to what used to be his hairline.

At that point, Dad realized that Eugene was none other than the adult version of the boy who had collided with John during the baseball game twenty years before. After all those years and all the changes that had occurred in both men since they had been together in high school, John had immediately recognized the teammate whose skull had struck his own during that fateful game.

Eugene then recognized John and started grinning and shaking his hand: "John, how are you? It's great to see you."

"I'm good, good," he replied. "But let me see your head." He reached over to part Eugene's hair. On the left side of his head, the side opposite John's own scar, was an almost identical mark. "There it is!" John said. "We're practically twins!"

As the two men talked, John learned that Eugene had suffered no long-term negative effects from the collision. Both boys had spent the night in the hospital after the accident, but for Eugene, the injury had healed completely. John was glad to learn that and wasn't at all envious of his former teammate.

Before he and John left the store, my dad took a photograph of the two men together. Both are smiling—Eugene with a sort of shy grin, and John with his typical huge and generous smile, brought out by his having unexpectedly run across the man who had inadvertently helped determine so much of his life. It's a wonderful picture.

When I heard about the meeting, I started laughing in delight. It seemed to me that this was the icing on the cake. If God had wanted to top off the nearly unbelievable series of events with something sweet and ironic, how could He have made a better choice than to set up this unlikely meeting that hearkened back to the beginning of John's epilepsy?

To me, it was almost as if He were saying, *Melinda, I know John has epilepsy. And I know it has been a huge problem. But see how something happy can come out of even that fact? Just continue having faith.*

Maybe I'm reading too much into the incident. But when added to everything that had been occurring for the past couple of weeks, it seemed to be just too unlikely for a mere coincidence.

But then something happened that didn't fit the recent pattern. A day or two after we arrived back in California, I received a letter from Slifer Designs. I tore it open, fully expecting a job offer to be inside. There was none. Instead, the letter said that at that time they were unable to offer me a position.

The series of happy events appeared to have abruptly ended. Slifer had seemed the perfect company for me, and I had thought I did well on the interview. I couldn't understand why God wouldn't want me there and had apparently closed that door. I could only conclude that He had something different in store for me.

At any rate, job or no job, we were still on our way to Colorado. And John would soon be on his way to Germany. I talked to Dr. Scheller several more times, and we began making the arrangements for the trip over and for the stem-cell treatment. The doctor forwarded some preliminary medications along with dietary advice that would help John prepare for the therapy. It wouldn't be long. John would leave for Germany along with his parents in mid-March, less than a month away. He would be there for three or four weeks.

While John was gone, Blake and I would do the bulk of the packing and would close down our lives in Orange County. We would probably complete the move to Colorado by ourselves in early April. That meant that when John arrived back in the States, he would be coming home to an entirely new environment.

For now, I was continuing to investigate other job possibilities in the Vail Valley, but I had made little progress when I received a phone call from Slifer in early March. I had put the company far in the back of my mind. Why would they be calling me at that point, I wondered.

I quickly learned, to my joy, that they were calling me because they had had a sudden influx of business. They wanted to know if I would like to take on a temporary six-month appointment with them. After that, they might be able to offer me a permanent position depending on how much work was then available.

I was ecstatic! The job, though temporary, would give me the opportunity to show them what I could do, and the pay they were offering was reasonable. I accepted their offer right away, and a few days later I got a contract by mail and signed it. With that, the very important question of employment in Colorado was answered. There had been some squeaky hinges to this particular door, and it had taken a while to open fully. But eventually, I had gotten not only a job, but one with the company I wanted to work for.

Once again, God had answered my prayers.

———

Over the next couple of weeks, John and I talked almost daily about his trip and what he might expect in Germany. I hoped that the repetitions would take root in his memory so that when it came time for him to leave, he would be clear on where and why he was going. But the news that he would soon be on his way overseas for stem-cell treatment continued to be fresh information for him each day when I brought it up.

The plan we had decided on was for him to first fly to St. Louis, where his parents would pick him up. Then, after a few days with them in Cape Girardeau, they would all take off for Germany. I worried about his being alone on the plane to St. Louis. My concern wasn't so much about him having a seizure, because his epileptologist had prescribed medications that would make it very unlikely that he would have an attack while on the flight. I was more worried about him being alone, forgetting why he was on the plane, and becoming frightened. I explained his disability to the airline people several times, and they promised they would take special care of him, but I still worried that something would go wrong.

In fact, as John's departure date neared, I had increasing doubts about the entire venture. The fact that Rock and Judy would be paying for the trip and the treatment and would be with John in Germany had made it easier for me to agree. But in the final analysis, those were relatively minor aspects of the undertaking. What was more important was that stem-cell therapy was still in the experimental stage and John would be in some danger. I found myself asking the same basic question that had gnawed at my mind before telemetry: *Was it worth the risk?*

As with telemetry, here too John had decided that yes, the risk was worth taking. And whenever I reminded him of where he would be and what he would be doing in just a few weeks, he reconfirmed that decision. We were playing out the same pattern as before. Again, he was choosing to live. And again, it was my part to support him, even through my apprehension.

It helped me to accept what was about to happen when I reflected that God seemed to have opened this new door for us. But I wasn't as certain about that as I was about the rightness of moving to Colorado. In the end, I could only trust that our Lord would watch over John in Germany and that if no improvement resulted, at least no harm would be done.

Departure day came quickly. Blake and I took John to the airport, where I again talked to the airline people. I had made sure that his cell phone was charged up and that he had on his person medications with instructions, as well as papers with explanations, addresses, and phone numbers.

As we waited for the plane, he maddened me by saying, "Where are we going now?"

"St. Louis! And it's only you going. Your mom and dad will pick you up there."

"Why aren't you coming?"

"Because next week you're going to Germany for stem-cell treatment. Your mom and dad will fly with you. Blake and I have to stay here."

"Okay," he said, looking puzzled.

"You silly goose!" I said. "I love you! I just want you to be safe. Don't lose your cell phone. If there's any trouble, or you feel odd, tell the in-flight service people right away."

A few minutes later he was on his way to board the plane. He had taken all of his medications on schedule, including one that should help him sleep on the flight. We waved goodbye to him as he disappeared through the boarding door.

I felt a little sick as Blake and I returned to our car.

What have I agreed to? I asked myself. Here we were, chasing another rainbow, except this time we would not be together for the chase. Instead, John would be thousands of miles away, with someone we barely knew trying to put a pot of gold into his head.

Despite all of the progress we had made over the past six weeks, I felt very unsure of everything at that moment. Again, as I was learning more and more all the time, the best I could do was to have faith in the Lord and hand it all to him.

Please God, I prayed through the roar of airliners taking off for distant places and daring ventures, *hold him safely in Your hands.*

CHAPTER TWELVE

A MILLION BLANK SLATES

John arrived safely in St. Louis and spent several days in Cape Girardeau with Rock and Judy while they prepared for the trip. They left together for Germany on the last day of March. At the St. Louis airport on the way out, John talked with an elderly man who was flying to Peru to visit an elderly lady he had met on the Internet. When the man learned the reason for John's trip overseas, he remarked to John, "You'd better watch out for those German doctors. They'll turn you into a Frankenstein."

Judy relayed that story to me by e-mail soon after they had arrived in Munich. I realized that John had probably enjoyed the joke, but the dark humor struck a little too close to home for me.

When I talked to John soon after he had landed in Germany, I could tell he was homesick, but he was committed to going through with the treatment. I didn't mention the fact that he had arrived on April Fool's Day, another dark joke. There was a car and driver waiting for them at the airport, and they were quickly swept away to a small private hospital in the Bavarian Alps, where they would stay for the next few weeks.

In the meantime, Blake and I were wrapping up our lives in Las Flores. After John left for Missouri, we began packing up our household and saying farewell to friends. It was hard to leave some very special people I had grown close to over the past several years. Blake, too, found it difficult to part with some of her classmates. But there was no avoiding it, and the proof that we were actually leaving came at the end of the month when the movers picked up our furniture and half a truckload of boxes. For the next several days, we lived a Spartan existence until it was time to board our own plane for Colorado.

My cell phone was an indispensable blessing during the move. Even with the gap resulting from telephones being disconnected at one house and connected at another, John and I were able to talk daily. I also received e-mail updates from Judy and Rock as I tried to stay abreast of what was happening in Germany.

During John's first week at the hospital, Dr. Scheller and several other doctors worked with him. Their main objective at that point was get him as healthy as possible before injection of the stem cells. He was a little overweight at the time, and the doctors wanted him to lose a few pounds. No wiener schnitzel and beer for him, but rather a healthy diet with lots of vegetables, along with a daily exercise regimen. The idea was to flush his body of any toxins and to create the optimum physiological environment so that the stem cells would have the best chance of successfully taking hold.

A couple of days after his arrival, he was transported temporarily to a Munich facility for a PET—positron emission tomography—scan. By providing a metabolic profile of his neural activity, the procedure would show which areas of his brain were malfunctioning.

When the doctors got the results of the scan, they were surprised by the extent of the injury John's brain had suffered. Based on his ability to function on several cognitive levels, they had expected much less damage. In fact, they thought it remarkable that he was doing as well as he was, given how much of his brain had atrophied.

Rock called me to report the results of the scan. Before going ahead with the treatment, the doctors wanted to make sure that I still agreed to it, given what they had discovered about how much damage they were dealing with.

"Do they still think the stem cells will help and not harm him?" I asked. Rock.

He explained that Dr. Scheller seemed confident that there was little danger of anything going wrong. The doctor also still believed that the treatment would significantly benefit John. But there were no guarantees.

"How does John feel about the therapy now?" I asked.

"He's ready to go ahead with it," Rock replied.

"Then I'm still on board. Let's pray they know what they're doing."

Blake and I arrived at our temporary home across from Jill's house on the fourth day after John had landed in Germany. The moving van showed up soon after, and we spent the next few days arranging furniture, emptying boxes, and storing other boxes. We took a few breaks, though, making time to visit with Jill and Augie and to explore the area.

This was Blake's first encounter with Eagle, and she learned quickly that we were a far cry from populous Orange County. But she also discovered that there were actually schools, stores, and restaurants in town, and a cinema only a few blocks from our house. One of our most important discoveries was the local lending library. That humble institution provided a sense of familiarity to the new area, which I knew Blake appreciated. She was also glad to find the library for the simple reason that it would help feed her voracious appetite for reading.

While we were gaining our Rocky Mountain legs by setting up house and exploring Eagle and the larger town of Vail, thirty miles up the highway, John was following his new regimen in Germany. Despite the troubling PET scan results, the doctors seemed satisfied with his progress, and they chose April ninth as the day on which to perform the main part of the stem-cell therapy.

Since my initial contact with Dr. Scheller, I had learned considerably more about how the treatment would proceed. But it wasn't until John was actually in Germany that I found out that the doctors would definitely be using embryonic stem cells. I think that up until then I had been trying to avoid that issue, hoping they would use adult stem cells, which are found in adult humans. Still, I had agreed to the therapy knowing that there was a possibility that the embryonic type would be used. Now that that was confirmed, I worried whether God would approve of the treatment.

I understood the controversy better by then because I had spent a lot of time on the Internet researching stem cells. The dispute, I knew, revolved around the source of the embryonic variety, which are undifferentiated cells that occur in embryos. As an embryo grows, most of its stem cells develop so that they can perform some specific function. For example, a particular cell may become a muscle cell, a blood cell, or a cell of some other kind. In this way, stem cells are like blank slates. Just as a blank slate can record any of a number of messages, a stem cell can develop into any of several specialized forms.

It's this "blankness" of stem cells that makes many researchers think that they hold great promise for treating a wide range of serious ailments, from heart problems to Alzheimer's disease. The general idea behind such treatment is that when the stem cells are injected, they can travel to a part of a person's body that has been injured in some way. There, they can take on the characteristics of cells in that part of the body and replace the damaged ones. For example, stem cells might help a person with an injured spinal chord by traveling to the area of the injury and then developing into healthy nerve cells that can replace those that have died or been damaged. Most of this promise is still unrealized, but research is being done throughout the world to find ways to fulfill it. And in some places, such as at Dr. Scheller's clinic in Germany, treatment techniques are already being applied.

The controversy about the use of embryonic stem cells arises from the belief that human life begins with fertilization, so that an embryo is already a human being. Many people argue that using embryonic stem cells amounts to using part of one human being to repair another. While this might be fine in cases where the donor is a freely choosing adult, they believe that it is not right to use embryos as donors because they have no choice in the matter.

On the other side of the coin, many believe it to be immoral *not* to use embryonic stem cells to try to help people who are suffering from serious illnesses. They say that the embryos from which the stem cells are obtained are not viable and would only be discarded. They think it is better to use stem cells from such embryos to decrease suffering in people than for the cells to go unused.

I was not sure which side of this debate was right. Though my church was against the use of embryonic stem cells, I had been impressed with the arguments of people like Nancy Reagan, who thought that research in this area should move forward. For several years, she had watched her husband, former President Ronald Reagan, become more and more out of touch with the world and his family as his brain succumbed to Alzheimer's disease. Though Mrs. Reagan probably knew that any advances in stem-cell therapy would be too late to help her husband, she supported research that might help other families escape the ravages of Alzheimer's disease.

I thought I knew how she felt. To see someone you love lose a substantial part of his mental powers is a truly difficult reality to face. If there was a treatment that provided a reasonable chance for John to recover some of those lost powers, it was difficult for me to believe that God would not want us to pursue it. I knew I might be wrong, and I couldn't be certain that supporting embryonic stem-cell treatment for John was the right thing to do. All I could say for sure was that in agreeing to the therapy, I made what I thought was the best decision at the time, and I prayed for God's blessing.

I was able to speak with John on the day before the treatment. With the eight-hour time difference, it was near noon for me and evening for him. I wished I could fly to Germany to hold his hand during the therapy, but all I could do was encourage him: "You're going to be fine, Love. I know it. Just relax and follow their instructions, then call me as soon as you can after it's done."

The treatment began, I found out later, with the doctors strapping John down and placing his head in an apparatus that insured little movement. Then, using multiple needles, they injected the stem cells into his brain along the scar that had resulted from the baseball accident. They didn't have to administer an anesthetic, because there are so few nerves in the area of the skull that very little if any pain resulted from the procedure.

The purpose of administering the stem cells at the point of the original injury was that it allowed easier entrance of the needles into John's skull, and it was very close to the atrophied areas of his brain. Even so, there was no guarantee that all of the stem cells or even the majority of them would travel to or stay in the damaged areas, which were in his cerebral cortex. There was some possibility that they might travel to other parts of his body where different kinds of cells may have been damaged for one reason or other. But the doctors considered that to be unlikely because John was in such good physical health, especially after his diet and exercise program. They seemed confident that the majority of the stem cells would travel to the injured sections of his brain, would take up residence there, and would develop into healthy neurons that could replace the ones that had been damaged.

Because of the time difference, I was asleep while the procedure was being done, but I woke early in the morning, anxious and hoping for a call. A little later, Rock phoned to tell me that the injections had been made and everything had gone well. I breathed the proverbial sigh of relief, but I was still eager to hear from John.

Later that morning, he called.

"How do you feel, Babe?" I asked.

"You mean from the stem-cell treatment? Weird. I don't remember much of it, but I do remember being strapped down. Then they stuck needles in me. Now they have my head bandaged."

"Did it hurt? Do you think it went all right?"

"I guess it went okay," he replied. "That's what everyone says. I don't remember anything hurting. It doesn't hurt now. I think they got the needles out. Ugh!"

I couldn't blame him for finding the thought of what had happened to him, especially its invasive nature, so distasteful. The idea of needles sticking into his brain made me cringe, too.

"Do you feel any different?" I asked.

"Not as far as I can tell. Should I?"

"Probably not," I replied. "Doctor Scheller said it might take several weeks for any improvement to show."

"Will I be going home soon?"

"I think they're going to keep you for another week or so. Then you're coming home."

"It won't be soon enough," he said. "I'm tired of people asking me questions."

"Are they getting on your nerves?"

"They're all nice. Maybe too nice. I'm sick of doctors, needles, the whole lot of it. I just want to go home."

"That's where I want you, too, John. The sooner the better."

That the procedure had gone off without a hitch was confirmed over the next week, as John remained healthy and alert. This indicated that his body had not had a negative reaction to the stem cells. The treatment itself was not yet over, though. The doctors were keeping him on the health regimen and were developing mental exercises that he could do once he got back home. The exercises were supposed to stimulate growth of new neurons and help him improve his cognitive function. The doctors were also injecting small additional doses of stem cells into the fatty tissue of his stomach area. This would continue for more than a month even after he arrived home. Twice a week, with my help, he would inject himself with stem cells that he would bring back with him from Germany.

The fact that he had come through the treatment so far with no ill effects was a relief. Still, a very large question remained: was the therapy going to work?

The first accounts were promising. Soon after the initial injection was completed, I started receiving e-mails from Judy indicating that they were already seeing improvements in John's memory. The messages were vague, though. I wanted to hear specific stories about cognitive feats that John was performing, but for the most part, the e-mails said only that he was improving. Otherwise, they provided few details.

The most specific occurrence mentioned was that one morning John and Rock had a conversation about a movie they had seen the night before. Supposedly, John remembered details of the movie during the conversation.

But I knew how easy it was to lead John by suggesting details of some experience that he didn't actually remember. And I wasn't sure that in discussing the movie, Rock didn't help John to "remember" by unconsciously giving clues to the movie's content.

When I talked to John, I kept listening for signs that would indicate a definite improvement in his short-term memory. But nothing had changed as far as I could tell. I didn't hear anything that led me to conclude that the stem cells were doing what they were supposed to do.

One part of me wanted to be hopeful. It would have been a beautiful treat to believe that once John was home, each day would find the stem cells replacing more and more of his damaged neurons. But I recalled how I had gotten my hopes up before telemetry and what had happened when they came crashing to the ground. I didn't want to do that again. If it was in God's will for John's memory to improve, it would happen. At that point, we would celebrate like never before! In the meantime, I thought my most reasonable approach was to take a wait-and-see attitude.

That also went for the possibility that the stem cells would heal John's epilepsy. The doctors were telling Rock and Judy that they expected the therapy to result in John having no more seizures. That in itself would be a wonderful outcome. But I tried not to allow myself to get caught up in longing for it.

It wasn't that I was pessimistic about the results. The recent door openings had made me hopeful again about the future, and I still felt that the stem-cell treatment might be God's answer to my many prayers for John's healing. But I didn't want to take the Lord for granted. Eventually, the doors to Colorado had opened wide in many ways, but the same could not yet be said about John's health. Yes, an opportunity for him to undergo an unorthodox treatment had opened up, but whether that would prove to be the door to improving John's memory function or healing his epilepsy was still not clear. That was up to God, and it was for me to wait until He made His will evident.

In the meantime, there was another issue that concerned me, and it was one that I might actually be able to do something about. This was the fact that when John returned to the United States, it would be to an unfamiliar house and town. He was homesick in Germany, and I knew he was missing not just me and Blake, but also his normal environment—our house that we had left behind in California, our neighbors, and our other friends there. Though he might not be able to describe our old house if someone were to ask him, he had lived there for nearly a year after the *status* seizure, and I knew it would feel familiar to him if he were to step inside. But when he returned to the United States, he would not be going back to the place he had left. Instead, he would find himself in Eagle, Colorado, in a house he had never set foot in before, and with no friends there other than Jill and Augie.

I wanted to soften that transition for him, so I often talked with him in our phone conversations about our new home. I hoped that somehow he would retain the information so that when he returned, he wouldn't wonder why he was getting off the plane in Denver and wouldn't be disappointed when he found himself in a house that was unfamiliar to him. It seemed unlikely that he would be able to retain the information; but if the stem-cell treatment was working, maybe he would.

"I think you're going to like our new home for the next few months," I would say to him.

"What new home?"

"In Eagle. Just across from where Jill and Augie live."

"Is that where you are now?'

"Yes. And that's where we're all going to live until we move into the new house in August."

"Another new house?"

"We're staying in a rental until our new house is completed. You're going to love both places."

"Well, I don't care which house it is or where it is. I just want to get out of here and back to my own bed!"

"That I can arrange," I said. "We brought out our big leather sleigh bed that we had in California. It's right here waiting for you to return. And it's awfully empty without you."

It was true. I was very lonely for my husband. I had missed his presence and help and input throughout our move to Colorado. I was also lonely for our life together back in California. My concerns about him missing his old environment may have been partly a projection of the fact that I missed it myself. Jill and Augie were great, and I would be starting work soon, but I knew I would feel unsettled until John returned and we could be a real family again.

Blake began school, and I began work at Slifer, about a week after we arrived. For both of us, there was the usual period of adjustment to new faces, locales, and expectations. Blake was still missing her friends, and I regretted not having more time to spend with her before I started work. In the morning, I dropped her off at school, and I didn't usually get home until after five. I didn't like it that she was alone for several hours after her classes, but I did like the fact that she could walk home from school through quiet and peaceful neighborhoods, and that Jill was just across the street.

As for me, I could tell right away that my new job would be very demanding. It was also, as I had expected, almost ideal for my skills and interests. I couldn't help but worry about the long hours, though, not only for the sake of my daughter but also for John's well-being when he returned. On weekdays, he would often be alone while I was at work and Blake was in school. That was why it had been so important to find both a temporary and a permanent home close to Jill. She had her own work, but she did much of it out of her house. That would give her some time to spend with John, which was a main reason she had wanted us to move nearby.

But even with Jill's gracious help, John would be alone a good portion of the time, and that concerned me. What he would do with his days when no one else was around for company was an issue we had not had to deal with since he had left CMS. But we would soon have to face the problem squarely.

Of course, if the stem-cell treatment worked well enough, he might be able to go back to work, perhaps even get back into the financial planning field that he so loved. If so, he wouldn't have to spend time home alone. But if there was no improvement in his memory function, then it was difficult to see what kind of work would be suitable for him. Having to take a menial job was out of the question. He remembered well that he had earned a JD and an MBA, and that he had been a lawyer and a successful financial planner. And he was very proud of those accomplishments. It was important that he be able to retain his pride and not have to take what he would consider a big step down.

But with no work to do, how would he spend his days? From the time he left CMS to when he took off for St. Louis, I had spent most of every day with him. We talked, went places together, played card games, watched television, shared life in many ways. This helped him to stay engaged with the world. But even with Jill visiting him often and Blake being there in the afternoon, there would be less input to keep him mentally active. One possibility would be for him to find a hobby in which he could invest his time and energy. But I had no idea what kind of hobby would interest him and be doable if his short-term memory continued to fail him.

My birthday, Easter, and the first anniversary of the *status* seizure all came and went with John still in Germany. Together with his parents, he was now making brief forays away from the hospital to explore some of the surrounding towns and countryside. He had purchased a video camera and was taking it with him everywhere to make a record of the excursions. I continued to receive vague reports of substantial memory improvement, but I continued to take them with a grain of salt. I would wait until I could see for myself.

Finally, a week and a half after the main treatment had been completed, John boarded the plane that would bring him back to America. He spent a couple of days in Missouri with his folks, then flew on by himself. I met him at the Denver airport on April twenty-fifth.

As I walked toward the arrival gate, I was totally beside myself, like a kid waiting to see Santa Claus fly in with his reindeer. But the only gift I wanted this Santa to bring was himself. And maybe, hopefully, just possibly, he would also bring with him one other very special present—a gift mainly for himself but also for the rest of us who loved him—a healthier brain function.

I wondered if he would know me after our having been apart for a month, but I needn't have doubted. He recognized me right away.

"The world traveler is back!" I said as I ran up to him.

"My beautiful wife!" he said as we hugged. "It seems like a long time."

"It has been a long time. But I've been waiting here patiently while you went gallivanting around the world."

"What do you mean around the world?" he asked.

"You were in Germany for three weeks."

"Was I? I thought I was in Missouri."

"You were," I replied. "But before that you were in Germany. Oh, never mind. It's great to have you back. Let's just go home."

Already, the conversation was going the same way that many of our conversations had gone over the past year. I was surprised at how disappointed I felt at this evidence that so far there had been no memory improvement. I had apparently allowed my hopes to rise higher than I realized.

On the way home, I talked to John about how long he had been away and about the stem-cell treatment he had undergone. I also reminded him that we had a new temporary house that would be unfamiliar to him.

"I figured as much," he said. "This is Colorado, right? If this is where we're living now, then we must have a new address."

After we arrived, he spent some time exploring the house. "What's this?" he asked, pointing to a two-foot long contraption that sat on a small table in our bedroom.

"It's an oxygen machine. Your epileptologist back in California suggested that we get one for you because of the high altitude here—over eight thousand feet. It's for you to use at night."

"You mean I have to wear a mask and breathe through a tube while I sleep?"

"Yes, but with the way it's set up, I don't think it will be uncomfortable. And the oxygen will help your blood flow and keep you breathing evenly. It should also give the stem cells their best chance of developing in the right way. I bought the machine so it would be here for you as soon as you got back."

He was not happy with this news. "Any other surprises?"

"Well, your therapy is supposed to continue here for several weeks," I said. "You should have some vials of stem cells with you in a cold-storage container in your baggage. In fact, we need to get them out now to put in the freezer. They're for you to inject yourself with a couple of times a week."

"I thought you told me I already had the treatment."

"You had the main part of it over two weeks ago in Germany. But we need to follow through with it here to give it the best chance of working."

"Sounds like a fun thing to do."

"I'll help you with the injections. It's all for a good purpose."

"To make me well?"

"Yes."

"Do you think I'm better?" he asked.

"I don't know. How do you feel?"

"Compared to what? I don't feel like I can remember much, if that's what you mean. I vaguely remember being somewhere. You say it was Germany. I got off a plane earlier today, so maybe it was. But I don't remember it."

"Somewhere in your baggage is a video recording you made of some outings you took in Germany," I said. "Judy told me it was your video scrapbook. Maybe it will refresh your memory."

"Really? Let's get it out now. I want to see."

I helped John find the videotape and set it up for viewing, then I got the stem cells into the freezer. I made us some coffee, and when I returned he was engrossed in images of storefronts in some small German town, interspersed with brief segments of Rock and Judy smiling for the camera.

"Do you remember being there?" I asked as I sat beside him.

"I'm not sure," he replied.

As the video continued, there were scenes along a highway showing gorgeous hills and mountains in the background.

"Very impressive," I said.

"That's where I was?" John replied.

"Yep. They're your pictures. You took them yourself."

"At least I have something to show for my trip. But I don't remember any of it so far. Maybe if I keep on watching, it will jog my memory."

For another fifteen minutes we viewed small towns, restaurants, highways, lakes, and snow-capped mountains. Much of it looked beautiful and inviting, but we might as well have been watching a travelogue on television made by a stranger except for the fact that occasionally John, Judy, or Rock would make a brief appearance on the tape. John made no sign that he remembered any of the scenes.

"I've had enough of this for now," he said finally. "I'm tired. I think I'll go for a nap. Where's our bedroom?"

"Just to the right at the top," I said, pointing to the stairs. I didn't mention the fact that he had been in the bedroom half an hour before.

"You want to join me?"

"Absolutely," I said. "Go ahead. I'll straighten up and be there in a minute."

As I retrieved the tape and took the coffee cups into the kitchen, I could still feel my disappointment. I had been with John for almost three hours now. Nothing he had said so far led me to believe that his short-term memory had improved one bit over what it had been before he left. And his reaction to the recording only confirmed that conclusion. But the main part of his therapy had occurred two full weeks ago. Surely, I thought, if there was going to be any improvement, there would be some sign of it by now.

As I climbed the stairs, I wondered how I had once more allowed myself to start expecting too much. Now I was starting to pay the price again, in disappointment.

When I got to the bedroom, John was already asleep, most of his clothes still on. I briefly considered waking him so he could go onto the oxygen machine, but he seemed to be breathing easily. *I'll let him rest,* I thought, as I lay down with him. *Maybe I can have a nap as well.*

Sleep wouldn't come. My mind was racing too fast. Gradually, though, as I listened to John's steady breathing, I started calming down. *How can I draw any conclusions at this point?* I thought. *The therapy is ongoing. Just because nothing much has come from it yet is no sure indication of what will happen in a week or a month. Wait and see, Melinda. Just wait and see.*

At least there was one thing I didn't have to wait for any longer. My husband. The adventurer had returned to where he belonged. *Thank you, Lord, for bringing him back safe.*

And now here we were in Colorado, together at last in the house that God had led us to. Like so many other times since the *status* seizure, I lay close to my husband, luxuriating not only in his warmth but in the precious fact that he was there with me, alive, healthy except for his poor dear brain, and doing the best he could.

Finally, I thought, *this little house can be a home.*

CHAPTER THIRTEEN

THE FLOOD

Why had I worried so much about John feeling out of place in our new location? I should have realized that with his happy memories of living in Colorado before we were married—memories he still retained—he would feel comfortable in Eagle. More than that, he embraced the area. It was springtime in the Rockies, and though there was still snow on the ground here and there, it was rapidly melting as the days turned mild. He immediately began taking advantage of the fair weather by exploring the neighborhood.

Sometimes I walked with him, but he often went off by himself while I was at work. I was apprehensive at first about his solitary excursions, and I did my best to make sure that his cell phone was always charged up and that he carried enough cash to pay for a taxi. But I needn't have worried on that account, either. By this time, he knew his memory limitations well, and he took his initial explorations slowly. After a few days I relaxed somewhat, thankful that the question of what he would do with his time alone at home was being answered. The answer was that he had little such time available. He was too busy finding his way out in the world.

Gradually, as he somehow got a feel for how to navigate in the neighborhood, he expanded his jaunts. A couple of times he called and asked me to pick him up, but he never sounded panicked on the phone, or even anxious. He might be a mile or two away from the house, unsure of exactly where he was and doubting his ability to retrace his steps. But he was never truly lost. He was always able to describe his surroundings—a store, a street name, or some landmark—well enough for me to know where he was.

Back in California, after the *status* seizure, he had never ventured out into the world on his own. With the exception of the incident on the tollway when his frustrations led him to climb the embankment and leave me behind, he would not go anywhere alone. I wondered if his new penchant for exploring his surroundings was a sign that his memory was starting to return to normal. Were his walks enabling him to develop a cognitive map of the neighborhood, one that was slowly etching itself into his memory? If so, that would be a powerful sign that the stem-cell therapy was working.

An incident that occurred soon after his return seemed to support the idea that the stem cells were beginning to take effect. Ironically, the event concerned a new doctor that he had begun going to. At my request, Augie had suggested a naturopathic practitioner for John, and I had made an appointment for him to see this new physician on the Monday after his return. Because of my work, Jill was the one to drive him to the appointment, so I didn't get to meet the doctor immediately. And later that day, when I asked John about the visit, he couldn't tell me any of the details.

The next evening, we went out to dinner. Shortly after we sat down at our table, John said to me, "I know that woman."

"What woman?"

He turned and pointed toward a middle-aged woman and man at a table ten feet behind him. "That one just back there."

"You don't know that woman, you silly goose," I said, thankful that the couple hadn't seemed to notice John gesturing toward them. "You just got into town. You don't know anyone here except me, Blake, Jill, and Augie."

"I do know her," he replied. "I'm sure of it."

This was beginning to sound far too much like the beginning of some of those conversations we had had shortly after the *status* seizure, the ones in which John had misidentified people, swearing that he had known them from his childhood. And just as back then, he wouldn't let it drop. Several times as we waited for our food and then after it arrived, he stole peeks at the woman and again swore that he was sure he knew her. Each time, I tried to ignore his comments and to steer the conversation in another direction.

Then, in the middle of our dinner, the other couple rose to leave. As the woman neared our table, John turned to her and said, "Excuse me for not remembering your name, but don't I know you?"

The two people stopped, and I felt my cheeks beginning to flush as I waited for the woman to reply—not rudely I hoped. But she said, "Oh, Mr. Wilferth. Yes, we do know each other. We met at my office yesterday." She turned to her companion and explained that John had just become her patient. I realized then that she was John's new naturopath.

After introductions all around and a few pleasantries, the couple went on their way.

"See, I told you so!" John said, obviously proud of his achievement. "I didn't remember her name, but I knew I had met her."

"I admit it, you were right on the mark," I replied, also excited about this success. "Next time I'll listen to you when you say you remember someone."

"I really feel I'm getting better," he said. "I'm going to get even better by my birthday. I just know it."

The incident was encouraging, but I soon decided that it was an anomaly. As the days moved on, there were no other signs that John's short-term memory was improving. At home, he still had to be reminded of where things were located, and of what had happened the previous day or even an hour earlier. Our conversations about ongoing issues still had to begin with me setting out the basic terms of the issue and what we had said previously in regard to it. If we went for dinner or to enjoy some other event, we still had to replay the experience repeatedly in our conversation to prevent John from quickly forgetting most of it.

Even in regard to his excursions, I decided that his ability to find his way back home wasn't actually based on an improved memory function. If I asked him a question such as how far the library was from our house or in which direction the main part of town was, he wouldn't know the answer. I concluded that he wasn't actually constructing a cognitive map that represented various locations in relation to each other. Or if he was, he wasn't able to bring it to his conscious mind. Whatever was enabling him to navigate outside the house didn't seem to be based on his having developed an improved conscious memory.

Nevertheless, we continued with his stem-cell treatment. Twice a week I injected him with the stem cells he had brought from Germany. He also worked daily on the cognitive exercises that the German doctors had designed for him, with Jill coming over many days to help him do the exercises while I was at work. Several of his former doctors in California had felt that performing mental exercises would not significantly benefit him because the necessary brain hardware just wasn't there. But Dr. Scheller thought that the exercises would help him to develop parts of his brain that had not been injured. He also seemed to think that they would help John to develop new hardware by stimulating the stem cells to grow into healthy neurons.

But as a week and then another passed with no apparent memory improvement, I began seriously wondering whether there had been any value in the stem cells, the exercises, or any part of the treatment. As for the doctors thinking that the stem-cell therapy would heal John's epilepsy, that was also called into question when he had a focal seizure a few days after returning. I kept telling myself that we should keep at it; but in reality, I felt that we were only going through the motions in completing the treatment.

About two weeks after John had arrived home, though, another tantalizingly suggestive incident occurred that seemed to indicate that his short-term memory was improving. One night after work I noticed that a phone number had been written on the calendar under the day's date, along with the word "Wain," apparently a reference to John's old friend from California.

"John, did you put Wain's name on the calendar?" I asked.

He walked over, looked at where I was pointing, and said, "Oh yeah, he called me today."

"That was nice of him," I said. "What did you guys talk about?"

"He told me he's put together another company in the credit card industry."

"Really? How's the company doing?"

"He's hoping to sell it," John replied. "For a million dollars."

"It sounds like he's doing well."

"He is. He said his house is worth over a million dollars now, too."

"When did you get the call?" I asked.

"This afternoon sometime."

That meant he had talked to Wain hours ago. "You mean you retained all that information since then? That's wonderful!"

"Yeah," John agreed. "I guess that is pretty good."

I asked him to tell me more about the conversation and he gave further details about what the two of them had talked about, leaving me thoroughly impressed by this unexpected feat of memory.

Later that night, though, the memory was already beginning to disappear.

"Was there something about a phone call?" he asked me at one point. "Were we talking about a phone call?" From his words and expression, it was clear that he was trying, as he often did, to re-grasp something that he felt was on the tip of his tongue, or of his mind.

"Yes," I replied. "You told me that you had talked to Wain on the phone earlier today."

"Yeah. I think I remember that now," he said. But if he did, the details and the clarity had apparently left. And by the next day, he seemed to have lost even a dim recollection of the phone call.

I didn't know what to make of the incident. I hadn't overheard the conversation, so I didn't know how accurately John had remembered it. Back in California, he had occasionally embellished a vague memory with his own imaginative construct. I wondered if that's what had happened in this case, but I didn't want to test it by calling Wain and asking him what he had told John. For one thing, that seemed as if it would be going behind John's back. For another, I wasn't in a hurry to find out that his brain had played tricks on him. By not knowing for sure, I could leave open the possibility that the episode was a sign that his memory was actually improving.

It wouldn't be long, though, before yet another event occurred that made it even clearer that something good was happening in John's head. When the evidence came, it did so in such convincing fashion, with such a flood of detail, that I found it difficult to doubt any longer that his short-term memory was getting better.

What made this incident even more heartening was that it happened in the midst of a family celebration. The celebration revolved around the wedding of my younger sister, Amanda. She had become engaged to a very nice man, Shelby, and they had decided on a May wedding, which was to be held back home in Sikeston. So in mid-May, just three weeks after John had returned, he, Blake, and I set off for Missouri to attend this very special event.

We only had a long weekend, so I tried to pack in as much visiting as I could with my family and old friends, while trying to do my part in helping to prepare for the occasion. Blake was excited because she was a bridesmaid and was also able to visit with her grandmother and grandfather Dame, my mom and dad, whom she had not seen for many months. John seemed to enjoy the festivities too, with my dad, as always, treating him like the son he had never had.

I was aware that some people who knew about John's condition and about the stem-cell therapy were curious about whether he had gotten better, and I was a little sad that he wasn't able to set them on their heels with a much-improved memory. But that wasn't an issue with Mom and Dad, or for Melanie and Amanda, who all knew that we were still waiting patiently for improvement. Like me, they were just glad that John was home from Germany, and that he was healthy and vital following the stem-cell treatment.

The wedding was gorgeous. Somehow, my beautiful baby sister had been able to stay single all those years until she found just the man for her, and she looked doubly beautiful in her happiness that day. Afterward, we all gathered for the reception, which was held outside at Mom and Dad's house. Though John seemed a little tired now and then, for the most part he had a good time throughout the afternoon and evening. It was quite late when we finally went to bed, and we both fell asleep immediately.

About eight the next morning, John burst awake so suddenly that he pulled me out of sleep at the same time. He sat up and leaned against the headboard, seeming agitated.

"What's wrong?" I asked, as I sat up too.

For a moment he didn't answer me. His eyes were open wide, but he didn't seem to be focusing on anything in the room. It was more as if he was looking inside, calculating something. Then he said, "I remember!"

"What? What is it?"

He grabbed my arm and looked at me, his eyes even wider: "I remember! I remember! Let me tell you what I remember!"

Words started tumbling out of his mouth. "We were at the wedding yesterday. For Amanda and Shelby. And we went to the reception after the wedding. It was outside. There was a big tent. And your dad gave a speech. I don't remember exactly what he said, but I do remember that he was very stoic when he gave it. And sentimental, too. It was a nice speech."

"That's right!" I said. "Stoic and sentimental describes his speech exactly. Do you remember anything else?"

"I remember a lot. I remember I split the seam in the arm of my suit before the reception, and I had to go change. And I remember that Joe and Anna were there, and I danced with Anna. I danced a lot. I got very warm and sweaty while I was dancing. And I remember falling on the dance floor at some point. Maybe I had too much to drink."

He went on to tell me even more details about the reception. He spoke of a woman he had met there, and of the woman's father. He didn't remember their names, and at first I didn't know whom he meant. But then he described the woman, including what she was wearing, and I immediately recognized her.

I sat there rapt and amazed as he continued to describe people and events at the reception in detail. When he finally seemed to run out of memory gas, I said, "John, do you know where we live?"

"Sure. We live in Eagle. In Colorado."

"Do you know what kind of house we live in?"

"Yeah. It's a small two-story. Right across from Jill and Augie."

"That's right!" I replied.

"Hey!" he said. "Do you know what else I remember?"

"What?"

"I remember taking videos at the rehearsal dinner the night before the wedding."

"That's two nights ago!"

"I remember it clearly," he said.

"What else?"

He seemed to be searching his mind again, then he said, "Well, I remember having trouble last night with my mouthpiece. I got up at some point to change it." He was referring to the mouth guard that he sometimes used to keep his teeth from grinding.

We must have spent more than half an hour sitting there in bed, the morning sun spilling through the window, as John recounted his memories to me. During that time I tried to be careful to ask few questions and none that might be leading. Everything he said that he remembered came directly out of his own mind, and every detail that I too had witnessed was precisely on target.

Taken all together, John's report amounted to a veritable flood of recent memories that went far beyond what he had previously been capable of since the *status* seizure. I didn't know what was the cause—the stem cells, the cognitive exercises, the combination of the two, or something else—but it seemed obvious that something had changed for the better in John's brain.

Yet, in spite of the joy we felt as words of recollection poured from his mouth that morning, a familiar pattern quickly reasserted itself. The pattern I'm talking about consisted of a sudden high peak of improved memory function (this one had been the highest so far) being followed by a much longer period during which his short-term memory seemed no better than before. The down part of the pattern began that afternoon when I asked him about the morning incident. He didn't recall it. He didn't remember waking up excited, with memories practically exploding out of his head. He recalled the wedding and the reception in only the most general terms, and he remembered none of the specific occurrences that he had reported with such relish just a few hours before.

When I reminded him of what he had accomplished earlier, he seemed to regard the incident as if it were an impressive achievement done by someone else. I know he wanted to believe me, but I'm not sure he did fully. It was like telling a man whose legs were amputated a year ago that they had suddenly grown back that morning. Maybe the man wants to believe you, but it's not so easy if the legs have again disappeared and he can't recall their having been back for that brief while.

I tried not to let my earlier enthusiasm plummet into dull disappointment. After all, *I* remembered it. *I* knew the rush of memories had occurred. And I was convinced that it couldn't have been a fluke, that it was bound to happen again. So, after we returned to Eagle and as we finished injecting the last of the stem cells, I kept expecting John to have more outbursts of memory. But they didn't materialize. In fact, nothing seemed to have changed. His present continued to be almost totally cut off from his recent past.

I didn't understand it. The awakening in Sikeston had been so dramatic, so detailed and far ranging, that I couldn't believe it was accidental. But why had it been only an isolated event? If there was something good hapening inside John's head, some new growth of nerve cells or reallocation of resources, it was certainly taking an idiosyncratic course. I prayed that whatever key had unlocked the floodgates of memory that morning was still somewhere in his brain, only temporarily misplaced.

As spring progressed, John got out of the house even more. He now had a bicycle, which took him not only around town but up into the nearby mountains. Sometimes he took his walking stick with him, parked his bike, and hiked into the hills. I was still puzzled about how he managed to navigate, but when he returned from one of his excursions and I asked him where he had been, he could usually give me only the vaguest of itineraries.

One evening, though, he told me about a tall, steep hill that he had climbed that day. He described how he had gotten to its summit and had been worried about how he was going to get back down the precipitous path he had taken. He told me how he had then finally managed to find a more gradual trail than the one he had ascended and had followed it back down. His rendition of the trek was very detailed, which was again remarkable in the context of his many short-term memory failures. But it answered no questions. It only reinforced the puzzling pattern of sudden brief peaks of memory rising out of long valleys of forgetfulness.

I started wondering what I should be looking for in terms of his getting better. Was I focusing on the wrong thing? My idea of memory improvement was for him first to be able to consistently remember much of what had happened several hours previously. Further advancement would mean his being able to recall much of what he had done the day before, then the day before that, and so on. And it seemed to me that this would all take place at a gradual, steady rate of progress. But that's not what was happening. The signs of memory improvement that he occasionally displayed were striking, but they were erratic and followed no step-by-step progression. I decided that maybe I was expecting the wrong thing. If so, then perhaps he was actually showing more improvement than I realized.

After all, there were his excursions, on which he never seemed to get lost. I still didn't know how he did that, but it represented a big advance in his ability to be aware of his geographic location. He also had a better understanding of where he was in time. Back in California, he had sometimes looked at his watch and said things like, "It's October?" betraying the fact that often, he had not even a vague idea of his temporal location. Now he was typically aware of the month and the season, and often even of what day it was. He was also a lot more confident out in the world, with a better comprehension of his surrounding environment. Surely, I thought, when taken all together, these added up to a significant advance for John.

On the other hand, I wondered whether I was fooling myself. Was I misremembering the way he had been six months previously? Did he really have a firmer grasp on his surroundings? If so, why was his short-term memory still mostly failing him? I found myself going back and forth on whether his memory and cognitive functioning were actually getting stronger, but I couldn't come to a firm conclusion. There just wasn't enough evidence one way or the other.

Then something happened in June, six or seven weeks after John's return, that was even more telling than his flood of memories in Sikeston had been. It was an achievement that required accurate short-term memory, but that went far beyond memory in what it demanded of John cognitively. And it was something that he would have been totally incapable of doing before the stem-cell treatment.

The incident occurred in relation to an ongoing legal issue that we were dealing with at the time. The issue involved what we considered unfair treatment of John in a position he had had several years previously. We had hired a law firm to represent John's interests, and it had been pursuing the case for at least two years. But in June one of the lawyers there wrote to inform us that the firm believed it was going to be difficult to move forward with a strong chance of success.

John, when he read the letter, was upset. As an attorney himself, still licensed to practice law in Missouri, he believed that there were solid legal grounds to continue pursuing the matter. We discussed the letter and how we should reply, and he kept insisting that we should not give up on the issue. Instead, we should respond to the law firm by laying out the reasons for moving forward with the case and continuing to seek justice.

"I'll do it," he said.

"Do what?"

"I'll write back to them and make the argument to move ahead."

"Do you think you can do that?" I asked.

"I'm a lawyer," he said as he took the letter and headed for the computer room. "That's what I'm trained to do."

All through the evening he remained at the computer. Whenever I went to ask him how he was doing, he either ignored me or shooed me away. Sometimes when I entered, he seemed to be reading the letter we had received from the lawyers. At others, he sat staring at the screen and the new letter he was trying to compose. But each time, he seemed to have made little progress on the project.

When it got to be eleven, I went in and gave him a kiss. "It's getting late," I said. "Do you think it would be a good idea to go to bed and continue tomorrow?"

No answer.

"Your mind might be clearer in the morning."

"I want to finish it tonight," he replied.

"It looks like you have a long way to go."

"I'll go to bed when I get it done."

"Okay," I said, "but first you should take your medicines."

He capitulated enough to allow me to get his anticonvulsants and help him to take the proper dosages. Then he was back at the computer.

"I'll be waiting for you," I said, but he was again totally engrossed in his project.

As I lay in bed, it was almost as if I could hear him thinking through the walls. I worried about him, not so much that he was up late but that he might be overworking his brain. Surely, I thought, he must be getting more frustrated by the moment. I knew he had a good legal mind, but I had no faith that he would be able to get his thoughts together enough to compose an incisive letter addressing the complicated legal problem that he was dealing with. I could barely believe that he had even been able to continue focusing on the problem for the last four hours. I didn't know what to expect as a result.

I woke a couple of times and rose to find him still working. "When I'm done," he said each time I invited him to bed.

Finally, at three or four a.m., I opened my eyes to find him undressing. "Did you finish the letter?" I asked.

"Yes."

"How did it turn out?"

"I don't know. I'll look at it in the morning. I'm exhausted."

"Don't forget your oxygen."

"Got it," he replied. He attached the breathing tube, flipped the machine on, then collapsed onto the bed and was asleep right away.

A few hours later he was up with me. After a quick wash, he went to the computer. A few minutes later, he was hurrying back to the bedroom, holding a sheet of paper. "Look at this!" he said. "Read this!"

I took the letter and read it. It consisted of only a few paragraphs, but within that brief space John had composed an articulate, well argued, and thoroughly professional reply to the letter we had received from our lawyers. The argument made several cogent points for pressing on in the case, and it did so with what I thought was wonderful clarity.

"This is a great letter!" I said.

"Glad you think so," he replied, beaming.

"Well, it should be," I said, ribbing him. "It took you most of the night to do it."

"Some work while lazier ones sleep," he replied. He held out his hand: "Give it to me."

"Are you going to mail it now?" I asked, as I handed the letter back to him. "Be sure to sign it." He turned and went back into the computer room without answering me.

I continued getting ready for my day, marveling at John's accomplishment. For seven or eight consecutive hours he had focused on the task. During that entire time, his short-term memory and his long-term memory had had to work together to clearly articulate a difficult and complex train of thought. Throughout, his brain had been required to continuously remember what he was doing, why he was doing it, and what his objective was. Yes, the job had taken much longer for him to accomplish than it would have before the *status* seizure. But the final product was something that millions of intelligent people would not have been able to do as well even if they were given a longer time. To me, his accomplishment seemed nothing less than phenomenal.

I stopped what I was doing as I heard what sounded like something knocking against a wall somewhere in the house.

"John?" I called. "Is that you?"

No answer.

I hurried downstairs and found him in the living room, turning away from the front door, where a single sheet of paper was plastered to the frame with a couple of staples. In one hand he held a staple gun. In the other he clutched several more sheets of paper.

"What are you doing?" I asked.

"I made some copies of the letter. I'm putting them up on the walls."

"Why in the world would you do that?"

"So I'll keep seeing them right in front of my face. That way I won't be able to forget what I did last night."

I laughed. "Well that's logical. But don't get carried away. I hope you don't staple them everywhere."

"Only a few more." He was already at one of the living room walls. He quickly attached another copy of the letter there, then went to the kitchen, where he stapled a third one onto the wall near the refrigerator. I followed him back upstairs where he put a fourth copy up in the computer room.

He turned to me: "Finished," he said.

"So, are you proud of yourself?"

"Yeah, I am," he replied.

"That's makes two of us," I said as I gave him a hug. "You're getting better. It's so clear now."

"I know I am," he said. "And we're going to beat this. I know it! I know it!"

He was wise to put up the copies. They enabled him to luxuriate in his accomplishment for much of the day. But even with the evidence plastered on the walls, he was already regarding the letter as something separate from himself by evening. He was still proud of it, but he couldn't recall the effort he had put into composing it the previous night, and he had to reread the letter to remember what it was all about.

I was used to the peaks and valleys pattern by this time, so I wasn't surprised when he again found himself in a valley. Nor was my enthusiasm dampened. His forgetting didn't cancel out his accomplishment, nor did it even take away from the promise of what he had done.

That promise was one of continued improvement. That's what I decided. And if the progress was occurring in fits and starts rather than in a steady, measured way, it didn't matter. More relevant was the fact that the peaks of his improvement were getting higher and higher. It seemed clear to me that it was only a matter of time before he would reach more, and even loftier, summits. While at the same time, there would be fewer valleys. Or the valleys would rise higher.

With all the bits of evidence that had come in since John's return—the excursions, the incident at the restaurant, Wain's call, the flood of memories in Sikeston, and now a letter that to me seemed almost miraculous—I was convinced of it.

Whether the improvement was due to stem cells or something else I didn't know. In my view, the ultimate source was God, but how He was doing His work I couldn't say. Nor did I know how long that work would take. It might be months, maybe even a year or more, but in time John's short-term memory would surely be restored. Not necessarily all of it. Maybe he would never be at the same functional level as before the *status* seizure. But much of his ability to remember would return, and all the while he would get better, and better, and better.

I was certain of it.

But as I should have learned by now, God's plans are not always so easy to understand. Over the next several months I would re-learn that lesson as I discovered, yet again, how wrong I could be. And how right.

CHAPTER FOURTEEN

AT HOME IN THE HERE

Summer passed with no more big memory surprises. There were no happy recognitions of faces met just the day before. No exhuberant morning awakenings with a fountain of memories flooding the bedroom. No triumphant letters stapled to the walls.

The erratic improvement in John's memory function had come to a halt. Occasionally he retained a memory of something that had occurred several hours before. Now and then he even remembered a few facts about what had happened the previous day. But there was still no rhyme or reason to it. And it was only the odd detail, or some vague sense of what had happened, that he recalled.

"Did we do something special yesterday?" he might ask.

"Yes, we did," I would reply. "We drove over to Vail Village and looked around the shops. We had a nice dinner. It was a beautiful day."

"I thought I remembered something like that. Did we buy anything?"

"No, just window shopped. In one store you were trying on cowboy hats, of all things! And checking out belts with big brass buckles."

"Did we look at any horses?"

"Not this time," I laughed.

"Good. Else I'd be getting worried."

"Do you remember any specifics of the day?" I would ask.

"Just a feeling that we did something nice. I'm glad we had a good time."

"Me too."

After a while I stopped expecting further evidence of improvement. I still didn't know if it had been the stem cells or something else that had brought on John's occasional bursts of memory soon after Germany. But whatever it was, it had stopped working.

Not that he seemed to mind so much. At least not like he had back in California. Though he still got down about his memory, he didn't pace the floor as often as before, searching for some tool to lever open the bars to his mental cage. Instead, he did more and more of his pacing—and his biking—outside, in the surrounding hills and mountains, often taking along his fly rod as he headed up some dirt road that might take him into the next county.

He had always loved fly fishing, since his early days in Colorado as a young man, and there were many places nearby where he could now practice the sport. Forested hills and ridges started barely two hundred yards from our house, and a small creek ran nearby. Farther on into the mountains were places like Roaring Fork River, Eagle Creek, Frying Pan Lake, and many other bodies of water fed by the high Colorado snows. In that vastness there was no end of possibilities for a man who loved the outdoors.

His ability to find his way around in the mountains continued to mystify me. He didn't carry a compass, but instead determined directions from the movement of the sun. He took maps with him on his journeys, everything from a Colorado state road map to topographic maps of nearby areas. Sometimes they gave him at least a rough idea of where he was, if he remembered to mark where he was going before he went, but I'm not sure they helped a lot. When I asked him how he managed to avoid becoming lost, he explained that one main strategy was to keep people-related landmarks in sight if he got off the road. As long as he could see a house, a car, or someone else fishing, he knew he could get directions if he needed them.

Nevertheless, he sometimes wound up in locations where there was no one else around and his cell phone didn't work. Finding himself in that position was the only thing that frightened him about being out on his own. Not the possibility that a bear or a cougar or a rattlesnake might cross his path—which is what would frighten me—but the realization that he didn't know his way back home or how to find it. It was the sudden sense of being lost in a here that felt wild and faraway.

Thankfully, he quickly learned methods to help overcome the fear when it came, and to calm his mind so that he could figure out what to do next. I started finding that out one evening, after one of his early trips into the mountains. I had been asking him about his day and had so far learned that he had been fishing at some lake, but that he didn't know quite where.

Then he said, "It was a great day, except some people who were fishing nearby left, and there was no one else around. I got more and more worried about finding my way back. It started feeling very weird. Scary. I didn't know what to do."

He seemed to remember this part of his day clearly. Maybe his fear had burned the experience more deeply into his brain than usual.

"Were you able to use your maps?"

He shook his head. "Here's what I did. First, I found some rocks." He paused for a second or two, trying to pin down the memory. "I asked myself, what can I throw them at? Then I saw a tree and started trying to hit it." He paused again. "I wanted to get focused on the tree. Do you follow me?"

"I think so."

"I kept doing that. Just throwing rocks and thinking about hitting the tree. And it worked. Pretty soon, the negative thoughts went away. After that, I sat down and cleared my head. I started keeping track of the sun, to find out the direction it was moving. When I figured that out, I knew which way was south on the road, and I was pretty sure I had come north. So I went south and pretty soon hit a highway. It was easy after that."

I felt proud of him for finding a way to control his emotions and calmly figure out what to do. But I still didn't understand how, even with the sun, he was able to navigate using only the most ephemeral memories and without a detailed map in his head. Trying to understand, I asked him one day how he was able to bike from our house to downtown and back.

"It's different from how you do it," he replied. "I try to use landmarks. Like that tract of expensive houses on the ridge over there. Or maybe a building. They help orient me. So if I'm downtown, I might think that our house is in the opposite direction from the tract of expensive houses. That way, I have a rough idea of which direction to go. After a while, I might see a church and feel like I'm getting closer to our house. Maybe I remember it a little. So I keep going. Then I might see our street name on a sign. It doesn't always work, though. Sometimes I just go around in circles, and I have to ask."

The more I thought about John's explanation, the more amazing his ability to navigate seemed to me. For most people, it's easy to get from point

A to point B only a mile or so away. They don't think about how they do it because they have a cognitive map that matches the world outside. They just know where B is and go right there. But the route isn't imprinted in John's mind, so he has to use clues to figure out a path every time he wants to get to B. And then he has to use clues again find his way back. What's amazing is that he can often do that even with his short-term memory deficit. He's able to use his faculties to reason out and accomplish the same thing that people with normal memories can do without really thinking about it.

I wondered whether John's learning how to navigate by using landmarks was due to new circuits developing in his brain to make up for the damage. Whatever it was, his ability to find his way out in the world, including up in the mountains, often made it look like he could remember just as well as anyone else.

I knew that was far from the truth, though, so I always worried if he was out while I was at work. At the same time, it made me happy to picture him wandering the mountains at his own pace. And happy to know that anyone he met would probably find a man feeling strong and joyful in his freedom.

On one particular day, I knew that he had planned on going biking, but I hadn't heard from him for hours and was getting anxious as my workday wrapped up. I kept trying him on both our home line and his cell phone, but there was no answer. I assumed he was still out, probably somewhere unreachable by his cell. I kept trying him as I drove home, but with no success, every unanswered ring leaving me more worried. Finally, soon after I arrived, I got a call from him. He told me he was in a town that I knew was twenty miles away. He said that some friends were getting ready to drive him home.

"Are you okay?" I asked.

"Yeah, I'm great."

"Who are the friends?"

"A couple I met today. I'll tell you all about it when I get there."

About an hour later, an SUV carrying three people pulled up in the driveway. John and the driver, a man I had never seen before, got out and retrieved John's bicycle and fishing gear from the back of the vehicle. Then the driver quickly got back in and John waved at him and the other passenger, a woman, as they drove away.

"Were those the friends you made?" I asked John when he came inside.

"Yeah," he said. "We spent all day together. Look at all the notes I took."

Out of his pockets he drug various pieces of paper—napkins, folded sheets of notebook paper, an envelope—all with copious amounts of information written on them.

John had always been a big note taker, even before the *status* seizure, but more recently he had done it even more as a way of trying to make up for his faulty memory. He thought that by writing events and experiences down, he would be able to imprint them better into his brain, and later he could refer to them to help spark his memories. So when he was out and something happened that he thought it was important to remember, he often grabbed whatever piece of paper was available—an envelope, a napkin, even a page out of a telephone book—and asked to borrow a pen or a pencil from whomever he was with to write down the experience. The practice had gotten so common, and he seemed to believe in its efficacy so much, that I had tried to get him to take a small notebook and a pen with him wherever he went. But he seldom remembered to do so.

On this day, as usual, the notes he had taken were on whatever bits of paper he could beg, borrow, or steal. He started reading through them so he could piece together what he had experienced and tell me about it. Though there was some initial confusion about what had happened before what, he was able to give me a good picture of what his day had been like.

Apparently, he had been heading somewhere to fish, and upon entering the town of Edwards had decided to stop in at a restaurant for a snack. Once inside, he had begun talking with a man and woman who became fascinated with him. It turned out that the couple owned a nearby ranch and were well known in the area, and after a while they took him into town to meet some of their friends. Then they invited him to their home and gave him a tour of their ranch. John's notes were full of details about the ranch—how many acres, how many head of cattle, what kind of feed. After that, they all hung out together for the rest of the afternoon.

"They were nice people," John concluded.

"Well, they were certainly very nice to give you a ride home."

"It was getting so late, they didn't like the idea of letting me bike all the way back to Eagle," he said.

That wasn't the only adventure John got involved in on his journeys. One day, he came across a motorcycle accident before any police or paramedics had arrived, and he stopped to render aid. I met the person involved and his partner several weeks later, and they told me what a great guy John was and how appreciative they had been of his help.

I knew he was a great guy, but it was sweet music to hear his praises from others. It was sad, though, that he almost immediately forgot incidents such as helping at an accident scene and making new friends at a restaurant. And notes didn't help. The day after the restaurant incident, he remembered none of it. When I told him what he had told me about the day before, it was as if he were listening to a story about someone else. And when I showed him the notes he had taken, they struck only the vaguest chords of memory. He knew that he was the one who had done those things, but he couldn't experience the pleasure of actually remembering them.

This was doubly sad because being able to recall such occasions might have done wonders for his outlook. It would have given him a fuller picture of who he was, and of the fact that there were so many people out there who liked him and appreciated him once they met him. Instead, he woke each morning with barely a glimmer of a memory of what he had been the previous day.

As summer faded and we got into the early fall, John thankfully had no major seizures, although his focal seizures returned at the same rate as before, which was about once a month. When I realized that the focal seizures were going to continue and the memory improvements had stopped, I felt the old anxieties returning about his health. Again, I started wondering what more we could do toward his healing.

Whatever that might be, it would probably cost considerable money, and I had no idea where that would come from. We wouldn't even have health insurance once John's insurance through CMS lapsed in a few months. After that, to get insurance under the government's COBRA plan would be so expensive—about $2,000 per month—that I didn't know how we would be able to afford it. Following a two-year mandatory wait after John was declared officially disabled in the fall of 2003, Medicare would kick in during the fall of 2005. But that was a year away, and as we'd learned over and over, a lot can happen in a year.

Our best chance to get insurance in the near term would be for me to purchase it through my work at Slifer. So far, I hadn't been able to do that because I was only on temporary assignment as an independent contractor. But I was hoping that after my first six months were up, they would decide to take me on as a full-time employee. In that event, I would be able to get insurance through their health plan, which would take a huge worry off my mind. As the date for my six-month evaluation drew near, I prayed hard that Slifer would recognize the benefit of offering me a position as a regular employee.

But when the evaluation came, the company didn't see things in the same light that I did. They were certainly happy enough with my performance to keep me on as an independent contractor and to give me plenty of work to handle. But for some reason, they weren't prepared to offer me a full-time position with the firm. That meant no health insurance, which in turn meant that soon we would be not only physically, but also financially hostage to John's illness.

After long consideration, I decided that it was time for me to seek a new opportunity. Somehow, I believed, there was a way for me to make a decent living for our family and not have to worry constantly about huge monthly insurance payments on the one hand or enormous medical bills on the other. When I told John about what I wanted to do and explained my reasons, he agreed. Soon after, in October, I handed in my resignation.

Though I had agonized about the decision, once it was made I felt liberated and energized about being on the job market again. There was another design firm interested in my services, and I planned to talk with them about the possibility of joining their staff. But then I hesitated. Maybe I shouldn't rush immediately into taking a job with someone else. Why not work for myself? Maybe start my own business? I had been in business for myself off and on for years, and had had some success. Even my brief stint at selling insurance, which had relied very much on my being a self-starter, had gone well. With that kind of track record, would I be making the wrong decision if I hooked on as an employee with another firm immediately?

Of course, going into business for myself would take money. But we had managed to move into our new home the month before and still had much of the profit from the sale of our house in California. If I could find a promising business in which I could invest some of that money, and then was able to add my time, energy, and talent to the enterprise, maybe I could bring in enough income so that the high COBRA insurance payments would be in the realm of possibility for us.

With those thoughts in mind, I started looking for a business opportunity. I talked to John about it as much as possible, asking for his thoughts and any advice he might have. But it was mostly up to me to locate an opportunity that was based on a sound business plan, had considerable promise, and didn't require too heavy an investment.

I soon located what seemed to be just the thing. It was a franchise opportunity developed and backed by the hugely successful online auction company eBay™. The idea, which was already being put to work successfully in many locations in the country, was for a business that would take care of auctioning individuals' goods through the eBay Web site. Instead of having a garage sale, or trying to auction off their goods themselves, people would bring them to my store. I would take care of auctioning the items, ship them to the buyers, and collect the payments. For providing those services, I would retain a percentage of the purchase price.

The more I learned about the idea, the more excited I became. I would have my own protected territory, which would include the town of Edwards and nearby environs. And the business seemed to have almost unlimited potential. I knew that eBay had become tremendously popular and that thousands of individuals had gone into business for themselves simply buying and selling through their Web site. In fact, more than a few had become very successful. That was nice to know, but wealth wasn't my goal. I decided that I would be happy if I could just achieve an income that would allow us to live reasonably comfortably and afford health insurance.

I talked not only to the people at the main offices, who were friendly and receptive, but to several individuals who had already gone into the business in other locations in Colorado. I visited their stores, and everything I saw convinced me that the business plan was good and the opportunity was there. After a few weeks of investigation, I sat down with John one evening to talk with him about what I had learned.

"I've been looking into the eBay opportunity, and I think it's a good one."

"What eBay opportunity?"

I explained to him again what it was all about. After a few questions and my answers, he said, "Where are your customers going to come from?"

"Advertising, and word of mouth."

"Do you think there's a market for it?"

"Look at how many people have garage sales to sell things they don't want or need any more. The sale takes up the entire weekend, and they end up giving half the stuff away. How much easier would it be to just load the items up, bring them to me, and wait for a check?"

"That's probably what I'd do. Then spend the weekend fishing."

"And everyone knows eBay. It has a great reputation. This way, people can surf the eBay wave without even getting wet."

"I don't know," he said. "It still sounds pretty chancy to me."

Given the fact that John had always been a risk taker, I was surprised by that reaction. I talked to him more about it, but he was lukewarm at best about the idea. I didn't know if it was because he didn't fully understand the concept or because he felt like he wasn't in control of the business, but it wasn't the reaction I was hoping for.

Still, I was convinced that it was a good idea and that it had superb backing. So not long after, I told the people at eBay that I was ready to get serious. Soon, I had signed a contract and was hunting for a suitable storefront for my March opening.

At first I was full of enthusiasm. But as the search for a store location continued over several weeks into December and I learned more and more about the business I was getting into—advertising, accounting, store operations, marketing strategies—I began realizing just how large was the project I had bitten off for myself. John would be there as a sounding board, though at that point he remained somewhat skeptical of the idea, but he wouldn't be able to help in running the operation. Its success or failure depended solely on me.

And if I failed, what then? Not only would we not be able to afford health insurance, but most of our savings would be gone. And me without a job. We wouldn't be back to square one; we would be at square minus one.

My anxiety only increased after I got back, in January, from a one-week company training in Pasadena, California. It wasn't that the instruction wasn't great. It was. And it wasn't that I didn't feel competent to take on the various aspects of the challenge. I did. It was just that so much depended on the success of the business that I found myself continually worrying that something I couldn't control would go wrong. Maybe there wouldn't be enough customers. Or what if John had a major seizure and I had to delay the opening? Or suppose something else bad happened?

Soon after I got back from Califonria, something bad did happen: John experienced his first major seizure for over a year. It wasn't as severe as most of his others had been, and certainly not as bad as the *status* seizure, but it made me question my decision all the more.

By the time March came, only a few weeks from my grand opening, I was a basket case. I couldn't sleep, I was constantly anxious, and all I could think about was the risk I was taking and the possibility of failure. That was exactly the wrong attitude to have when opening a new business, and I knew it. But I didn't know how to get out of it.

Then one day I was talking by phone to an old friend who had noticed how apprehensive I seemed, and he asked me if I had been going to church.

"Not enough!" I replied. "I've only been a few times over the last couple of months. I feel guilty!"

"Have you been talking to God in your journal?"

"Not for a while. I ran out of pages in my old one and I can't locate another like the ones I've always had. I've bought a couple, but they don't look right. They seem ugly to me."

"But journaling is your main way of praying, isn't it?"

"Yes. And I know I should just use whatever I have."

"Maybe so. Maybe it's time to get back to your roots."

Afterward, I thought hard about that conversation. What my friend had guessed was right. Recently, I had allowed myself to put God and prayer on the back burner. No wonder I felt so alone.

But why hadn't I been praying? I didn't really understand my behavior. Was it because I was so worried? Before, I had always turned to God with my troubles. So why wasn't I turning to Him now, when it was so obvious I needed His strength?

Was I angry at Him? Maybe angry that John hadn't gotten better? No, I decided, that wasn't it. At least not quite. It was more like disappointment, I realized, disappointment that some of the doors God had seemed to be opening for us when we were in California—doors that appeared so promising—had not led us far. Ultimately, John's stem cell therapy had apparently not made a large and lasting difference in his memory function. Nor had it healed his epilepsy. And the job at Slifer—it had seemed such a wonderful sign of God's grace on our family, but it had not developed into the answer to our financial problems.

What happened to all those doors that opened for us? Those new pathways? In the end, what good came from them?

That's what had been going on my mind recently, I realized—questions like that nagging at me. For months I had been doubting God instead of praying to Him. The result was a mental state that was growing more negative by the day.

At that point, I started turning the questions on myself instead of God. *What right do I have to mistrust the Lord?* I asked myself. *What right to second guess Him?* And anyway, wasn't I being myopic to think that the doors had not led anywhere? How about the move to Colorado? Wasn't that the thing that had allowed John to regain some autonomy? How would he have ever gotten any part of his freedom back in Southern California, with all of its people and highways and cars? Where are the trout streams in Orange County? The quiet roads on which he can bike in safety for twenty miles? The mountains where he feels so at home? What would life be like for him if he still had to depend on me for every trip away from our house?

As for the stem-cell therapy, how did I know it had no value? Maybe it had helped John just enough that he was able to navigate better in the mountains. I didn't know. No one did except God.

And the job at Slifer—hadn't it kept us going for six months? Maybe it didn't prove to be everything I had hoped, but was I expecting God to set us on Easy Street for the rest of our lives? Besides, if it was time for me to start my own business, then I should be thankful that the other job hadn't been perfect.

And there were also other blessings. For instance, in early February, John had made a new friend, Virgil, a man who had previously worked with brain-injured people. They had become pals and had already gone out together several times, including to a fitness center to work out, shopping for Valentines Day presents for me and Virgil's wife, and even scouting for elk.

Not all was rosy, of course. Is it ever, for anybody, for long? Still, when I looked at everything together, it seemed ridiculous that I should feel any complaint toward God. My second-guessing of Him started seeming thankless and short-sighted. I remembered the minister in my old church who had said that my faith was immature. Was it ever!

You've been acting like a spoiled kid, Melinda, I told myself. *God puts what He feels is best for you on your plate. If it seems tasty to you, you eat it. If not, you turn your nose up at it. Then you blame Him for not giving you everything just the way you like it. And if He doesn't hop to it, you start doubting Him.*

Suddenly, I understood. On a deeper level than ever before, I comprehended what it is to give it all to God. Previously, I had thought that it means putting my faith in Him, trusting in His wisdom and grace. And so it does. But the question is, trusting Him to do what? Just what I want? That's what I had been doing, I realized—thinking that if I kept praying and was patient, I must eventually get what I prayed for. Then, when the problems persisted, I stopped trusting, stopped praying.

But that couldn't be right. God isn't my servant. He's not there to grant every wish I might have, no matter how much I want it. He's there to listen to, understand, and care for me in His own fashion. And anyway, I thought, look what He *has* given me! My daughter and my husband. My parents, two beautiful sisters, and good friends. The opportunity to love, to grow, to wake in the morning to sweet mountain air. My life!

Much of what is on my plate is truly wonderful. And, wonderful or not, God has given me that plate. To trust Him, I realized, is to accept what's on it fully. It's all right to want some of what's given me to be different, but not all right to whine or feel fretful about it. Rather, it's for me to savor every morsel set before me the best I can. To get the most out of every day, every triumph, every trial.

That night I got out one of those new journals and did something I had not done for months. I put my pen on the paper and talked to God. I asked His forgiveness for my neglect and misunderstanding, His help on my new business venture, and His blessings on us all. I also asked again, as passionately as ever, for John's full healing. But my request was with a new understanding: even if God's ultimate answer to that prayer turned out not to be what I asked for, I would, with His grace, accept it fully.

Did everything immediately start turning out hunky-dory after that? No. While skiing with John one Saturday in March, I took a bad fall and dislocated my shoulder, which required an operation a few weeks later. Then John had another major seizure just a few days before my grand opening in April.

In spite of it all, we continued moving forward, in faith and love. And I with a new understanding.

Now here we are, already late spring 2005. Not long ago, we celebrated the second anniversary of John's Easter *status* seizure. It felt like a time of rebirth, and so it was, with spring beginning to waft through the Rockies. I had to delay the opening of my new business by a few weeks, but it's now going full speed ahead. I'm busier than ever, but the initial returns are promising. With God's blessing, I will do my very best to make it a success.

My beautiful daughter Blake is doing well, too. She wanted to spend some time with her father and is currently with him in St. Louis, excelling in school. We talk every day on the phone, and I'm hoping she will be able to spend a good part of the summer and perhaps the next school year with us.

As for John, I expect him to become even more of a mountain man this summer. He will probably sometimes have the company of his new friend. Only God knows what adventures he may find in his travels. One thing is certain, though: whoever crosses his path and spends a few minutes with him will discover a remarkable, courageous, engaging man who is far from being defined by his disability.

What else the coming days will bring us, I don't know. But I believe with all my heart that God wants us to continue striving for the best we can, and that He will hold us in His loving hands while we do so. I have great hope for the future, especially when I think back on the last two years. Through all of the setbacks and tears, we have managed not only to survive, but also, somehow, to grow a bit and even to thrive. Problems may remain, yet our blessings are many.

This was proven to me again, in a funny and most memorable way, by an incident that happened just a few weeks ago. I want to tell you about it, because it may help you understand why I am so hopeful, and even often joyful about what is given me. It may also explain, better than anything else I've told you so far, who this man John is, how smart, unstoppable, and full of life, and why I love him so much.

The incident happened the evening after my birthday. John and I went out with friends to celebrate, and during dinner one of them mentioned a write-up about my new business in the local newspaper. I hadn't seen the article, so on the way back we stopped by a coin-operated dispenser less than a mile from home to get a copy of the paper.

But as I was getting out of the car and fumbling for some quarters, my purse tipped and a container of pain pills that the doctor had prescribed after my shoulder operation rolled out and fell through a curbside drain below the car door. Worse, when I lunged for the pills, my new cell phone also tumbled out and into the opening.

A teenaged girl coming from the movie theater a few doors down was walking by and saw it happen. "Oh, bummer," she said, raising her eyebrows, and walked on.

I won't repeat what I was saying as I bent over the grate and peered into the darkness, trying to see what had become of my pills and phone. John pulled the car forward, and a nearby streetlight made enough light for us to spot the items. There, eight or so feet below, were the two wayward travelers, lying in water that looked to be an inch or so deep, taunting us to come and get them.

I was beside myself. I would surely need the pain pills later that night, and there would be no pharmacy open until tomorrow. I also needed my cell phone, whose number was listed on my ads and cards, for my business. My clumsiness meant I would have to take time off—time I didn't have—to locate an outlet for my cell phone company and get the phone replaced. "It had to be those two things!" I said. "Not my lipstick, eyeliner, tissues, pen, or any of the other dozen doodads lying around inside my purse, but the most important two items there. Now, they're gone!"

"Oh we can get them," John said as he bent down beside me. He was examining the grate, which consisted of crisscrossing iron bars that created open squares a few inches on each side. Squares just large enough for a pill container and a cell phone to squeeze through. After a moment, he gripped the bars on one end of the grate with both hands and started pulling up. "You do the other side," he said. "Maybe we can lift it."

Feeling a little squeamish about sticking my fingers into the crusty grid, I did it anyway. Squatting down, I gripped the small bars on my end and pulled.

"Harder," John said.

"I'm doing my best! I still have a bad shoulder here."

After a few more seconds we gave up. The grate hadn't budged.

"There's got to be some way to get them," he said, rising.

"No there doesn't. We're never going to retrieve those things."

He seemed to be pondering, then he said, "I've got an idea. Let's go home."

"Suits me. I don't know what you're idea is, but I know I have to call up the phone company and see how to get a replacement phone."

Five minutes later, we were home. On the way, it occurred to me that the city might be able to help us out somehow, so as soon as we arrived, I called the police department, the only government agency that I thought might be open at ten at night.

"Has anyone ever dropped something important down into the street drainage system in town?" I asked. "Is there any way to get something like that out? Any way to get the grate off?"

"Yes and no," the woman on the other end of the line replied. "Yes, it happens occasionally, and no, there's nothing much to be done about it. The grates are cemented into the pavement."

"That's what I thought," I said. "Thanks anyway."

As I called the cell phone company, I wondered what had happened to John. I figured he had probably forgotten all about the problem and was upstairs getting ready for bed.

I learned from the cell phone people where I would have to go to get a new phone and how much it would cost. As I was hanging up, the door to the garage opened and John came through it, loaded down with a hodgepodge of implements—a garage broom handle, another long handle of some sort, a square of cardboard, a roll of duct tape, and a tool box. Backlit from the garage light, he looked like an unearthly explorer heading for some odd Rube Goldberg rendezvous.

He stopped and looked at me, a puzzled expression on his face. "What are we supposed to be doing now?"

"What!?" I blurted out. "You're not still thinking about going to get the phone and the pills are you?"

"Yeah, that's it! Let's go. I'm ready."

"What is all that stuff you're carrying?"

"It's so we can get your phone."

"We can't get it. I just talked to the police. There's no way to get down there."

"Yes we can, Melinda. Let's go back there now. I'm going to do this."

I saw that there was no talking him out of it, so I asked him to wait while I called the police again to tell them what we were about to do. I didn't want anyone to think we were out there on the street at night casing a bank.

"We'll send somebody by to look in on you," the woman said.

I hung up and turned to John. "Okay, if you're set on it, let's go." But I was sure we were embarking on a classic wild goose chase.

Once there, John removed all of his accoutrements from the back of our SUV and spread them around the drain opening. A moment later, a patrol car pulled up in front of us and a policeman got out.

"Good evening, Mr. and Mrs. Wilferth," the officer said. "John, isn't it? I was at your house a few weeks ago when you had a seizure. Looks like you're doing much better."

"Hanging in there," John replied.

"They radioed that you folks were trying to retrieve a cell phone."

"Yeah," said John. "We need to get that out. Melinda needs it for her business." He had started taping the two poles together.

"I lost a prescription down there, too," I said. "John insists that he can get both of them out."

"Well, as far as the cell phone goes, my advice is to cancel your service," the policeman said. "There's no way you're going to get it out of there. We cement those grates into the pavement just for that reason—so people can't remove them. It's not going to budge."

"That's not how I'm going to do it," John replied. "Don't worry, I'll get them out."

With the officer unable to dissuade John, I wondered if he was about to order us to stop fooling around with the city's drainage system. But he only told us to pull all of our gear up onto the sidewalk. "I'll check back with you after a while to make sure you're all right. All I can say is good luck. You'll need it." He shook his head skeptically.

After the man had gone, I was feeling thoroughly dejected, and I let John know it. It was cold, my shoulder was hurting, and it was getting late. I would have to get to work early in the morning and make time to call the doctor to get a new prescription, go to the pharmacy, and drive to the phone store. I just wanted to go to bed.

No doubt tired of listening to me moan, John said, "You go home. I'll stay and get it out."

"I'm not going to leave you out here on the street at night," I said. "Anyway, you need me to hold the flashlight if you're going to try to fish them out somehow." I still didn't understand just what kind of apparatus he was putting together.

After a few more minutes, the tool became clear. He had taped the two handles securely together to make an eight—or nine-foot long pole. He had then shaped a piece of the cardboard into a narrow scoop, no more than a couple of inches wide, and had taped the cardboard to one end of the pole. Finally, he had snipped off a length of picture wire and created an arm-sized loop near the opposite end.

The contraption looked to me like it would fall apart at any moment, and I was still doubtful as he carried it the couple of feet to the drain, carefully stuck the cardboard end through a portion of the grid that stood near the big drain opening in the curb, and pushed most of it through.

"Now grab hold of it," he said, offering me the pole. After I did, he lay down on his stomach half over the grid, stuck his entire right arm through the curb opening, snaked it around down below the grid, inserted it into the wire loop, and grasped the pole from below.

By this time, I too was half lying on the filthy grid, my feet out into the street. I held the flashlight as I watched John navigate the apparatus so that the cardboard hit the wet concrete below. He then guided it toward the vial of pills and slid beneath it. Caught by the lip of the cardboard, the container rolled around a bit but stayed in the scoop as John carefully pulled the pole up until its end popped up again through the grid.

"Take hold of it," he said. I did, and he pulled his arm first out of the loop, then out of the side hole. He took the pole from me, stood, and pulled it up until the pill container was just under the grid and I could reach my fingers through and grab it.

During this time, though the street was nearly dead, several cars had passed by, and I had vaguely heard a few of them slow down. I knew they must be gawking at us, wondering what in the world this man and woman were doing lying on top of a drainage grid at eleven at night. But though I had felt foolish to begin with, I was now starting to feel elated.

We immediately went through the same procedure to try to capture the cell phone. The only difference was that at one point, John lost his handhold on the pole. But that only served to show his foresight in making the wire loop. The pole stayed on his arm, and he was able to grab it again. A moment later, the flashlight beam showed him scooping up the phone and starting to pull it up.

"You genius!" I said as my fingers reached through the grate and grabbed the phone. "You did it, you did it, you did it!" We both stood up, grimy and wrinkled, and gave each other high-fives.

"I told you I was going to get that stuff," John said.

"I know, I know! I should have believed you."

I dried off the outside of the phone, but I didn't dare try it until it had had a chance to dry inside too. I found out a few hours later that it was working fine. As for the pills, my shoulder pain had disappeared in my excitement, so I wouldn't be needing them as quickly as I had thought. I wanted to use John's cell phone to call someone and tell them what had just happened, but it was eleven o'clock, a little late to be waking people up to share our story. I did call the police station, however. I asked them to say thank you to the officer who had stopped, and to pass on the information that John had totally succeeded in his objective.

I was so excited by John's—and our—success after we got home, that I had a hard time falling asleep. I kept thinking about how he had figured out in the first place just how to retrieve the phone and the pills, and how he had gathered precisely the tools he needed—down to the wire loop—to do the job. And I kept remembering how everyone—me, the woman at the police station, and the policeman—had doubted that he could do what he said he was going to do. And how he hadn't let it sway him one bit.

So now you know my beautiful, irrepressible John just a little better, and you know that indeed I do have much to be thankful for. And maybe you will understand me better now when I say that of all our many blessings, one of the greatest is simply the fact that John is gradually finding himself more and more at home in the here.

As am I.

Epilogue

A few months after this book was completed, on May 4th, 2006, John R. Wilferth passed away in his Colorado home following a final seizure. His body is resting in the family farm graveyard near Cape Girardeau, Missouri. He was forty years young.